dBASE III Plus®
SmartStart

Ralph Duffy
North Seattle Community College

dBASE III Plus SmartStart.

Library of Congress Catalog No.: 93-86971

ISBN: 1-56529-410-6

97 96 95 4 3 2

Interpretation of the printing code: the rightmost double-digit number is the year of the book's printing; the rightmost single-digit number, the number of the book's printing. For example, a printing code of 94-1 shows that the first printing of the book occurred in 1994.

Screens reproduced in this book were created using Collage Plus from Inner Media, Inc., Hollis, NH.

dBASE III Plus SmartStart is based on dBASE III Plus.

Publisher: David P. Ewing

Director of Publishing: Michael Miller

Director of Operations and Editing: Chris Katsaropoulos

Book Designer: Amy Peppler-Adams

Production Team: Gary Adair, Jeff Baker, Angela Bannan, Danielle Bird, Paula Carroll, Charlotte Clapp, Kim Cofer, Stephanie Davis, Meshell Dinn, Terri Edwards, Brook Farling, Carla Hall, Jenny Kucera, Bob LaRoche, Beth Lewis, Nanci Sears Perry, Caroline Roop, Michael Thomas, Lillian Yates

Dedication

To Andy, Chris, and Tim Cashman—The Finest Nephews.

Editorial Director

Carol Crowell

Managing Editor

Sheila B. Cunningham

Senior Editor

Jeannine Freudenberger

Editors

Don Eamon
Mary Anne Sharbaugh
Phil Kitchel

Editorial Coordinator

Elizabeth D. Brown

Formatter

Bryan Bird

Composed in *Garamond* and *MCPdigital* by Que Corporation

About the Author

Ralph Duffy holds a B.A. from the University of Michigan and an M.S. from Pennsylvania State University. He has worked as a statistical consultant and programmer/analyst for Pennsylvania State University, the Indiana University School of Medicine, and Purdue University. He is currently an instructor in the Computer Information Systems Department of North Seattle Community College.

Mr. Duffy also is the Director of the IBM Technology Transfer Center in Seattle. This Center, in coöperation with Microsoft Corporation, provides training in computer applications for the faculty and staff of colleges throughout the Northwest, including the University of Washington and Seattle University. Mr. Duffy is the author of *Excel 4 for Windows SmartStart* and *Paradox SmartStart* and coauthor of *Paradox for Windows SmartStart*, all published by Que College.

# Acknowledgments

I would like to acknowledge Betsy Brown for her competent handling of all the details, Don Eamon for his editing and assistance, and Jeannine Freudenberger for her excellent work.

Que College is grateful for the assistance provided by the following reviewers: Bill McTammany and Michelle Poolet. A special thanks also to our technical editor, Michael Regoli.

Trademark Acknowledgments

All terms mentioned in this book that are known to be trademarks or service marks have been appropriately capitalized. Que cannot attest to the accuracy of this information. Use of a term in this book should not be regarded as affecting the validity of any trademark or service mark.

dBASE III Plus is a trademark of Borland International. Paradox is a registered trademark of Borland International, Inc. Microsoft and MS-DOS are registered trademarks and Windows is a trademark of Microsoft Corporation.

Contents at a Glance

Introduction 1

1 An Overview of dBASE III Plus 5

2 Designing and Creating a Database File with dBASE III Plus 21

3 Adding and Editing Database Records 49

4 Using Dot Prompt Commands to Display Your Database Records 81

5 Restructuring a Database File 107

6 Sorting and Indexing Database Files 135

7 Working Efficiently with Large Databases 163

8 Printing Reports and Mailing Labels 189

9 Retrieving Data from Multiple Linked Databases by Using Views and Joins 219

Index 247

Table of Contents

Introduction 1

Who Should Use This Book 2
How This Book Is Organized 2
Where to Find More Help 3
Conventions Used in This Book 3

1 An Overview of dBASE III Plus 5

Objectives 5
Objective 1: To Understand What a Database Is 6
What Is a Database? 7
Relational Databases 8
Objective 2: To Understand the Main Features of dBASE III Plus 9
Program Features 9
Using dBASE III Plus 10
Sorting and Indexing Your Data 11
Searching a Database 13
Creating Reports and Mailing Labels 14
Retrieving Related Data from Multiple Databases 16
Modifying the Structure of a Database File 16
Creating Custom Data Entry Screens 17
Chapter Summary 18
Testing Your Knowledge 18
True/False Questions 18
Multiple-Choice Questions 19
Fill-in-the-Blank Questions 20

2 Designing and Creating a Database File with dBASE III Plus 21

Objectives 21
Objective 1: To Understand How DOS Organizes Disk Storage 22
Drives and Directories 23
Objective 2: To Start dBASE III Plus 24
Exercise 2.1: Starting dBASE 25
Objective 3: To Understand the dBASE III Plus Assistant 26
Exercise 3.1: Exploring the Assistant Menu 27
Objective 4: To Create a Database File's Structure 28
Specifying the Field Name, Type, and Size 28

The Database File 28
Creating the Structure of Your First Database 29
Exercise 4.1: Creating a Database File 30
Objective 5: To List On-Screen and Print the Database File's Structure 34
Exercise 5.1: Listing the Structure of Your Open Database File on the Screen 34
Exercise 5.2: Listing Your Database File's Structure On-Screen and on the Printer 35
Objective 6: To Exit from dBASE III Plus 36
Exercise 6.1: Quitting dBASE 36
Objective 7: To Understand the Rules for Naming dBASE III Plus Files and Fields 37
Naming the Database File 37
Naming Fields 38
Objective 8: To Understand the Types of dBASE III Plus Fields 39
Specifying a Field Width 40
Objective 9: To Understand the Guidelines for Designing a Database File 40
Planning the Database File Structure 40
Setting the Database Objective 41
Analyzing the Current System 41
Describing Desired Outputs 42
Small Is Better 42
Chapter Summary 43
Testing Your Knowledge 43
True/False Questions 43
Multiple-Choice Questions 44
Fill-in-the-Blank Questions 45
Review: Short Projects 45
Review: Long Projects 46

3 Adding and Editing Database Records 49

Objectives 49
Objective 1: To Open a Database File 50
Exercise 1.1: Opening a Database File 51
Objective 2: To Add Data to a Database File by Using the Append Command 53
Exercise 2.1: Selecting the Append Command 54
Exercise 2.2: Adding Data Records to the Customer Database File 55

Objective 3: To Display Data by Using the List Command 58
Exercise 3.1: Listing Your Open Database File On-Screen 58
Exercise 3.2: Listing Your Open Database File On-Screen and on the Printer 60
Objective 4: To Edit Data by Using the Edit Command 61
Exercise 4.1: Editing Data with the Edit Command 61
Objective 5: To View and Edit Data by Using the Browse Command 63
Exercise 5.1: Editing Data Using the Browse Command 64
Objective 6: To Delete and Recall Records 65
Exercise 6.1: Marking a Record for Deletion Using the Browse Command 66
Exercise 6.2: Marking a Record for Deletion Using the Delete Command 67
Exercise 6.3: "Unmarking" a Record Using the Recall Command ... 69
Exercise 6.4: Deleting by Using the Pack Command 71
Chapter Summary 71
Testing Your Knowledge 72
True/False Questions 72
Multiple-Choice Questions 72
Fill-in-the-Blank Questions 73
Review: Short Projects 73
Review: Long Projects 75

4 Using Dot Prompt Commands to Display Your Database Records 81

Objectives 82
Objective 1: To Begin to Use Dot Prompt Commands 82
The Use Command 83
Exercise 1.1: Opening a Database File 83
The List Command 84
Exercise 1.2: Listing the Database File in Use 84
Exercise 1.3: Listing the Structure of the Database File in Use 84
The Append Command 84
Exercise 1.4: Adding Records to the Database File in Use 85
The Edit Command 85
Exercise 1.5: Editing Records in the Database File in Use 86
The History Command 86
Exercise 1.6: Using History to Access a Previous Command 86
Exercise 1.7: Using List History to Access a Previous Command ... 87
The Clear Command 87

Exercise 1.8: Using the Clear Command 87
The Delete, Recall, and Pack Commands 87
Exercise 1.9: Using the Delete Command to Mark a Record for Deletion 87
Exercise 1.10: Using the Recall Command to Unmark a Record 88
Objective 2: To Use the List Command 88
Exercise 2.1: Listing the Student Database 89
Exercise 2.2: Using the List Command to List Specific Fields 90
The List Files Command 91
Exercise 2.3: Using the List Files Command 91
The List Status Command 91
Exercise 2.4: Using the List Status Command 92
Exercise 2.5: Using the Display Status Command 93
Objective 3: To Use the List For Command 94
Establishing Conditions That Must Be Met before a Record Is Listed 94
Exercise 3.1: Using the List For Command 95
Exercise 3.2: More Practice Using the List For Command 95
Exercise 3.3: Using Date Type Fields in the List For Command 97
Multiple Selection Conditions in List For Commands 97
Exercise 3.4: Using .AND. in a List For Command 98
Exercise 3.5: Using .OR. in a List For Command 98
Using the Comparison Operators in List For Commands 99
Exercise 3.6: Using a Comparison Operator in a List For Command 99
Objective 4: To Print by Using the List Command 100
Exercise 4.1: Using the List to Print Command 100
Exercise 4.2: Using the List to Print Command with Selection Criteria 101
Exercise 4.3: Using the Full List to Print Command 101
Objective 5: To Use the Set Commands 101
The Set Default To Command 102
The Set Bell Off Command 102
Exercise 5.1: Turning Off the Bell 102
Objective 6: To Quit dBASE from the Dot Prompt 102
Exercise 6.1: Using the Quit Command 103
Chapter Summary 103
Testing Your Knowledge 103
True/False Questions 103
Multiple-Choice Questions 104

Fill-in-the-Blank Questions 105
Review: Short Projects 105
Review: Long Projects 106

5 Restructuring a Database File 107

Objectives 107
Objective 1: To Understand dBASE's Rules for Restructuring a File 108
Objective 2: To Copy a Database File 110
Exercise 2.1: Making a Backup Copy of the Student Database File ... 110
Objective 3: To Change a Database File's Structure 111
Following the Recommended Procedure When You Restructure 111
Exercise 3.1: Beginning the Restructuring of Student 112
Adding Fields 113
Exercise 3.2: Adding a New Field to the Database File 113
Deleting Fields 114
Exercise 3.3: Deleting a Field from the Structure 114
Moving Fields 115
Exercise 3.4: Moving a Field in the Structure 115
Changing the Size of a Field 116
Exercise 3.5: Changing the Width of a Character Field 117
Changing a Field Type 117
Exercise 3.6: Changing the Type of a Field 118
Exercise 3.7: Restructuring the Student Database file 119
Exercise 3.8: Viewing the Restructured Student Database File 120
Changing the Name of a Field 120
Exercise 3.9: Changing a Field Name 120
Objective 4: To Use Logical and Memo Fields 122
Understanding the Logical Data Type 122
Understanding the Memo Data Type 122
Understanding Memo Files 123
Using Memo Fields 123
Exercise 4.1: Adding Logical and Memo Type Fields to a Database File Structure 124
Entering Text into a Memo Field 125
Exercise 4.2: Adding Data to Logical and Memo Type Fields 126
Listing the Contents of Memo Fields 127
Exercise 4.3: Listing Logical and Memo Type Fields 128
Objective 5: To Rename a Database File 128
Exercise 5.1: Renaming the Stubak Database File 129

Objective 6: To Delete a Database File 129
Exercise 6.1: Deleting a Database File 130
Chapter Summary 130
Testing Your Knowledge 130
True/False Questions 130
Multiple-Choice Questions 131
Fill-in-the-Blank Questions 132
Review: Short Projects 132
Review: Long Projects 132

6 Sorting and Indexing Database Files 135

Objectives 136
Objective 1: To Understand How dBASE Sorts Character, Date, and Numeric Fields 137
Sorting on a Character Type Field 137
Sorting Numeric and Date Type Fields 138
Objective 2: To Sort a Database File Using One Sort Field 139
Sorting Database Files 139
Exercise 2.1: Sorting the Student Database File by Using the CITY Field 139
Objective 3: To Sort a Database File Using Multiple Sort Fields 140
The Major Sort Field 141
Exercise 3.1: Setting Up Ties in the Student2 Database File 141
Exercise 3.2: Sorting Using Two Fields 142
Objective 4: To Sort a Database File in Descending Order 142
Ascending and Descending Order 142
Exercise 4.1: Sorting a Database File in Descending Order 143
Saving the Sorted Database Files 143
Objective 5: To Understand the Problems Created by Sorting 144
Problems Created by Sorting Database Files 144
Index Files 145
Objective 6: To Understand What Indexing a File Does 145
Exercise 6.1: Printing the Customer Database File 145
Exercise 6.2: Manually Indexing the Customer Database File on the LAST Field 146
Exercise 6.3: Manually Indexing the Customer Database File on the CITY Field 147
Maintaining Index Files 148
Objective 7: To Index a File on One Field 148
Exercise 7.1: Creating an Index Using the LAST Field 149
Exercise 7.2: Creating an Index Using the CITY Field 150

Objective 8: To Use Index Files 152
Exercise 8.1: Working with Indexes 152
Exercise 8.2: Activating Multiple Indexes When You Are Going to Modify a Database 154
Objective 9: To Index a File Using Multiple Fields 156
Exercise 9.1: Creating a Multiple-Field Index 156
Chapter Summary 157
Testing Your Knowledge 158
True/False Questions 158
Multiple-Choice Questions 158
Fill-in-the-Blank Questions 159
Review: Short Projects 159
Review: Long Projects 160

7 Working Efficiently with Large Databases 163

Objectives 164
Objective 1: To Use the Goto Command 164
Exercise 1.1: Using the Goto Command 165
Objective 2: To Use the Insert Command 166
Exercise 2.1: Using the Insert Command 166
Objective 3: To Use the Delete For Command 168
Exercise 3.1: To Use the Delete For Command 169
Exercise 3.2: Using the Delete For Command with Date Type Fields 169
Objective 4: To Use the Recall Command 170
Exercise 4.1: Using the Recall For Command 171
Exercise 4.2: Using the Recall All Command 171
Objective 5: To Use the Replace Command 172
Exercise 5.1: Using the Replace Command 172
Exercise 5.2: Using the Replace All Command 173
Exercise 5.3: Using the Replace For Command 174
Objective 6: To Use the Count, Sum, and Average Commands 175
The Count Command 176
Exercise 6.1: Using the Average, Count, and Sum Commands 176
Exercise 6.2: Using the Average For, Count For, and Sum For Commands 177
Objective 7: To Use the Find Command 178
Exercise 7.1: Using the Find Command 179
Using the Find Command to Find and Display All Records with a Particular Value 179
Exercise 7.2: Using the Find Command and the List Next Command 180

Exercise 7.3: Using Both the Find and List While Commands 181
Objective 8: To Use the Seek Command 182
Exercise 8.1: Using the Seek Command 182
Exercise 8.2: Using the Seek Command with Date Type Fields 183
Chapter Summary 183
Testing Your Knowledge 184
True/False Questions 184
Multiple-Choice Questions 184
Fill-in-the-Blank Questions 185
Review: Short Projects 186
Review: Long Projects 186

8 Printing Reports and Mailing Labels 189

Objectives 190
Objective 1: To Create and Use a Mailing Label Form 191
The Create Label Command 191
Exercise 1.1: Using the Create Label Command to Access the Create Label Screen 192
Exercise 1.2: Using the Create Label Screen to Select a Standard Label Size 193
The Label Contents Menu Box 193
Exercise 1.3: Using the Create Label Screen to Define the Contents of a Label 194
Printing Your Labels 197
Exercise 1.4: Displaying and Printing Your Labels 197
Objective 2: To Modify a Mailing Label Form 198
Exercise 2.1: Modifying a Label-Form File 198
Exercise 2.2: Displaying and Printing Your Modified Labels 200
Objective 3: To Create and Use a Report Form 201
Building the Report Format 202
Exercise 3.1: Adding More Data to the Customer Database 202
Exercise 3.2: Setting the Options 203
The Columns Menu 204
Exercise 3.3: Defining the First Column in the Report 205
Exercise 3.4: Defining the Second Column in the Report 207
Exercise 3.5: Defining the Remaining Columns in the Report 208
Exercise 3.6: Printing the Report 209
Objective 4: To Modify a Report Form 210
Exercise 4.1: Modifying the Report-Form File 211
Printing Your Completed Report 212
Exercise 4.2: Printing the Report 213

Chapter Summary 214
Testing Your Knowledge 214
True/False Questions 214
Multiple-Choice Questions 215
Fill-in-the-Blank Questions 216
Review: Short Projects 216
Review: Long Projects 216

9 Retrieving Data from Multiple Linked Databases by Using Views and Joins 219

Objectives 220
Objective 1: To Understand the Concept of Related Database Files 222
Relational Databases 222
Relationships among Data Files 222
Using a Primary Key Field as a Link Field 223
Retrieving Related Data from Multiple Databases 224
Objective 2: To Use the Select Command to Open Multiple Database Files Simultaneously 224
Select Areas 225
The Current Select Area 225
Exercise 2.1: Using the Select Command to Open Multiple Database Files 226
Exercise 2.2: Using the Select Command to Move between Work Areas 227
Exercise 2.3: Using the Clear All Command to Close All Open Database and Index Files 228
Objective 3: To Create a View File 228
Exercise 3.1: Naming the View File 229
Exercise 3.2: Selecting the Database Files to Link and Their Index Files 229
Exercise 3.3: Using the Relate Menu to Define the Linkage between the Two Database Files 231
Exercise 3.4: Selecting the Fields to Include in the View 232
Exercise 3.5: Saving the View 234
Objective 4: To Use a View to Retrieve Data from Two Linked Files 234
Exercise 4.1: Using the View File 234
Objective 5: To Modify a View File 236
Exercise 5.1: Modifying the View File 236
Exercise 5.2: Using the Modified View File 238

Objective 6: To Create a New Database File by Using the Join Command 238
Exercise 6.1: Joining the Student and Courses Databases 239
Exercise 6.2: Joining Student and Courses in a New Database with Three Fields 241
Chapter Summary 242
Testing Your Knowledge 243
True/False Questions 243
Multiple-Choice Questions 243
Fill-in-the-Blank Questions 244
Review: Short Projects 244
Review: Long Projects 245

Index 247

Introduction

If you are new to dBASE, or to database programs in general, this book will give you a flying start. You can use *dBASE III Plus SmartStart* in a class or as a self-teaching guide. This book is designed for a hands-on computer course in database management, enabling an instructor to structure topics within the time frame of the curriculum. Whether you are a novice or have used another version of dBASE, this *SmartStart* is one of the easiest and fastest ways to master dBASE III Plus.

dBASE III Plus SmartStart uses an easy-to-grasp, hands-on tutorial style that leads you through the essential parts of the program. You will quickly grasp the essentials of databases and structures and learn the fundamentals of sorting, indexing, querying databases, linking database files, printing mailing labels, and producing reports. Illustrations are plentiful throughout the book and supplement the basic information in the text.

This book takes you through dBASE III Plus with step-by-step exercises within the chapters, describing all the fundamentals you need to know. Each chapter begins with an overview and lists the objectives and key terms to be covered in each chapter. At the end of each chapter, you can test your knowledge by completing questions and projects to reinforce the material covered in the chapter. dBASE III Plus is a large and powerful database program, but *dBASE III Plus SmartStart* will get you up and over the learning curve quickly by enabling you to master the basic concepts. *dBASE III Plus SmartStart* will provide you with a solid background in dBASE III Plus and in the concepts of computerized database management.

Who Should Use This Book

dBASE III Plus SmartStart is designed primarily for new users of dBASE III Plus, but you can benefit from it even if you already know something about database management programs. If you want to master the basics of dBASE III Plus quickly, this book is for you.

This book assumes that the dBASE III Plus software is already installed on your hard disk.

How This Book Is Organized

The chapters in *dBASE III Plus SmartStart* are arranged so that you learn the basic tasks and then proceed to the more complex procedures.

Chapter 1, "An Overview of dBASE III Plus," introduces the subject of databases. You then quickly tour the main features of dBASE that are covered in this text.

Chapter 2, "Designing and Creating a Database File with dBASE III Plus," shows you how to start the dBASE III Plus program, explains what you will see on the screen as you begin to use dBASE, demonstrates the creation of a database file, and explains how to exit dBASE III Plus.

Chapter 3, "Adding and Editing Database Records," explains how to add data to a database file's structure, edit this data, delete records, view the data, and then print the data.

Chapter 4, "Using Dot Prompt Commands to Display Your Database Records," shows you how to issue commands to dBASE so that you can work more efficiently.

Chapter 5, "Restructuring a Database File," covers changing the structure of a database file and gives methods for avoiding the loss of data when you restructure. This chapter also explains the use of Logical and Memo type fields.

Chapter 6, "Sorting and Indexing Database Files," explains how to sort a database file in ascending or descending order using one sort field or multiple sort fields. This chapter also discusses the creation of indexes and some of their advantages over sorting.

Chapter 7, "Working Efficiently with Large Databases," deals with special commands designed to help you maintain large database files and rapidly locate information in a database. The Average, Count, and Sum commands are also discussed

Chapter 8, "Printing Reports and Mailing Labels," explains how to design, save, and print custom reports and mailing labels using the data in your table.

Chapter 9, "Retrieving Data from Multiple Linked Databases by Using Views and Joins," covers two techniques for joining related data from two different database files.

Where to Find More Help

This book concentrates on the most important and frequently used dBASE III Plus functions. After you learn the fundamentals presented in this book, you may want to learn more advanced applications of dBASE III Plus. Que Corporation has a full line of dBASE III Plus books you can use. A more advanced text is the *dBASE III PLUS Handbook*, 2nd Edition, from Que Corporation.

Conventions Used in This Book

Certain conventions are used throughout the text and graphics of *dBASE III Plus SmartStart* to help you understand the book.

References to keys are as they appear on the keyboard of the IBM Personal Computer and most IBM-compatibles: ↵Enter. When two keys appear together, for example, ⇧Shift+F2, you press and hold down the first key as you also press the second key. In numbered steps, these keys appear in blue: Alt.

To select a menu option means to highlight the option and press ↵Enter. Information that you type, such as **NAME**, appears in blue and boldface in numbered steps and in boldface in regular text.

DOS commands, dBASE commands as typed, and field names are written in all capital letters. Other dBASE commands and options and names of databases are written with initial capital letters. Messages and exact quotations from the computer screen are printed in a `special typeface`.

An Overview of dBASE III Plus

1

One of the most useful features of a computer is the capability of storing large amounts of data in a database. By using a database, you can consolidate all your data into a few files; this capability helps you become organized and efficient because your data is not scattered in different locations. When your data is stored on a computer, you can retrieve this data or selected parts of the data quickly and without error. To perform this task, the computer must run a piece of software known as a *database management system* (or *database program*). dBASE III Plus is a popular database program used on personal computers.

Objectives

1. To Understand What a Database Is
2. To Understand the Main Features of dBASE III Plus

1

Key Terms in This Chapter	
Database	An organized collection of related data.
Database program	A computer program, such as dBASE III Plus, that enables you to create, maintain, and use a computer database.
Database file	A disk file, created and maintained by dBASE III Plus, that contains a database made up of records and fields. Your data is stored in database files. The first step in creating a database file is to define a structure; you then fill the structure with data.
Record	A set of information on one person, place, thing, or event. Records are stored in a database file.
Field	A field contains one data item. Records consist of fields. All the records in a database file contain the same fields, although the data in the fields differs.
Structure	The way in which a database file is organized. Consists of the field names, type (such as alphanumeric or date), and size of the field.
Key field	A field that contains a unique identifier, such as a Social Security number, that identifies a particular record in a database file.
Link field	A field that occurs in more than one database file. You can use a link field to match (join) related records in two or more different database files.
Relational database	A group of database files that can be linked together (joined) by using a shared link field or fields.

Objective 1: To Understand What a Database Is

Before learning dBASE III Plus's capabilities, you should first consider the broader topic of databases in general. After you understand the concept of a database, you can move on to learn how this concept is implemented in dBASE III Plus. This chapter introduces databases, and then the text explains them in greater detail in following chapters.

What Is a Database?

A *database* is a collection of information organized in a logical way. You probably already are familiar with common examples of databases maintained manually on paper. The card file—the reference document that shows the book collection in a library—is a database. A dictionary is a database containing information about the meanings of words. A telephone book is a database of names, addresses, and phone numbers.

The Rolodex and files maintained in an office are other kinds of databases. Business databases usually contain information on employees, payrolls, customers, products, inventories, and sales. Databases in schools contain information on courses, students, teachers, and student grades. Real estate databases contain information on listings—the price, location, square feet, number of bathrooms, and so on. Figure 1.1 shows registration information from a college database.

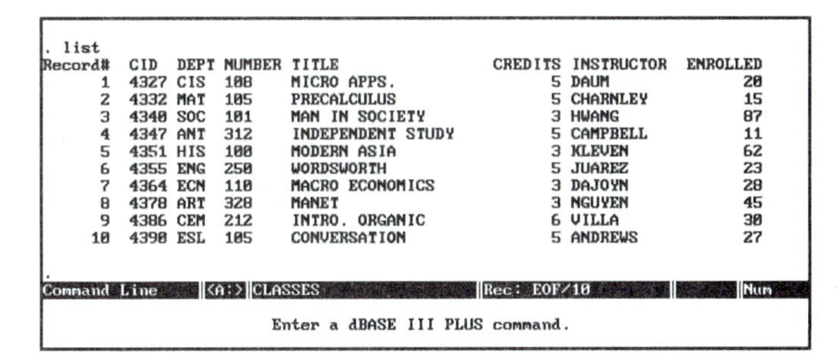

. list

Record#	CID	DEPT	NUMBER	TITLE	CREDITS	INSTRUCTOR	ENROLLED
1	4327	CIS	108	MICRO APPS.	5	DAUM	20
2	4332	MAT	105	PRECALCULUS	5	CHARNLEY	15
3	4340	SOC	101	MAN IN SOCIETY	3	HWANG	87
4	4347	ANT	312	INDEPENDENT STUDY	5	CAMPBELL	11
5	4351	HIS	100	MODERN ASIA	3	KLEVEN	62
6	4355	ENG	250	WORDSWORTH	5	JUAREZ	23
7	4364	ECN	110	MACRO ECONOMICS	3	DAJOYN	28
8	4378	ART	328	MANET	3	NGUYEN	45
9	4386	CEM	212	INTRO. ORGANIC	6	VILLA	30
10	4390	ESL	105	CONVERSATION	5	ANDREWS	27

Command Line | <A:> | CLASSES | Rec: EOF/10 | | Num

Enter a dBASE III PLUS command.

Fig. 1.1
Part of a college database.

You can keep a database on paper, but computers provide the most useful databases. To set up a database on a computer, you need a database program such as dBASE III Plus.

dBASE stores a database in a database file. A database file is similar in layout to a spreadsheet or a table of data. Database files also are organized in rows and columns. When you store data in a database, the database program places a record in a single row of the database file. For example, a record in a database file that contains information about a business's customers usually contains one customer's first name, last name, address, and phone number. Each customer record occupies one row in the database file. This method is the same method of storing data used in a spreadsheet or in a table of data.

Each database file record is divided into fields. Fields are similar to the columns in a spreadsheet or a table of data. When you begin to create a database file, you first must define a structure for the file. The exact layout of a record in a database file is determined by that database's *structure*. The structure lists the order in which fields occur in a record and the name, type, and size of each field in the database file.

All the records in a database file contain the same fields. A field contains one piece of the data belonging to the record. In a database of customers, for example, the customer's first name is field 1; the last name, field 2; the street address, field 3; and so on. When a database file is displayed or printed, the records are the rows of the database file, and the fields are the columns.

Often, one field in a database file is designated as a primary *key field*. Keys are optional in a database file, but they do have advantages. Only one record in a database file can have a particular value in the primary key field. Therefore, primary key field values uniquely identify a record. In a school database, for example, information about you may be one record, and your Social Security number or student number uniquely identifies your record. In dBASE III Plus, a database file key can consist of several fields in combination, although the best design for a database file uses only one field as the key.

You have already learned that database files function as the structures in which data is stored. You can create, delete, and sort these database files as needed. dBASE III Plus can make backup copies of the database files on a disk. dBASE III Plus database files can contain many thousands of records, and dBASE III Plus has the capability of storing any numeric, date, or alphabetic data in fields. By restructuring an existing database file, you can add or delete fields, and you can change their width or type. You can add new records or easily change the data in existing records by using dBASE III Plus's editing capabilities. dBASE III Plus can create reports and print mailing labels from database file data.

Relational Databases

Modern computer database programs create relational databases. A *relational database* consists of one or more related database files. What does *related* mean? As an example of related database files, assume that you create a database file that contains a listing of the information about your customers and another database file that contains invoice information previously sent to these customers. These database files are related because the customers referenced in the invoice file are the same customers whose information you stored in the customer file.

You can link these two database files by using a field that exists in both database files. A relationship exists between records in the two database files if a field value in the first database file record also occurs in the other database file. If a customer identification number field is included in both database files, for example, you can extract the information about a specific customer from both the invoice database file and the customer database file.

By using this capacity for connecting different but related database files, you can keep small, simple database files, with each file containing a limited set of data. This method makes updating and changing the different database files in a database simpler and more efficient. Because you can retrieve related data records from linked files, the data is not fragmented into separate files that cannot be integrated.

Objective 2: To Understand the Main Features of dBASE III Plus

dBASE III Plus is a powerful program with a full range of database capabilities. Covering all aspects of dBASE III Plus, however, is beyond the scope of this text. This book concentrates on the most important and frequently used dBASE III Plus functions. If after finishing this book, you want to learn more about dBASE, a more advanced text is the *dBASE III Plus Handbook*, from Que Corporation.

Program Features

This section offers a preview of what you will learn. In the following chapters, you explore in depth the main features of dBASE III Plus. dBASE III Plus uses the Microsoft operating system, DOS. If you previously used another DOS-based word processing or spreadsheet program, you probably are familiar with the restrictions on file names imposed by DOS. When using dBASE, you don't actually interact with DOS except to start the dBASE program. The dBASE commands cause DOS to save, open, copy, rename, list, print, or delete files.

Using dBASE III Plus

When dBASE runs, you need to tell the program what you want it to do in either of two ways. If you are a new user, the easiest way to interact with dBASE is to use the Assistant. The Assistant enables you to communicate commands to dBASE by making selections from a series of menus. When you start dBASE, the Assistant is displayed on-screen (see fig. 1.2). Notice the explanation of the highlighted menu choice at the bottom of the screen and the word `ASSIST` at the lower left of the screen.

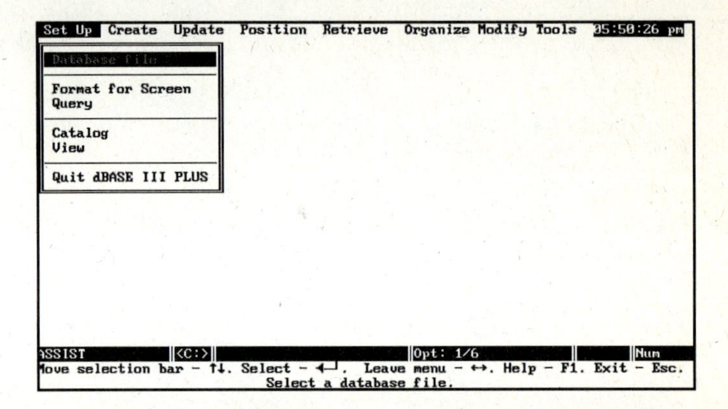

Fig. 1.2
The Assistant.

Each menu choice enables you to perform a different operation with dBASE. Because most students prefer to use the Assistant when studying dBASE, use the Assistant in the first exercises in this text.

The second method of interacting with dBASE is issuing commands by entering them directly at the dot prompt (see fig. 1.3). This prompt is displayed every time you leave the Assistant by pressing the Esc key. You find this key at the upper left corner of the keyboard.

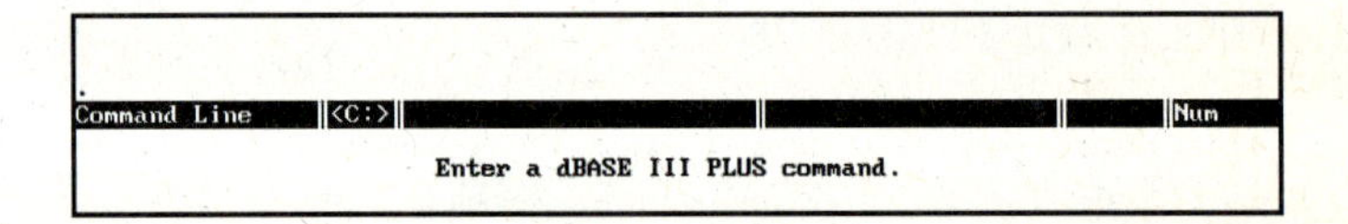

Fig. 1.3
The dot prompt.

At first, this method of using dBASE may seem strange, but remember what you are trying to accomplish. You want dBASE to do something for you. Therefore, you must give dBASE a clear, syntactically correct command that tells the program what you want done. You also need to know when dBASE has completed one task and is ready for another. To signal that dBASE is ready for your command, a dot followed by a blinking cursor appears at the lower left of the screen. This dot is the prompt to type a command. Notice also the message `Enter a dBASE III Plus command` at the bottom of the screen.

As you become more familiar with dBASE, you probably will want to enter the commands after the dot prompt. This method is faster than using the Assistant, and many more commands are available than are available in the Assistant's menus. A good way to learn commands is to watch the bottom of the screen as dBASE builds a command from the Assistant menu choices you select. If you want, you can return to the Assistant from the dot prompt by typing **assist** and pressing ↵Enter. As a shortcut, you can press F2 at the top of the keyboard.

By using the commands in the Assistant menus or by typing commands at the dot prompt, you can create, save, open, modify, print, and delete database files. These database files, in which all the data is stored, are the most important and fundamental part of a computerized database. After you create a database file, dBASE enables you to perform some useful operations with the data.

Sorting and Indexing Your Data

When you enter records into a database file, dBASE stores the records in the same order you entered them—from first to last. As databases grow larger, you may want to see the records in an order that differs from the original order. dBASE provides two ways to accomplish this reordering: sorting and indexing.

By using the SORT command, you can sort the records in a database. The SORT command, however, doesn't place the sorted records back into the original database file. Rather, when you tell dBASE to sort a database file, you also must provide the name of a second (new) database file. The new file has the same structure and contains the same records as the original file, but these records are in a different order. Figure 1.4 shows the records in the same database used in figure 1.1; however, the records now are sorted on the TITLE field.

1

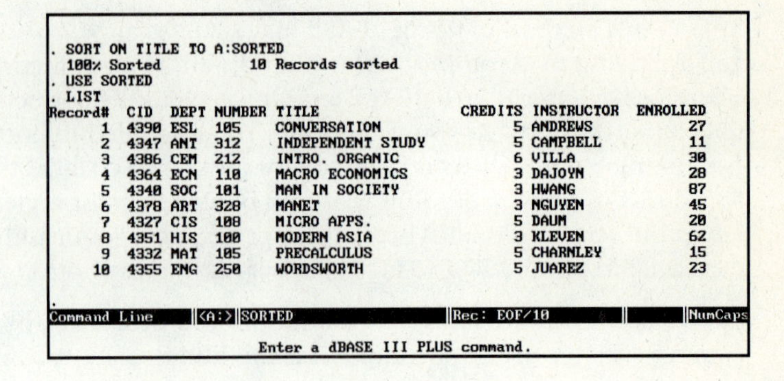

```
. SORT ON TITLE TO A:SORTED
  100% Sorted           10 Records sorted
. USE SORTED
. LIST
Record#  CID  DEPT NUMBER TITLE                        CREDITS INSTRUCTOR  ENROLLED
      1  4390 ESL  105    CONVERSATION                       5 ANDREWS           27
      2  4347 ANT  312    INDEPENDENT STUDY                  5 CAMPBELL          11
      3  4386 CEM  212    INTRO. ORGANIC                     6 VILLA             30
      4  4364 ECN  110    MACRO ECONOMICS                    3 DAJOYN            28
      5  4340 SOC  101    MAN IN SOCIETY                     3 HWANG             87
      6  4378 ART  328    MANET                              3 NGUYEN            45
      7  4327 CIS  108    MICRO APPS.                        5 DAUM              20
      8  4351 HIS  100    MODERN ASIA                        3 KLEVEN            62
      9  4332 MAT  105    PRECALCULUS                        5 CHARNLEY          15
     10  4355 ENG  250    WORDSWORTH                         5 JUAREZ            23

.
Command Line    <A:> SORTED            Rec: EOF/10              NumCaps

                    Enter a dBASE III PLUS command.
```

Fig. 1.4
The database file sorted by the TITLE field.

To illustrate the use of sorting, consider the kind of database that a college might maintain. A database file at a college usually contains student records in the order that the students registered at the school. By using the SORT command, the registrar can create two additional database files. The first file can contain the student records in order by name. The records in the second file can be sorted in Social Security number order. The registrar doesn't need to reenter the student data because the SORT command creates a new file from the records in the original file.

Sorting is a straightforward solution to the need for maintaining database records in different orders. However, sorting also can create some big problems. To understand why, suppose that a student comes to the registrar with a change of address. The registrar is busy and neglects to make the change to all the (sorted) files. Now, an error exists in the school's database.

Over time, this problem grows. Years of experience with databases have proven that people constantly forget to add records, delete records, or update records in one of the files. Eventually, several errors exist in each file, and no files are correct. In addition, accurate storage of data is one of the most important reasons that people use computer databases. Another disadvantage of sorting is that if you add new records to a file, you must sort the file again—creating a new file—and you must remember to delete the old file, because one or more records are missing. You will find that the files multiply rapidly and soon fill your disks.

Indexing is another way to maintain database records in different orders. Indexing involves creating an *index file* that tells dBASE the order in which you want to see the records in a database file. This method enables you to have, and update, just one database file but still see the records in different sorted orders. When you use a database with an index file, the database appears in order of the field used to create the index. Index files are not database files and are useful only when used with the database from which they were created. However, index files give you the same flexibility and functionality as the Sort command with none of the drawbacks. As you will see, indexes have an additional use when you need to find a particular record quickly in a large database. Index files are covered in detail in Chapter 6.

Searching a Database

When a database grows larger than about fifty records, asking the database program to search for records is more accurate and efficient than looking through the data yourself. Because most databases contain many hundreds or thousands of records, the capability of the program to find and display quickly an individual record or a group of records is essential.

dBASE has several ways to find records, which are explained in following chapters. You need to use the program to locate records in two general situations. The first situation occurs when you need to locate a particular record in the database only if this one record contains the information you need. This situation is analogous to searching for one book in a library. You also will search for a specific record when you need to delete the record or to modify the record's contents.

The second situation in which you use dBASE to search for data occurs when you need to answer a query. A query is a question you ask dBASE about the data in a database file—for example, "Which of our customers are located in Chicago?" To get an answer, you provide dBASE III Plus with a description of the information you need from a database file, and dBASE III Plus finds, extracts, and displays the information. In database terms, the preceding example question can be expressed as "List all the records in this database that have 'Chicago' in their CITY field." The requests you give dBASE for information must be constructed and entered exactly according to dBASE's command syntax, or dBASE cannot understand your request. How to construct requests is explained in following chapters. Figure 1.5 shows the result of requesting dBASE to show all the records of the instructor HWANG or VILLA. In this small database, only two records meet the requirements.

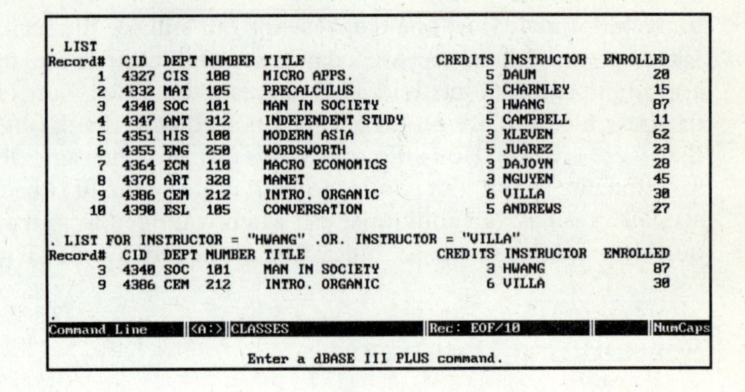

```
. LIST
Record#  CID  DEPT NUMBER TITLE                     CREDITS INSTRUCTOR  ENROLLED
      1  4327 CIS  100    MICRO APPS.                     5 DAUM             20
      2  4332 MAT  105    PRECALCULUS                     5 CHARNLEY         15
      3  4340 SOC  101    MAN IN SOCIETY                  3 HWANG            87
      4  4347 ANT  312    INDEPENDENT STUDY               5 CAMPBELL         11
      5  4351 HIS  100    MODERN ASIA                     3 KLEVEN           62
      6  4355 ENG  250    WORDSWORTH                      5 JUAREZ           23
      7  4364 ECN  110    MACRO ECONOMICS                 3 DAJOYN           28
      8  4378 ART  328    MANET                           3 NGUYEN           45
      9  4386 CEM  212    INTRO. ORGANIC                  6 VILLA            30
     10  4390 ESL  105    CONVERSATION                    5 ANDREWS          27

. LIST FOR INSTRUCTOR = "HWANG" .OR. INSTRUCTOR = "VILLA"
Record#  CID  DEPT NUMBER TITLE                     CREDITS INSTRUCTOR  ENROLLED
      3  4340 SOC  101    MAN IN SOCIETY                  3 HWANG            87
      9  4386 CEM  212    INTRO. ORGANIC                  6 VILLA            30

.
Command Line     |<A:>|CLASSES            |Rec: EOF/10          |     |NumCaps

                    Enter a dBASE III PLUS command.
```

Fig. 1.5
The result of a search of the Classes database.

Because your information needs can become complicated, dBASE has the capability of recognizing very complex queries provided that they are correctly expressed in a dBASE command. An example of a more complicated query is "Which customers located in Chicago, Detroit, or Indianapolis owe more than $10,000.00 and have a credit rating of Fair or Poor?"

As previously mentioned, the capability of a database program rapidly and accurately to search a large database is a major reason that organizations use computer databases. You will really appreciate database programs only when you have to make the complex queries your boss needs from the large databases found in your workplace. When you are learning to construct queries and locate or extract records in the small databases used in this book, you may become frustrated. You will correctly feel that "I can eyeball this data in less time than it takes me to enter these search commands."

That is the point. When you are learning to conduct a search (query) of a database, you can know that you did it correctly only if you can check the result by *eyeballing* the database—a check that is impossible with a large database. You must practice with this book's small databases and verify the results so that, in the "real world," you can have absolute confidence in the correctness of your dBASE search commands. If you enter the proper command, you can be certain that dBASE does not make errors.

Creating Reports and Mailing Labels

A useful capability in dBASE III Plus is the capability of printing reports and mailing labels. A dBASE III Plus *report* creates a printed document from the data in one or more database files. These reports are more professional and businesslike than a standard dBASE printout. With a report, you can print your database records formatted to look the way you want. Reports are useful because they present database file data in a form that everyone can understand. Reports can be distributed in an organization or mailed to other locations. Reports also are a printed record of the data contained in a database file on a certain date (see fig. 1.6).

```
Page No.      1
02/14/94
                                    CLASS  LISTING
                                 SPRING  QUARTER  1994
                                     QUE  COLLEGE

CLASS
 ID           COURSE                CREDIT   INSTRUCTOR        NUMBER
NUMBER        TITLE                  HOURS      NAME          ENROLLED


4327    MICRO APPS.                      5 DAUM                    20
4332    PRECALCULUS                      5 CHARNLEY                15
4340    MAN IN SOCIETY                   3 HWANG                   87
4347    INDEPENDENT STUDY                5 CAMPBELL                11
4351    MODERN ASIA                      3 KLEVEN                  62
4355    WORDSWORTH                       5 JUAREZ                  23
4364    MACRO ECONOMICS                  3 DAJOYN                  28
4378    MANET                            3 NGUYEN                  45
4386    INTRO. ORGANIC                   6 VILLA                   30
4390    CONVERSATION                     5 ANDREWS                 27
*** Total ***
                                        43                        348
```

Fig. 1.6
A simple report.

You create these reports by using the dBASE custom report designer. Creating a *report format file* with the dBASE III Plus report designer is a highly visual and interactive process. You see the layout of the report on-screen as you work. You can see how the report will look with the real data in your database file. When you finish this book, you will have created and printed several reports of your own.

You are familiar with computer-generated mailing labels. You see them on the letters, magazines, and advertisements that you receive in the mail. Usually, these labels are produced by using a database program, and dBASE can perform this task. You probably have already received mail addressed to you by dBASE. If you have a database file that contains names and addresses, dBASE III Plus can print each name and address on a separate mailing label. You explain to dBASE how to print the labels by creating a *label format file*. You then can print the data by using the format you defined. Of course, your printer also must be loaded with the standard-size sheets of detachable mailing labels available in office supply stores. In Chapter 8, you learn how to create a label format file and print names and addresses. For practice, however, you probably will use ordinary printer paper rather than special mailing label forms.

Retrieving Related Data from Multiple Databases

Previously in this chapter, you were introduced to the concept of relational databases. dBASE III Plus, as you now know, can link related records in multiple database files. For dBASE to link records, you must have designed your database structures with the appropriate common (link) fields. You can use these link fields in two ways in dBASE—you can use the dBASE Join command, or you can create a view.

When you use the Join command, you create a new database file. This file results from the Join operation and contains fields from all related records in the two original database files that you joined. You can use the resulting joined database file as you use other dBASE database files—you can even join the file to a third database if the proper link fields were designed into the databases. The design of link fields in database files is discussed in greater depth in Chapter 9.

A *view file* also can link two database files by using a common field. You can create and use the view file to display and edit records from more than one database file at a time. You can also print the view file data in a report. Views, however, are not databases. A *view* is a way of seeing the data in one or more files and cannot be joined with database files. In Chapter 9, you learn how to extract related information from multiple database files by using both the Join command and view files. You also see in greater detail how to design databases with link fields and what the term "related information in separate database files" means.

Modifying the Structure of a Database File

Creating a good database design often is a trial-and-error process. You must test your "first cut" at a database structure by adding data and then actually using the database. During this testing phase, you notice what you need to change in the structure. You may need to add, delete, or rename fields. The order of the fields in a record may not be the most useful order. You may need to increase the size of a field because the data items you need to store in the field are longer than expected.

dBASE enables you to make these kinds of changes to the structure of an existing database file, so you are not locked into your initial database structure. By fine-tuning a structure, you can develop a database that meets all your information needs. You restructure a dBASE database file by using the Modify Structure command. When you use this command, however, you must consider whether modifying the structure will cause data stored in the old structure to be lost. Chapter 5 explains how to restructure a dBASE database and how to avoid losing data you have already entered into the database.

dBASE includes some tools that may be useful when you are either modifying the structure of a database or modifying the actual data contained in a database. These tools are the Copy command and the Rename command. You learn how to use these commands later in this text, and you also learn why these commands are so useful.

Remember that a big advantage of databases is that you can consolidate all your data into a few database files. This consolidation helps you to be organized and efficient because the data is not scattered about in various locations. This centralization, however, has a potential downside—all your eggs are in one basket. You can retain all the benefits of a database *and* protect against a disastrous data loss by creating backup copies of all your database files. You can keep these backup copies on the same disk as the originals, or you can copy them to a different disk. To back up a database file quickly, you use the Copy command. To avoid duplicating a file name, you can use the Rename command.

Creating Custom Data Entry Screens

You enter data into a dBASE III Plus database file by typing data in a data entry form. By default, dBASE produces an on-screen data entry form every time you enter—either through the Assistant or the dot prompt—a command signaling dBASE that you want to add data. This form is taken from the structure of the database file you are using. After *you* create a database, you know what each field name means and what data needs to be entered in the field. However, the rules for naming dBASE fields, as you learn in the next chapter, limit the names you can use for fields. Other people—for example, other office workers—may be confused when they need to enter data or edit data in a database you created.

To make data entry and editing easier for others who use your database, dBASE has the Screen Painter. This feature enables you to create a customized on-screen data entry form for a database. You can use field names with which other office staff members are familiar. You can control the layout of the on-screen form. You can re-create on-screen a paper form used in your office, and your staff can fill in the blanks, just as they do with the old paper form. Using the Screen Painter to create custom on-screen forms is not discussed in this text. If you want to create a custom data entry screen, consult the dBASE III Plus documentation. Figure 1.7 shows a custom data entry screen created by using the Screen Painter.

1

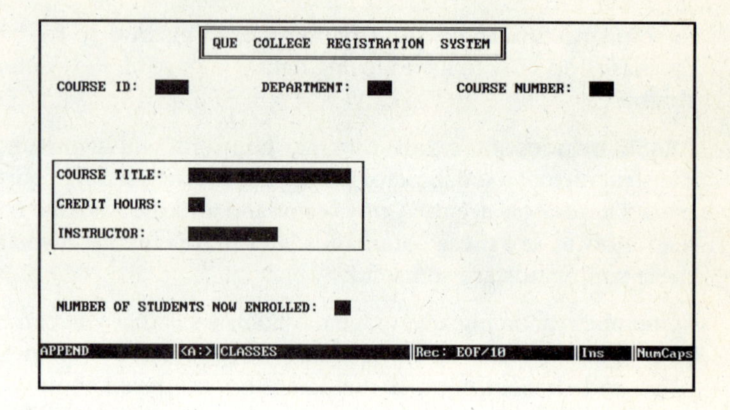

Fig. 1.7 A custom data entry screen for the Classes database.

Chapter Summary

This overview chapter introduces you to dBASE III Plus and some capabilities of this program. You have learned what a database is and what a database program like dBASE III Plus can do for you. dBASE III Plus is sophisticated and powerful with a myriad of capabilities. *dBASE III Plus SmartStart* introduces the main features of dBASE III Plus.

Now that you have read this overview, you are ready to learn more about the specific commands and features of the program. In the following chapter, you start dBASE. You then learn how to use the Assistant menus to create a database file structure and enter data into the database. Finally, you quit dBASE and save your data.

Testing Your Knowledge

True/False Questions

1. A database file consists of records that contain the same fields.
2. dBASE III Plus is referred to as a *hierarchical* database program.
3. Data in a dBASE III Plus database is stored in a query file.
4. dBASE III Plus can print reports that contain data taken from an index file.
5. After a dBASE III Plus database file is created, it cannot be restructured.

Multiple-Choice Questions

1. Custom data entry forms are created by using (the) _________.
   a. Screen Painter
   b. Form Generator
   c. CUSTOM command
   d. none of these answers
2. A(n) _________ can be used to display the data in a database file in a sorted order.
   a. query
   b. index
   c. view
   d. none of these answers
3. A relational database consists of a group of linked _________.
   a. extensions
   b. reports
   c. QBEs
   d. database files
4. Database files can be linked by a common ___________.
   a. object
   b. mode
   c. field
   d. record
5. The command that is used to link two database files that contain a common field is (the) ________.
   a. Query command
   b. Link command
   c. Match command
   d. none of these answers

1

Fill-in-the-Blank Questions

1. A _______ is an organized collection of related data.
2. The _______ is a system of menus designed to help you learn to use dBASE III Plus.
3. Each data item contained in a database record is stored in a ______.
4. Each record is one ______ of a database file.
5. The ________ of a database file defines the field names, field types, and field sizes.

Designing and Creating a Database File with dBASE III Plus

2

In Chapter 1, you were introduced to the concepts involved in setting up a database with dBASE III Plus. You also were given a quick overview of some dBASE III Plus capabilities and of the topics covered in this text.

In this chapter, you learn how to start dBASE III Plus, create a database file structure, and exit from dBASE. In Chapter 3, you add data to your database file.

Objectives

1. To Understand How DOS Organizes Disk Storage
2. To Start dBASE III Plus
3. To Understand the dBASE III Plus Assistant
4. To Create a Database File's Structure
5. To List On-Screen and Print the Database File's Structure
6. To Exit from dBASE III Plus

7. To Understand the Rules for Naming dBASE III Plus Fields and Files
8. To Understand the Types of dBASE III Plus Fields
9. To Understand the Guidelines for Designing a Database File

Key Terms in This Chapter	
DOS	Your computer's operating system, which loads dBASE into a computer's internal memory (RAM) and stores and retrieves disk files.
Directory	A specific location on a disk in which files are stored.
Default disk	The disk drive on which files are stored unless you specify another drive.
Default directory	The disk directory in which files are stored unless you specify another directory.
Menu	A list of options from which you select the operation or command you want.
Selection bar	A highlight that you can move in menus. When the selection bar is on a menu choice, pressing ↵Enter causes dBASE to execute an operation or command.
Link field	A field that occurs in more than one table and is used to extract (join) related records from the tables.

Objective 1: To Understand How DOS Organizes Disk Storage

Before you can use dBASE and save database files, you need to know the proper commands to tell the operating system to begin running the dBASE III Plus program. You also need to understand, after you created the file, the concept of disk drives and directories in order to save a database file. When dBASE was installed on your system or network, the person who installed dBASE placed dBASE on a disk drive in a directory.

The person who installed dBASE also established a default drive and directory in which to store files that you create. The installer can choose from many possible ways to place the program on your hard disk. For this reason, the manner in which you start the program or where you are supposed to store your files may not match the methods covered in this text. Your instructor can explain how dBASE was installed on your system. After you start dBASE III Plus, the program will run essentially the same regardless of the installation method.

Ask your instructor for the steps you follow to start dBASE and for the drive and directory where you should save files. For future reference, write this information in the space provided below:

You start dBASE by:

You save your files by:

Drives and Directories

DOS, the operating system that dBASE uses, organizes the storage space on a disk into areas known as *directories*. Properly used, directories can help you keep groups of programs and files separate and can impose order on the mass of files that you accumulate over time. When you are not the one who set up the directories on your hard disk, however, programs and files may be hard to find. You know that the program is on the computer and you saved the file—but you don't know where the file was placed.

To understand what a directory is, consider the following analogy: Consider a directory on a disk as one drawer in a filing cabinet. Suppose that you want to get a file folder at work. First, you have to find the correct file cabinet. Next, you must locate the correct drawer in the cabinet. Finally, you need to search the drawer for the file. Then, after you finish working with the materials in the file and you want to clear it from your desk and save it, you open the appropriate drawer and replace the file.

Computers have multiple disk drives (A, B, and C, for example) that function like separate filing cabinets. Often, the disk is subdivided into directories, like the file drawers in the analogy. On a computer disk, however, you can have directories (drawers) inside directories. Where your file is stored—often a series of directories inside directories—is referred to as the *path* to your file. Just as you cannot see where a file is in a file cabinet until you open the proper drawer, you cannot see a disk file until you look in the proper directory.

Occasionally, a disk may not have been subdivided into directories, and all your files will be stored in one common area. You may decide not to create, for example, directories on your personal diskette. Then you can indicate that you want a file only from the A or B drive without mentioning a directory. As I explain shortly, dBASE always signals which drive is the *default drive* (where your files will be stored).

If you need to change the default drive, you can select the Set **D**rive command. This command is found in the Assistant's Tools menu. When you select the Set **D**rive command, dBASE displays a list of the drives on your system. You can then use ↑ and ↓ to place the highlight on the correct drive. You press ↵Enter to make this drive the default drive. You can store the file in any directory you want when you name and save the file. But don't forget where you stored a file, because when you need to retrieve it, you must to tell dBASE where to look to find it.

Objective 2: To Start dBASE III Plus

Before you can use dBASE, you must ask DOS to load and begin to execute the program. Usually, dBASE is installed in a directory named DBASE on your computer hard disk drive. The hard drive is referred to by DOS as the C drive. Usually, instructors want their students to save all files on a floppy disk in drive A. This text assumes that you are saving files on drive A. If you are not saving to drive A, make sure that you substitute the proper drive designator in your commands.

If you use the A or B disk drives, before you start dBASE, make sure that you have a formatted disk in the proper drive. In a following section of this chapter, you print the contents of a database file. Make sure that the printer is turned on, on-line, and loaded with paper.

Exercise 2.1: Starting dBASE

To start dBASE, follow these steps:

1. Follow the instructions that your instructor gives you for starting dBASE.
2. If you started dBASE correctly, you see a short license agreement message from Ashton-Tate (see fig. 2.1). You then can press Enter, or wait about 10 seconds for the message to disappear.

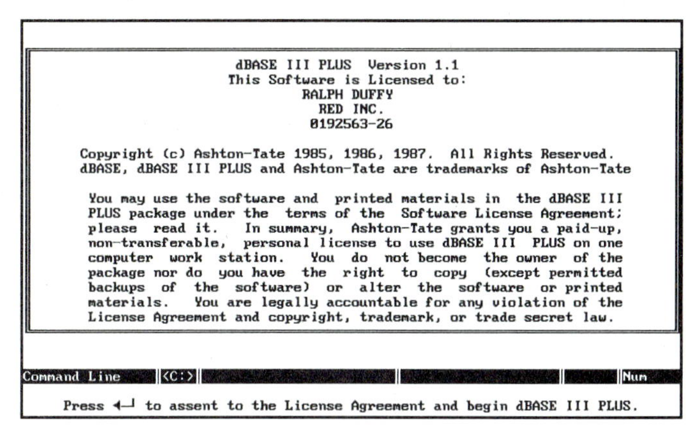

Fig. 2.1 The license agreement screen.

3. When dBASE is ready to use, the screen looks like figure 2.2.

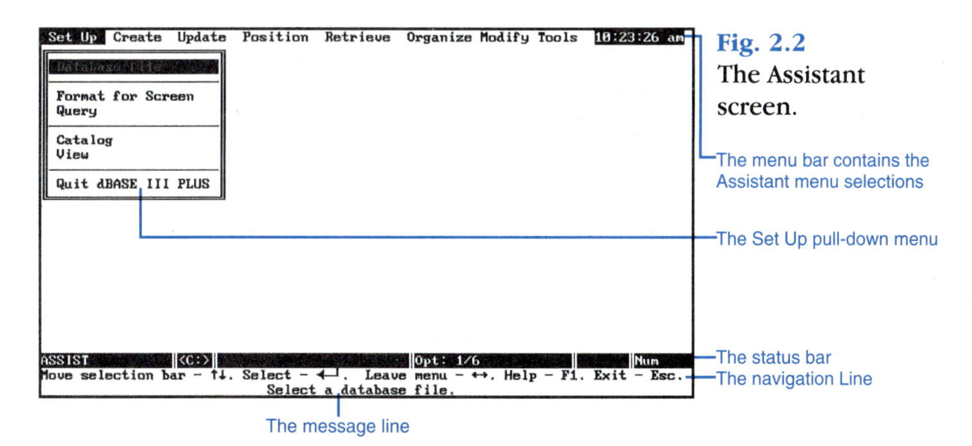

Fig. 2.2 The Assistant screen.

Objective 3: To Understand the dBASE III Plus Assistant

The Assistant is an optional system of menus that you use to create a database file, print the file, and quit dBASE (returning control of the computer to DOS). A *menu* is list of options from which you select the operation or command you want. You make the selection by using the arrow keys to place the highlighted selection bar on the menu choice. Then you press ↵Enter. The menu bar lists the names of the menus available in the Assistant (refer to fig. 2.2). Only one menu can be open at a time. All the Assistant menus are shown on the inside front cover of this text. You can use some menu choices only if you have opened a database file (in dBASE terms, if a database file is *in use*).

Pull-down menus are covered in this section. To open a menu, you move the selection bar highlight on to the choice. Notice that a highlighted selection bar appears over the Set Up choice in the menu bar (refer to fig. 2.2). This menu is now open, and you can see the related pull-down menu. All the choices in the pull-down menu are available. Notice that the selection bar highlight is on the Database File choice in the pull-down menu. This menu choice is discussed in Chapter 3, "Adding and Editing Database Records."

Remember that you can exit from the Assistant to the dot prompt by pressing Esc. If you accidentally switch to the dot prompt, you can display the Assistant again by pressing F2. If you accidentally quit dBASE, you have to start dBASE again before you can use the Assistant. If you make the wrong choice from an Assistant menu, pressing Esc usually "backs you out" from the choice. When you use the Assistant, remember that the function of the highlighted menu choice is explained in the message line at the bottom of the screen. When you first use the Assistant, you should work slowly and check the message line before you make a menu selection (press ↵Enter).

One of the most important on-screen areas to watch is the white bar across the bottom of your screen. This area is the status bar, which is always displayed in dBASE. In figure 2.2, you can see the message, `ASSIST`, on the far left side of the status bar. This area is the mode indicator which, at this point, tells you that you are in the Assistant. The mode indicator changes as you change modes in dBASE. In the next status bar section to the right, `<C:>` is displayed because, at the time the figure was created, the default (or active) disk drive was drive C. Unless you specified otherwise, dBASE saves on drive C a database file that you create. If you tell dBASE to open an existing file, dBASE looks for the file on drive C unless you specify another drive.

The area of the status bar just to the right of the drive indicator is where the name of the database file that you are using appears. Because no database file is currently open, this area is blank. The other area of the status bar that you will find useful is at the far right. In figure 2.2, the status bar contains `Num` in this area, which means that the keys in the numeric keypad at the right end of your keyboard will enter numbers when pressed. If the number lock is off, some of the keys in the numeric keypad function as cursor-movement keys. When Caps Lock is on, the word `Caps` appears at the far right of the status bar.

The action line is displayed immediately above the status bar (refer to fig. 2.4). The Navigation line and the message line are below the status bar.

Keep checking these areas of the screen as you work in dBASE. If you find yourself asking the following questions, you usually get the answers by looking at the four lines at the bottom of your screen:

- What do I do next?
- What mode am I in?
- What database, if any, is in use?
- What does this Assistant menu choice do?

Exercise 3.1: Exploring the Assistant Menu

To learn how to move through the Assistant menus, follow these steps:

1. Press → to highlight the Create menu. Notice that the message in the message line changes.
2. Continue to press →, noting which menu choices are unavailable because no database file is in use.
3. Keep pressing →, moving the cursor until it returns to the Set Up menu.
4. Press Esc. The Assistant menus disappear, and the dot prompt appears at the lower left of the screen.
5. Press F2 to return to the Assistant.

Objective 4: To Create a Database File's Structure

This section shows you how to get started quickly and easily with dBASE. You design a Customer database step by step. (The tasks and concepts to which you are introduced are discussed in greater detail in a following section of this chapter.)

Specifying the Field Name, Type, and Size

The dBASE field name, type, and width enable you to specify both the type of data a field can contain and, in some cases, the length of the data. dBASE uses the field type you specify in the table's structure to determine how to store and display the data you later enter in the field. These field types and the kind of data that you can store in them are described in a following section of this chapter.

The Database File

The basic building block of a dBASE database system is the database file. Without the database file, the other files, such as forms, views, and reports, are useless. dBASE stores data in database files. Each database file contains records, which are made up of fields. A dBASE database file is similar in structure to a spreadsheet or grid—all records are stored in rows; fields are stored in columns.

Entering information into a database file is similar to entering data into the columns of a spreadsheet or using a column format with a word processor. Before you can enter data into a dBASE database file (often referred to as a *table*), you first must name the table and create a structure into which dBASE can place the information. The *structure* of a database file tells dBASE how to store the data in the database file. The structure contains the names of the fields in the database file and tells dBASE what type of data can be stored in each field. To indicate to dBASE which type of data a field will contain, you enter a field type in the database file's structure. For some field types, you also need to indicate how long (how many characters) you want the data field to be.

The process of naming fields, indicating the type and (if necessary) the size of a field is known as *defining*, or creating, the database file's structure. dBASE database files can contain character (alphanumeric) data, numeric data that is used in arithmetic calculations, and dates. dBASE has five field types. These field types are discussed in detail in a following section of this chapter.

Creating the Structure of Your First Database

Now you are ready to create the structure of your first database file. Assume that the owner of a small mail order service wants to keep information about her customers. She wants to keep a record of the name, the address, the date of last purchase, and the amount of purchase for each customer. She decides to name the database file Customer. You already have designed the structure of the database that she will use (see table 2.1); you need only to create the file. In a later section of this chapter, you learn the rules for naming a database file and for naming fields. Later in this chapter, you also learn how to decide the type and the size of fields.

Table 2.1 The Structure of the dBASE III Plus Database File: Customer

Field	*Field Name*	*Type*	*Width*	*Dec*
1	LAST	Character	8	
2	FIRST	Character	6	
3	STREET	Character	10	
4	CITY	Character	8	
5	STATE	Character	2	
6	ZIP	Character	5	
7	DATE	Date	8	
8	AMOUNT	Numeric	6	2

For now, concentrate on learning how to create the structure of this database file. Work slowly and carefully. As with any unfamiliar computer program, avoiding mistakes is easier than correcting them. When you see a new display on-screen, take time to look around in the screen and become familiar with the display before you begin to work. As mentioned previously, this text assumes that your instructor wants you to save files on the A drive.

Exercise 4.1: Creating a Database File

Note: This exercise is long and has many steps. Please read through the exercise to make sure that you understand what you need to do before you begin this exercise. Make sure that you have a formatted disk in the drive on which you plan to store files.

To create the Customer database structure, follow these steps:

1. Move the menu bar selection bar highlight over the Create choice. The pull-down menu appears with the Database file choice highlighted (see fig. 2.3).

   The message line displays `Create a database file structure.`

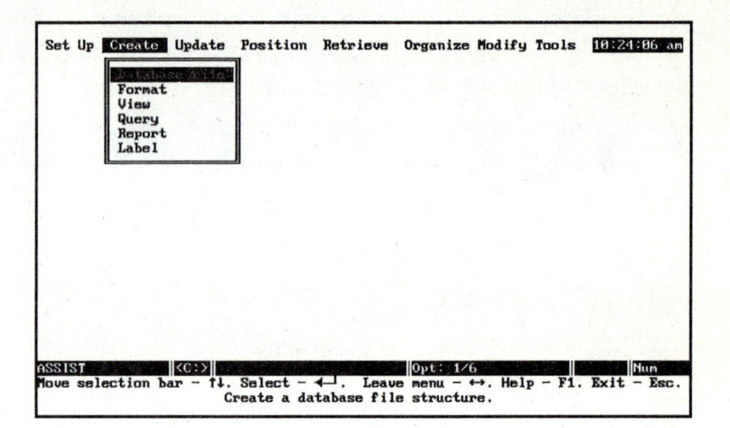

Fig. 2.3 The Create pull-down menu.

2. Press ↵Enter to tell dBASE that you want to create a database file.

   Now dBASE needs to know which disk drive you want to use. dBASE displays the drive selection submenu (see fig. 2.4). The disk drives listed in the submenu depend on the number of disk drives you have on your system.

3. Using the cursor-movement arrow keys, place the highlight on `A:` if it is not already highlighted.

   The message line displays `Select a disk drive to search.`

4. With the highlight on `A:`, press ↵Enter.

   Now dBASE needs to know the name of the file you are creating.

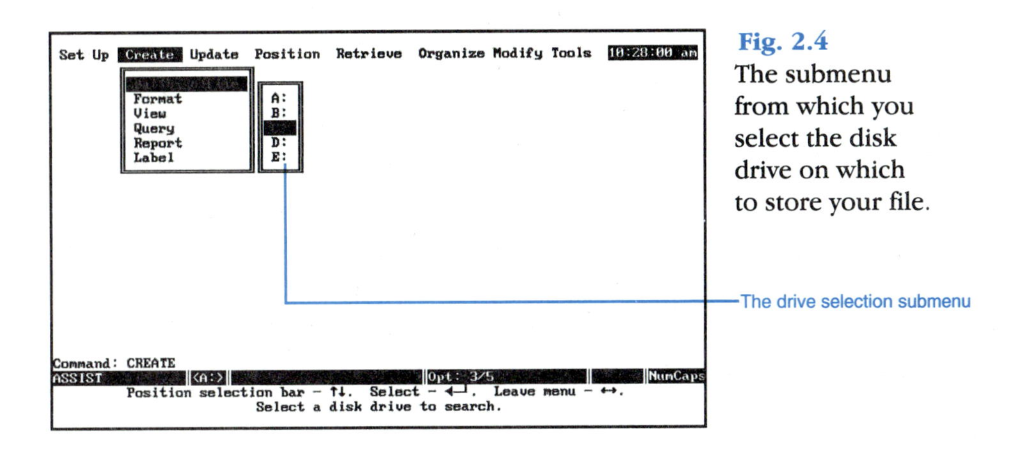

Fig. 2.4 The submenu from which you select the disk drive on which to store your file.

5. Type **Customer**. Check to see that you typed the name correctly. If you made an error, use ←Backspace to delete the error, and then retype the name.

   Notice the dot prompt command displayed in the action line. Your screen now should resemble figure 2.5.

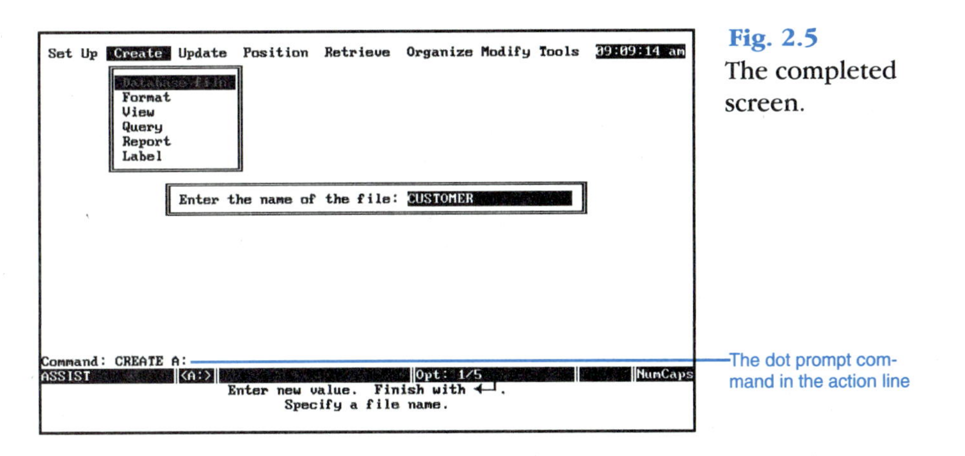

Fig. 2.5 The completed screen.

6. Press ↵Enter.

   The screen that you use to define the structure of the database file is displayed (see fig. 2.6). Notice that the status bar indicates that you are in Create mode, A is the active drive, and the database file is Customer. The display at the top of the screen lists some special keystrokes you may need to use.

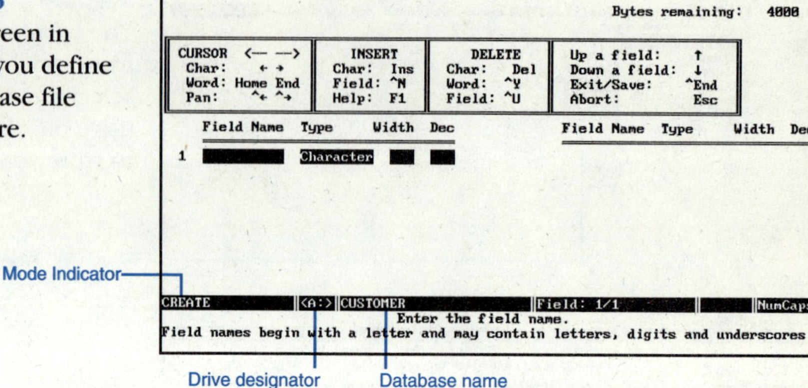

Fig. 2.6 The screen in which you define a database file structure.

The ^ that appears with some keystrokes means that you first press and hold down Ctrl and then press the second key. For example, after you finish defining the structure, you save it by pressing and holding down Ctrl and then pressing End. Then release both keys.

If you have problems defining the structure and just want to discard your work and start over, press Esc. dBASE asks whether if you want to abort the structure definition. Press the Y key and you return to the Assistant.

7. Type **LAST** and press ↵Enter.

   The cursor moves to the Type column.

8. This is a Character type field. Press ↵Enter to enter `Character` in the Type column.

9. The Width of this field is 8; type **8** and press ↵Enter.

   Your first field definition is complete. The cursor moves to the next line (see fig. 2.7).

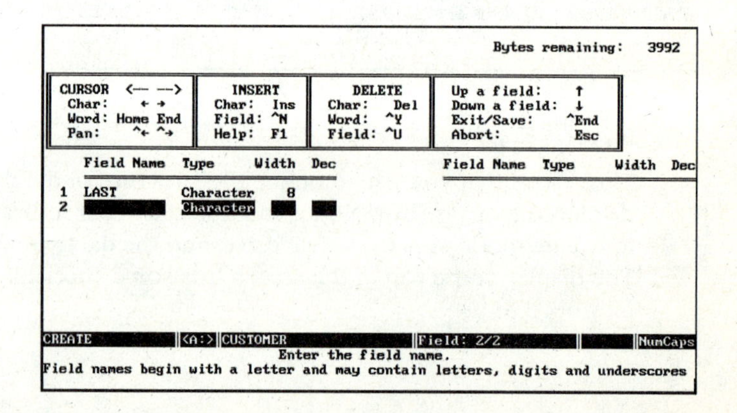

Fig. 2.7 The completed definition of the LAST field.

10. Use the same technique to enter the remaining five Character type fields shown in table 2.1.
11. For the 7th field, DATE, type the field name, and press ↵Enter just as you did for the previous fields. When the cursor moves to the Type column, press the Spacebar twice and the word `Date` appears in the Type column. Press ↵Enter to place `Date` in the Type column.

    Notice that typing a width for a Date type field is unnecessary; dBASE sets the width to 8. The cursor also should move down to the next field.
12. Type the field name **AMOUNT**, and press ↵Enter.
13. Press the Spacebar, and the word `Numeric` should move into the Type column. Press ↵Enter to place `Numeric` in the Type column.
14. Type **6** in the width column, and press ↵Enter. The cursor moves to the Dec (decimals) column.
15. Type **2**, and press ↵Enter.

    Now the screen should resemble figure 2.8. You have finished entering the structure and need to let dBASE know that you are done.
16. Press and hold down Ctrl, and then press End.

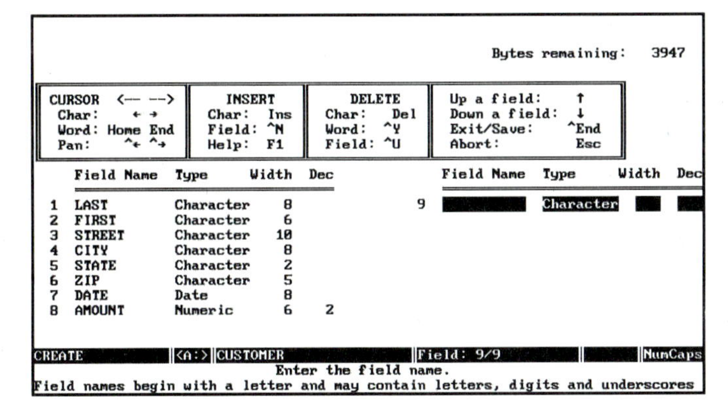

Fig. 2.8 The finished database file structure.

17. The message `Press ENTER to confirm. Any other key to resume` appears under the status bar. Press ↵Enter.

    The screen now should look like figure 2.9.

2

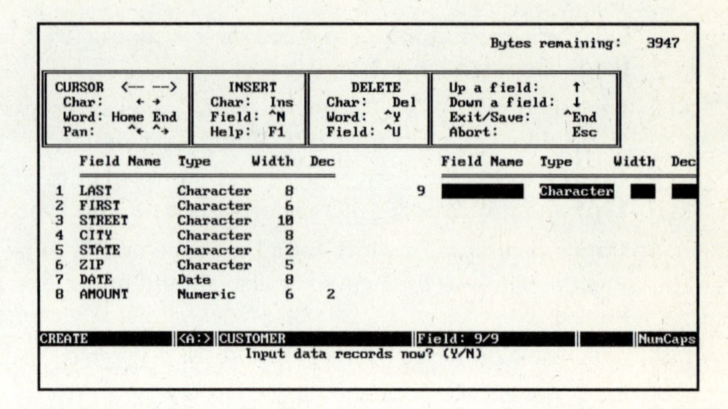

Fig. 2.9
The screen asking whether you have data records to enter.

18. You now have saved the structure of Customer. The message, `Input data records now? [Y/N]` appears. You do not yet have data records to enter, so press N, but *do not* press ↵Enter. When you press N, you are returned to the Assistant, but pressing ↵Enter makes a menu selection.

Objective 5: To List On-Screen and Print the Database File's Structure

In the following exercise, you display the structure of the database on-screen. You often need to do this to remind yourself of a field's name, type, or size when you work with database files.

Exercise 5.1: Listing the Structure of Your Open Database File on the Screen

To display the structure of the database in use (Customer), follow these steps:

1. Move the selection bar highlight to the Tools menu.
2. Move the highlight down to the List Structure command by pressing ↓ (see fig. 2.10).
3. Press ↵Enter to execute the command.

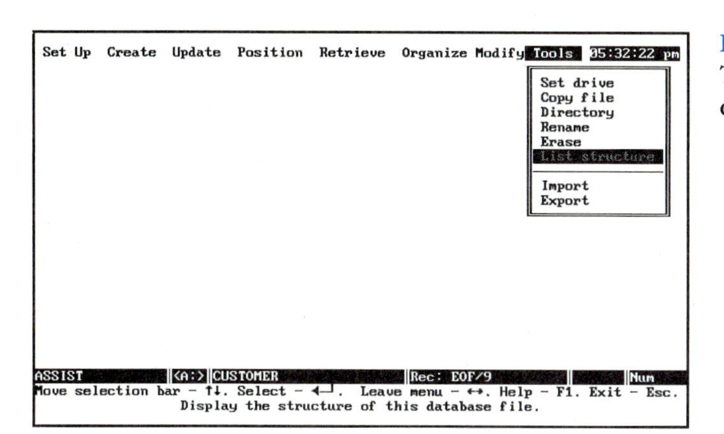

Fig. 2.10
The Tools pull-down menu.

4. The message, `Direct output to the printer? [Y/N]` appears. Because you don't want a printout yet, press N to display the structure on the screen; *don't* press ↵Enter (see fig. 2.11).

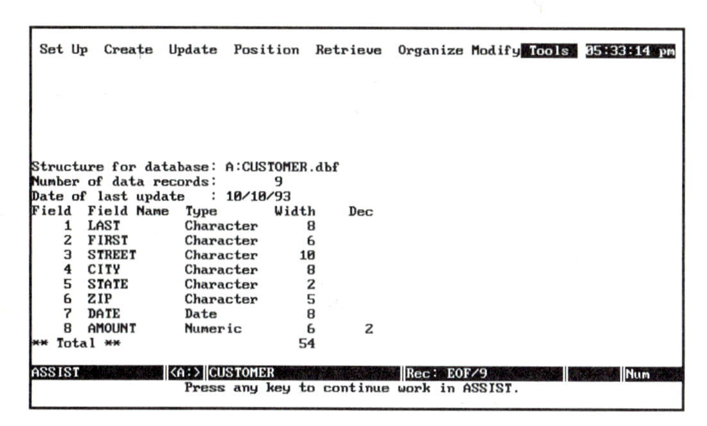

Fig. 2.11
The database file structure listed on-screen.

5. Press any key to clear the screen and return to the Assistant.

Exercise 5.2: Listing Your Database File's Structure On-Screen and on the Printer

Before you begin printing, check with your instructor for any special procedures for printing.

To obtain a printout of the structure of the database in use (Customer), follow these steps:

1. Move the selection bar highlight to the Tools menu.
2. Move the highlight down to the List Structure command by pressing ↓ (refer to fig. 2.10).
3. Press ↵Enter to execute the command.
4. This time, you want a printout. Press Y; *don't* press ↵Enter.
5. Press any key to clear the screen and return to the Assistant.

   Your printer probably cannot eject the page that you printed. You probably need to go immediately to the printer before someone else begins printing on your printout.
6. On the printer, press the On Line button. Press the Form Feed button, which should eject the printout. Press the On Line button again.

Objective 6: To Exit from dBASE III Plus

Now that you have finished your work, you need to exit from dBASE and return to DOS. When you exit from dBASE properly, your data is saved to the disk in drive A; you do not need to save the file with a special command. If you just remove the disk and leave or if you shut off the computer without first quitting dBASE, you probably will lose all or most of your data records.

Exercise 6.1: Quitting dBASE

To exit from dBASE, follow these steps:

1. Move the menu bar selection highlight to the Set Up choice (see fig. 2.12).
2. Use ↓ to move the Set Up menu selection highlight to Quit dBASE III Plus, and press ↵Enter.

   The database file's structure is saved, and you exit dBASE.

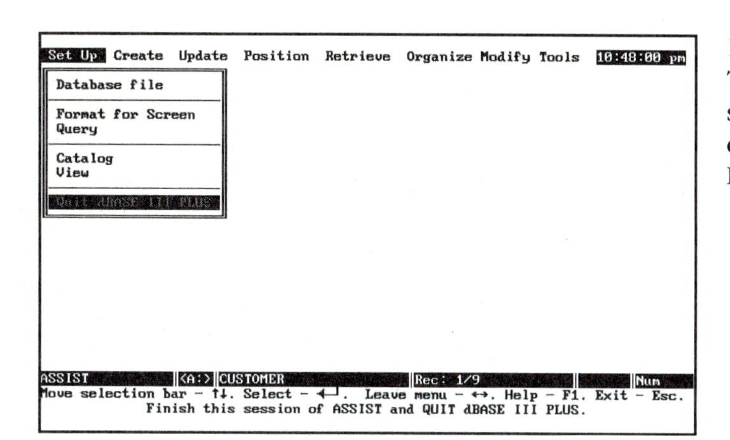

Fig. 2.12 The menu selection to exit dBASE III Plus.

Objective 7: To Understand the Rules for Naming dBASE III Plus Files and Fields

You need to name database files so that both you and the computer can distinguish each individual database. You also need to give names to the individual fields in a database structure just as you did when you created the Customer database. In this way, you can ask dBASE to display the data stored in a particular field because you can refer to the field by name. Field names also are useful column headings when you list the records in a database. dBASE places some restrictions on field names; these restrictions are discussed in the following section.

Naming the Database File

Giving a database file a name that suggests a specific purpose makes the bite much easier to find later on your disk and use. Database file names such as Customer, Invoice, Inventory, or Salary, are more descriptive than File1 or File2.

dBASE requires you to follow these normal DOS conventions when naming a database file:

- Use up to eight characters (the maximum), not including the file extension. By default, dBASE adds the file extension DBF.
- The name can include letters, numbers, and some special characters. Limit the special characters you use to $, &, #, and _.

- Do not use spaces or the following characters: ?, ., /, , or *. These characters are reserved by DOS.
- Do not use a name you gave to another database file. If you use the same name in the same directory, the new database file overwrites the existing database file.

Consult a DOS manual for a more complete discussion of DOS file names.

For the greatest ease of use of your database, store all related database files (linked databases) in one directory. You can retrieve a database file from another directory by typing the complete path and name of the database file's directory, however, if you type the command at the dot prompt.

Naming Fields

Names can have from one to ten characters and can contain letters, numbers, and the underscore character. Although the letter *X* is a valid name for a field, using a single-character name makes it difficult to remember what kind of data the field contains. Choose a field name that describes the data in the field. You also may want to insert an underscore to increase the readability of a name. You can name the inventory part number field Inv_num, for example, rather than Invnum. Do not include blank spaces in a field name.

Each field name in a database file must be unique in the database file; you cannot have two fields with the same name in one database file. You can have up to 128 fields in one database structure. Keep the following rules in mind as you create field names to help simplify your database:

- Make the name descriptive of the field's contents.
- A field name cannot start with a space. In other words, do not press Spacebar before typing anything else.
- A field name must begin with a letter.
- You cannot use two or more words for a field name unless they are separated by an underscore.
- You cannot duplicate a field name in the same database file. Adding spaces at the end doesn't make the names different.
- When creating a database structure, you can type field names in uppercase, lowercase, or mixed case. Field names will always appear in uppercase letters.

Objective 8: To Understand the Types of dBASE III Plus Fields

The field type tells dBASE III the classification of data stored in the field. You can choose one of five data types: Character, Numeric, Date, Logical, or Memo. The field types are listed in table 2.2.

Table 2.2 dBASE Field Types

Type	*Use*
Character	Can contain letters, numbers, and special characters (such as $, %, &). If you store phone numbers, ZIP codes, or Social Security numbers, these numbers contain parentheses and hyphens and should be stored in a Character field. Numbers stored in a Character field cannot be used in calculations. A size must be specified (1 to 254).
Numeric	Contains numbers used in calculations. A size of from 1 to 19 must be specified. The minus sign and the decimal place each occupy one position and must be included when determining the field size.
Date	Contains a valid calendar date. Use this data type for all dates. dBASE establishes 8 as the field width.
Logical	For True/False or Yes/No responses. You can type the data value as upper- or lowercase: T (True), F (False), Y (Yes), or N (No). dBASE establishes 1 as the field width.
Memo	Text information too long to be stored in a Character field. Memos are stored in a separate file. A memo field can contain 5,000 characters of data in the separate file. In the database file's structure, dBASE establishes 10 as the field width.

Specifying a Field Width

A field should be just wide enough to hold the largest possible value; otherwise, you waste space when you display data on-screen or print reports. Use the field width specification to indicate the maximum number of characters or digits a field can hold. You must specify widths for the Character and Numeric types; dBASE supplies the widths for the Date, Logical, and Memo fields. The following list shows the length requirements:

- *Character:* Enter a field width as narrow as 1 or as wide as 254. Field content can include any ASCII character.
- *Numeric:* Enter a field width between 1 and 19. Remember that the minus sign and the decimal place each occupy one position and must be included when determining the field size. For example, –987.65 requires a field width of 7. You must indicate the number of decimal places (Dec) for Numeric fields. The number of decimal places must be at least two places fewer than the specified width of the field.
- *Date and Logical:* dBASE III supplies a Date field width of 8 and a Logical field width of 1. Dates appear in the format *mm/dd/yy* (*month/day/year*), such as 01/24/94.
- *Memo:* dBASE III supplies a field width of 10. Although the field in the record displays only the word `Memo`, dBASE III can store a large document in a special memo file linked by dBASE to your database file. You can toggle between the two files when viewing or editing data. We explain how to do this in Chapter 5, "Restructuring a Database File."

Objective 9: To Understand the Guidelines for Designing a Database File

Planning the Database File Structure

The first step in implementing an electronic database management system is to design the database on paper, based on discussions with others who may use the system. Resist the urge to sit at the keyboard and begin creating the database structure before you plan carefully what you want to do with the data. This section discusses database design techniques that you can follow when creating a database structure.

As you begin the design process for a dBASE database, the first step is to think about all the information, or fields, you need in each record. Before you create the new database, plan the database file. Sit down with a pad of paper and a pencil and answer the following questions:

What information do I now keep? How is it used? How is it kept?

What problems am I now having with my information system?

Is updating or changing records difficult?

Do I have problems finding records?

Do I have a tough time consolidating information?

What information do I need from my data?

The answers to these questions and others you may think of can help you plan the database file's structure.

Suppose that you want to create a database to track vehicle sales to customers of a car dealership. You can think of obvious pieces of data (fields) to include in this database. A customer database obviously includes fields of names, addresses, vehicle descriptions, and amounts charged.

Setting the Database Objective

After consulting with end users of the proposed database, write a clear and concise objective statement that describes the purpose of the database. Try not to describe specific data items or output reports. Consider including who might use the data, what information needs must be met, and how timely the data must be.

Analyzing the Current System

If you already are using a paper or computer database system, use this system as a starting point. A system already in place can indicate what information, expected outputs, and data fields you must have in a similar dBASE III database. Your task may be as simple as automating a manual system with dBASE III or converting from an old computer or outdated software to dBASE III. Begin your dBASE III application error-free by making sure that the old system does what you want before you use it as the basis for the new database design. If the old system doesn't meet your needs, you probably need to redesign the system from scratch.

Describing Desired Outputs

The easiest way to know what data fields should be in a database system is to figure out what the end users want the database to produce. As a beginning, determine what lists, reports, and labels are needed. Writing a brief objective statement about each output can be helpful.

As you plan the structure of your first database file, look at your answers to the preceding questions. If you want to replace some of your paper files with your dBASE database, you can borrow much of your database file's structure from the existing paper forms.

As you design the database file, be thorough. Include all the necessary data, or fields, that you will need. Try not to keep fields you do not use. Remember that you can always modify the structure (restructure) later to add or delete fields.

Try to classify the data into groupings. In the Customer database file you built in this chapter, for example, you used several kinds of data, including name and address data and information concerning purchases. This database is already small, but—to illustrate this point—you can divide this information into two database files—a name-and-address database file and a purchases database file. With dBASE's linking capability, you can tie together two or more database files by using a common field. dBASE can join related information from the two linked database files.

Small Is Better

dBASE is a full-featured database program and has a vast capacity to hold information. As you create your first database, this capacity may tempt you to include all possible fields (pieces of information) in one large database file. When you actually use a database, however, you will find that accessing data is much easier if you have several smaller database files. With dBASE, you can link these database files together when you need to extract related information from two or more database files. Maintaining databases also is easier if the databases consist of several small database files.

The term *small* means that the database files contain only the necessary fields. Keep the design of your database files simple because dBASE has the capacity to link many small database files into a single database. The database file that you created in this chapter—Customer—has eight fields. You probably will find that you can design database files to have around ten fields. As a rule, if you have more than twenty fields in a database file, consider splitting the database file into several linked database files. This practice will make editing, listing, sorting, and searching the database easier for you, and dBASE will perform these operations faster on the smaller database files.

Remember that several small linked database files usually are more useful than a single large database file. Small database files also are helpful when you search for specific information or sort a database file because queries and sort operations work much faster on a small database file than on a large database file. Joining linked database files is discussed in Chapter 9.

As mentioned previously, when you start using a database file, you may see that your original dBASE database file structure needs fine-tuning. Altering the original design of a database file is known as *restructuring*. Although some limitations and cautions exist regarding restructuring a database file, you always can restructure a database file. You can add or delete fields as needed, or you can change field types. Restructuring is discussed in Chapter 5, "Restructuring a Database File."

Chapter Summary

In this chapter, you have learned the techniques of database design and ways to implement a design by using dBASE III Plus. The following projects will reinforce this learning. Many projects in subsequent chapters use the database files that you create here, and completing these projects is strongly recommended. In Chapter 3, "Adding and Editing Database Records," you learn how to enter, edit, and list the records in the Customer database.

Testing Your Knowledge

True/False Questions

1. Each column of a database file is one record.
2. Only numeric fields can contain digits like 98105.
3. The command that enables you to type the structure of a database file is found in the Set Up menu.
4. When possible, data should be stored in one large database file structure.

5. The command that enables you to print the structure of a database file is found in the Output menu.

Multiple-Choice Questions

1. Field type __________ can contain letters, numbers, and many other keyboard characters.
   a. Alpha
   b. Date
   c. Character
   d. none of these answers
2. Which of these field types should be used to store phone numbers?
   a. Character
   b. Number
   c. Memo
   d. Binary
3. dBASE can perform calculations by using the data in a(n) __________ field.
   a. Alphanumeric
   b. Number
   c. Character
   d. none of these answers
4. What is the width of all Date type fields?
   a. 8
   b. 10
   c. whatever you enter for the width
   d. none of these answers
5. To return to the Assistant from the dot prompt, press __________.
   a. F1
   b. F2
   c. Esc
   d. none of these answers

Fill-in-the-Blank Questions

1. A field that occurs in two related tables and can be used to tie together the data in the tables is called a _________ field.
2. A database file name can be a maximum of _________ characters.
3. A field name can be a maximum of _________ characters.
4. A field name _________ (can/cannot) be the same as another field name in a database file's structure.
5. A field name _________ (can/cannot) include spaces.

Review: Short Projects

1. Determining Invalid Database and Field Names
   a. List five database file names that are incorrect for five different reasons. Explain why these names are invalid.
   b. List four field names that are invalid for four different reasons. Explain why these field names are invalid.
2. Creating a Courses Database File for a College

   Create the following database file structure. Name the database Courses. Then print the structure.

Courses Database File			
Field Name	*Type*	*Width*	*Dec*
ITEM	Character	4	
DESCRIPT	Character	30	
ROOM	Character	20	
TAUGHT_BY	Character	30	
ENROLLMENT	Numeric	3	0

3. Creating a Student Database File for a College

   Create the following database file structure. Name the database Student. Then print the structure.

Student Database File		
Field Name	*Type*	*Width*
STUDENT#	Character	11
LAST_NAME	Character	15
FIRST_NAME	Character	10
STREET	Character	20
CITY	Character	15
STATE	Character	2
ZIP	Character	5
PHONE	Character	12
ITEM	Character	4

Review: Long Projects

1. Setting Up a Travel Agency Database

   Andy Cashman is just beginning to establish a Seattle travel agency. Wisely, Andy has decided to computerize the information system by using dBASE III Plus and has contracted you to set up the database.

   a. The first set of data Andy wants on the computer is a listing of the tours that were arranged. Assume that after a consultation, Andy has agreed on the following fields and tour data. You advise Andy that you should establish a link field (Tour Code) so that a table of Clients can be linked with this table, and you won't need to duplicate tour information on the Client records. Andy has written some sample data that will be stored in the completed Tours database file. The cost of the tour should be a Numeric type field. The data is shown in the following table:

The Tours Table					
Tour Code	*Destination*	*Departs*	*Depart*	*Return*	*Cost*
A102	Ireland	Boston	7/19/94	7/26/94	1422.00
A109	Singapore	Portland	6/01/94	6/05/94	1375.00
C101	Cozumel	New Orleans	1/17/95	1/21/95	1995.00

Your task is to establish the dBASE database file structure for Tours and then create the database file that contains the data shown. View the structure on-screen to make sure that the structure is correct. Then print the structure of Tours.

b. The Tours database file will be linked with a second, related file database, Clients, in Chapter 9. Note that the TOUR field in Clients is used to create a link with the Tours database file. The TOUR field is a link field and contains the tour code for the tour the client has booked. Use the following structure to create the Clients database file:

Structure of the Clients Database File		
Field Name	*Field Type*	*Size*
NAME	Character	15
TOUR	Character	4
ADDRESS	Character	15
PHONE	Character	14
INTERESTS	Character	20

View the structure to make sure that it is correct. Then print the structure.

2. Setting Up a Climate Database File

Andy finds that the clients often ask about winter temperatures and the amount of rainfall at their destinations. Andy supplies you with the following sample data and asks you to set up a database file that enables you to access this information quickly when a client requests it. Name the database file Climate. The temperature, precipitation, and elevation fields should be Numeric type fields. View the structure to make sure that is correct. Then print the structure.

The Climate Table					
Station	*Country*	*Jan. Max.*	*Jan. Min.*	*Annual Precip. (in inches)*	*Elevation (in feet)*
Addis Ababa	Ethiopia	75	43	49	8038
Buenos Aires	Argentina	85	63	37	89
Sydney	Australia	78	65	47	62

Adding and Editing Database Records

3

In Chapter 2, you learned about the concepts involved in designing a database using dBASE III Plus. You also created your first dBASE III Plus database file structure and exited from dBASE. In Chapter 3, you add data to the Customer database file that you created in Chapter 2. Then you learn how to list the contents of your database on-screen and at the printer. You learn how to make changes to the fields in your records and delete unneeded records. You find many of the commands discussed in this chapter in the Update menu of the Assistant because adding, editing, and deleting records all involve updating your database.

In this chapter, it is again important to notice the commands that you build as you make selections from the Assistant's menus. In Chapter 4, you leave the Assistant and issue commands from the dot prompt.

Objectives

1. To Open a Database File
2. To Add Data to a Database File by Using the Append Command
3. To Display Data by Using the List Command
4. To Edit Data by Using the Edit Command

5. To View and Edit Data by Using the Browse Command
6. To Delete and Recall Records

Key Terms in This Chapter	
Append	To add to the end; the command used to add records to the end (or bottom) of a dBASE database file.
Edit	To change the data currently stored in a record in the database.

Objective 1: To Open a Database File

When you create the structure of a database file and name the file, you create an organization or pattern for the records in whose fields you will enter data. In the preceding chapter, you created and then stored on disk the structure of the database file, Customer. Before you begin the next exercise, start dBASE by using the method given to you by your instructor. Make sure that the disk on which you stored the Customer file is in a disk drive and the Assistant menus are on-screen. Notice that the status bar shows that no database is in use (see fig. 3.1).

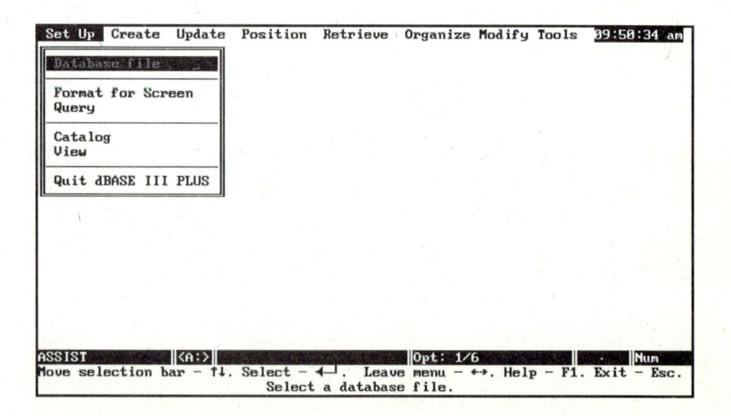

Fig. 3.1
The Assistant screen.

The command to open a database file is found in the Set Up menu. Because opening a database file that was stored on a disk is a common operation that users perform after starting dBASE, the Assistant always starts with this choice (Database File) highlighted (see fig. 3.1); you just have to press Enter.

Remember to look at the message line and the action line to see the command that dBASE is building from your Assistant menu choices. Soon, you will be entering these commands at the dot prompt.

Students often make two understandable mistakes when starting to use dBASE. The first mistake is that they try to use a Retrieve menu command to *get* their database file from storage on disk and open it on-screen. A second common mistake is to try to use the View command in the Set Up menu to see the data records in a file. Appealing as these choices seem, they don't work. To open a database file, you use the Database File choice in the Set Up menu; and, as you see in the following section, you use the List command to display or print database records.

Exercise 1.1: Opening a Database File

To open the Customer database file, take these steps:

1. With the selection bar highlight on the Database File choice (see fig. 3.1), press Enter.
2. dBASE now needs to know which drive the database file is on. So dBASE displays the drive submenu. Use ↑ and ↓ to move the selection bar to the proper drive, and then press Enter (see fig. 3.2).

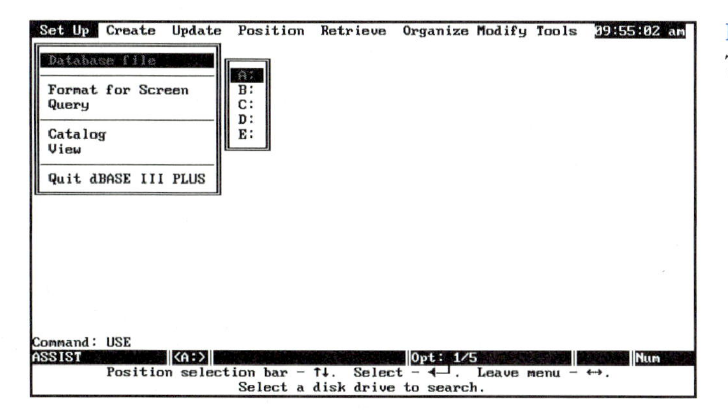

Fig. 3.2
The list of drives.

dBASE now lists the names of the database files located on the drive that you selected. So far, you only have one database file (see fig 3.3).

3. Place the selection bar on CUSTOMER.DBF. Press Enter.

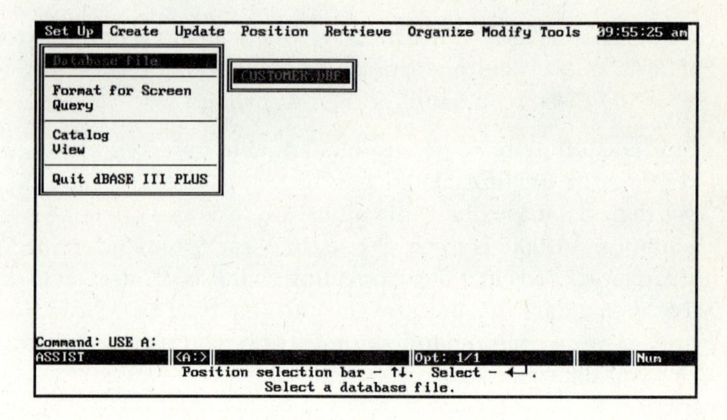

Fig. 3.3 The listing of database files.

Notice the command in the action line.

dBASE now asks whether this database has been indexed (see fig. 3.4). Until you learn about indexes in Chapter 6, always answer No to this question.

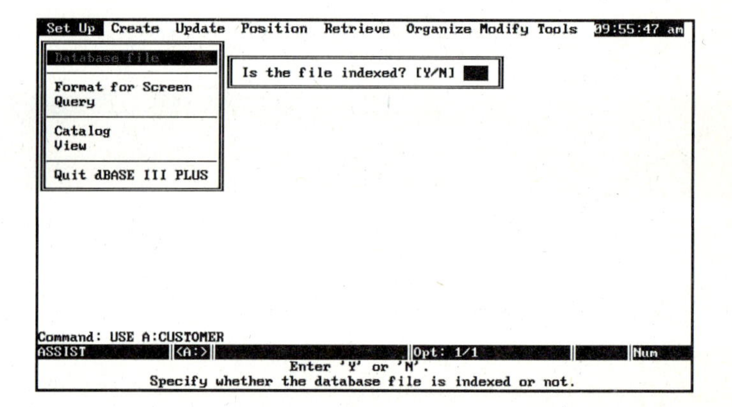

Fig. 3.4 dBASE asking whether the database file is indexed.

4. Type **N**. Do not press ↵Enter.

   The database Customer now is open (The status bar contains the name `CUSTOMER:`), as you see in figure 3.5. You also can see that no records exist in the file because the status bar contains `Rec: None`. You are ready to add some records now.

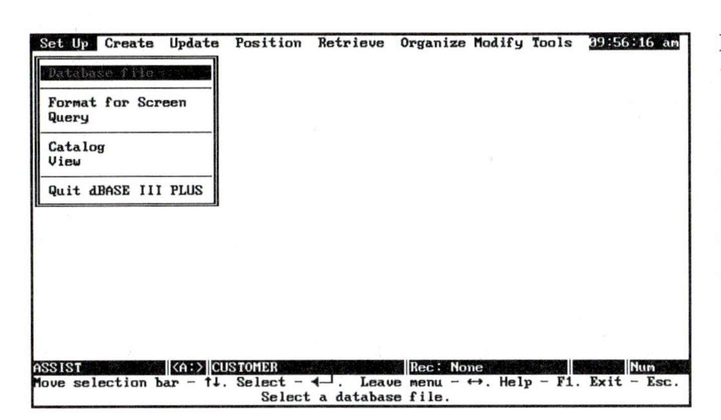

Fig. 3.5 The status bar indicates the name of the database in use and the number of records it contains.

Objective 2: To Add Data to a Database File by Using the Append Command

When you create the structure of a database file and name the file, you create an organization, or pattern, for the records in which you enter data. dBASE uses the structure to create a data entry screen to make entering data records easier. dBASE also uses the structure to perform some screening checks on the data you enter. For example, dBASE makes sure that only digits are entered in Numeric fields and that only valid dates are accepted into Date type fields. If no data is yet available for a field, you can leave the field blank.

A dBASE record can contain up to 128 different fields, and you can store thousands of records in a database file. dBASE's standard method of storing these records is to store each record in the order in which you enter the information. dBASE always remembers the order in which you entered the records by placing a record number (1, 2, 3, and so on) at the far left of a record. When you list the records on-screen or print the records, you see this record number. You can use the record number to refer to a particular record if you want to modify a record's data or to delete the record.

Remember that unless you specify otherwise (a technique you learn in a following chapter), new records are added (appended) to the bottom of the database file. Your Customer database file is empty so that the first record you add will be placed at the top of the file. In a following exercise, you enter nine data records into the Customer database file, which you created in Chapter 2.

3

Exercise 2.1: Selecting the Append Command

To get ready to add records to the Customer file, take these steps:

1. Move the selection bar highlight to the Update menu.

   The Append choice is highlighted (see fig. 3.6). Note the message displayed in the message bar; this option is the choice that you want.

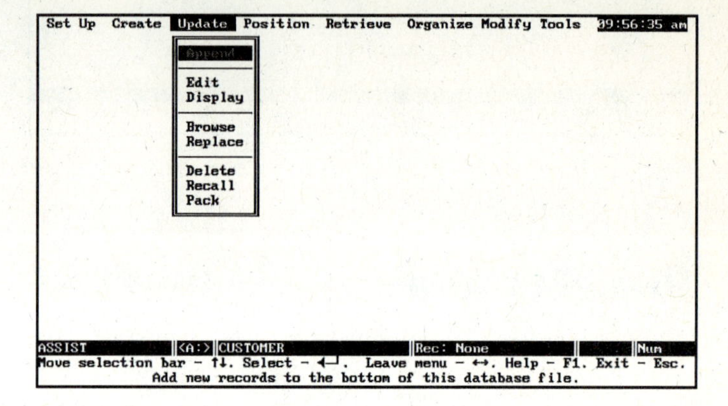

Fig. 3.6 The Update menu.

2. Press ↵Enter to signal dBASE that you want to add records to the database in use.

   The screen now should resemble figure 3.7. When you indicate that you want to append data, dBase displays this standard screen. Notice the word APPEND at the far left of the status bar, indicating the operation being performed.

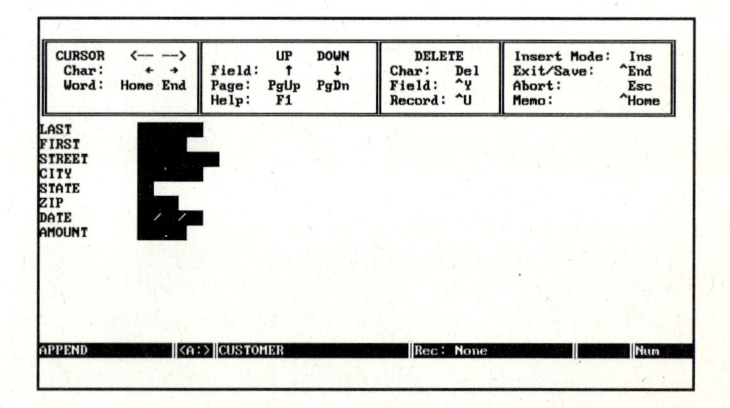

Fig. 3.7 The Append command data entry screen.

The list of keystrokes at the top of the screen indicates that ^*End* (pressing and holding down Ctrl and pressing End) saves the data. Pressing Esc returns you to the Assistant without adding data records to the database file. No matter which key you press, do not worry about losing your structure; it has been saved.

By defining the database file structure, you created your first database file. After creating the database file structure, you then enter the data. In the following exercise, you add nine records to the Customer database file. After you are done, you are returned to the Assistant.

Type carefully and don't work too fast. When you are just beginning to learn a program, avoiding making mistakes is better than trying to correct them. Before you begin, press Caps Lock. In a later chapter, you use this data, and all your data in this database should be in uppercase.

Exercise 2.2: Adding Data Records to the Customer Database File

To add data to your database, take these steps:

1. Check to see that Caps Lock is on and that the blinking dash cursor is in the far left of the white bar just to the right of the field name LAST. The ← and → move this cursor.
2. Type the last name of your first customer, **MILLER**, and then press ↵Enter. The cursor moves to the FIRST field.
3. Now type the following information in the remaining fields. Enter the date without typing the /; dBASE automatically supplies the slash. When you type the dollar AMOUNT, do not type the decimal; type **10095**. dBASE supplies the decimal.

   Press ↵Enter after each entry unless, as in the STATE, ZIP, DATE, and AMOUNT fields, the entry fills the field width. When you fill the field, dBASE beeps and drops the cursor to the next field. In the case of the AMOUNT field, the next field is the first field in the following record, and you see a blank data entry form for the next record on-screen.

FIRST	**GLEN**
STREET	**34 BRADY**
CITY	**EDMONDS**
STATE	**WA**
ZIP	**98600**
DATE	**10/20/94**
AMOUNT	**100.95**

4. You now should see a blank data entry form on-screen. To go back one record to see what you entered, press PgUp. If you made a mistake, move the cursor to the field by using the arrow keys. To make a correction, use ←Backspace or Del and retype.

   At this point, your screen should look like figure 3.8.

3

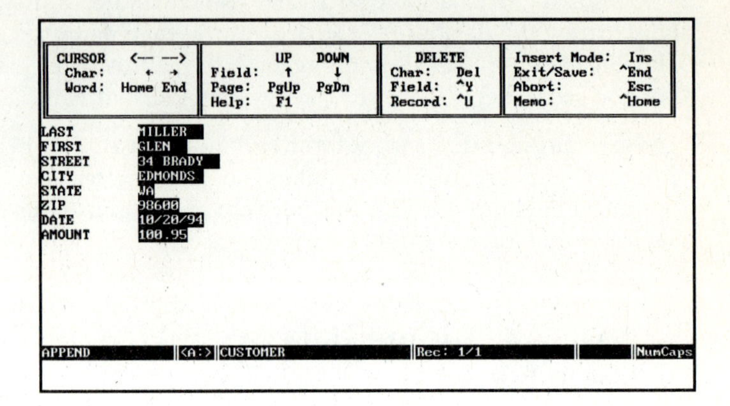

Fig. 3.8
The completed first record.

5. Press the PgDn key to move to the second record.
6. Now, using the same method you used for the first record, enter the following data. You do not need to use PgUp and PgDn; just type all the records. Only if you want to check for and correct mistakes do you need to use PgUp and PgDn.

LAST	**CHEN**	**LEAMER**	**PETERS**	**LOPEZ**
FIRST	**SUSAN**	**ED**	**KENT**	**MARIA**
STREET	**654 MAIN**	**12 VESTAL**	**81 HILL**	**33 WALNUT**
CITY	**MERCER**	**CAMAS**	**PORTLAND**	**EDMONDS**
STATE	**WA**	**WA**	**OR**	**WA**
ZIP	**98666**	**98654**	**97299**	**98622**
DATE	**10/12/94**	**10/18/94**	**12/10/94**	**11/17/94**
AMOUNT	**220.17**	**125.00**	**102.52**	**317.87**

7. Enter these remaining records into the database file:

LAST	IWASAKI	WILLS	THORPE	HUSAMI
FIRST	JULIE	BILL	TAMU	MIKE
STREET	1312 MAIN	312 JAMES	459 ELM	18 LEROY
CITY	MERCER	PORTLAND	ARBOR	SEATTLE
STATE	WA	OR	WA	WA
ZIP	98666	97211	98752	98156
DATE	10/27/94	12/11/94	10/18/94	11/21/94
AMOUNT	186.55	251.39	115.48	263.40

8. After you add the last (ninth) record, a blank form for entering a tenth record is displayed. Press PgUp to return to Mike Husami's record.

   Note: The reason that you return to the last completed data record before saving the database file is to avoid adding an empty 10th record to the bottom of the file. Later in this chapter, you learn how to delete unwanted records. For now, however, avoid adding the blank record in the first place.

9. When Mike Husami's record is on-screen, press and hold down Ctrl and then press End. Release both keys. This key combination signals dBASE that you have added your last data record. You have completed the append operation and will return to the Assistant.

   Now your screen resembles figure 3.9. You can see from the status bar that the database Customer from drive A still is open (in use) and that now nine records exist. `Rec 9/9` means that you are *on* the ninth record of a total of nine records. dBASE's current (or active) record pointer is on record number 9. This status bar feature is discussed in a following section of this chapter.

One characteristic of dBASE that, at first, frustrates and confuses students is that dBASE doesn't constantly show a database's records on-screen, a method that differs from word processing and spreadsheet programs. But the records are in the computer, as the `Rec 9/9` message in the status bar tells you. In the next section, you learn how to display your data records.

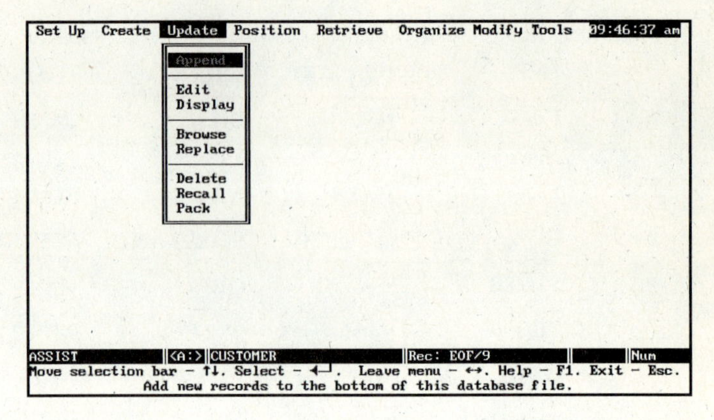

Fig. 3.9 The status bar now shows that nine records are in Customer.

Objective 3: To Display Data by Using the List Command

After you enter the records, you want to call them up on your computer screen and to list them on your printer. The next set of exercises explains this procedure, step by step.

Exercise 3.1: Listing Your Open Database File On-Screen

To list the records in the open Customer file, take these steps:

1. Move the selection bar highlight to the Retrieve menu (see fig. 3.10).

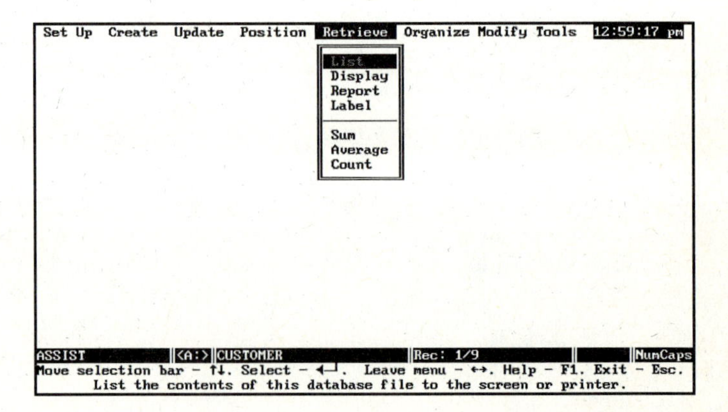

Fig. 3.10 The Retrieve menu.

Notice that the message line explains that selecting List from this menu lists the contents of the database in use (the open database file, Customer) to the screen or printer.

2. Press ↵Enter to select the List choice. The List submenu appears (see fig. 3.11). Notice the dot command displayed in the action line (also referred to as the command line) at the bottom of the screen.

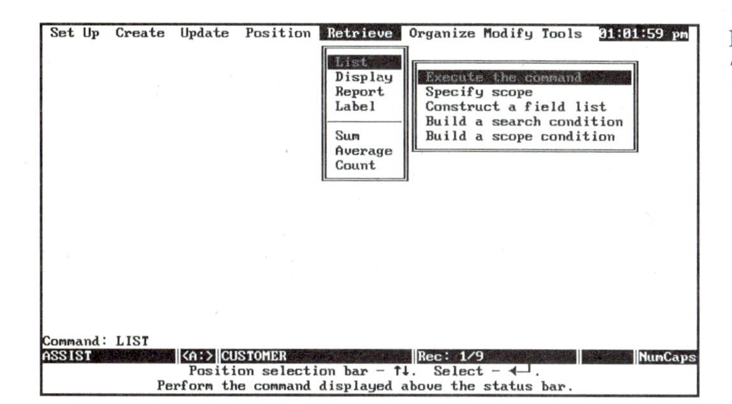

Fig. 3.11
The List submenu.

When the selection highlight in the submenu is on Execute the Command, pressing ↵Enter causes the command shown in the command line to execute.

3. Press ↵Enter to select Execute the Command.

   Now you have told dBASE that you want to see your data. When you use the List command, dBASE always lists the records on your screen. But you also have the option of obtaining an additional listing at the same time on your printer. So dBASE next needs to know whether you want only to see the data on-screen *or* you want both to see the data on-screen and also to list the data on the printer (see fig. 3.12).

4. Type **N**; *don't* press ↵Enter.

   The listing on-screen should resemble figure 3.13.

5. After you finish viewing your records, press any key—most people use ↵Enter or Spacebar—to clear the screen and return to the Assistant.

   Notice the contents of the Rec section at the right side of the status bar. The meaning of this information is explained later in the chapter.

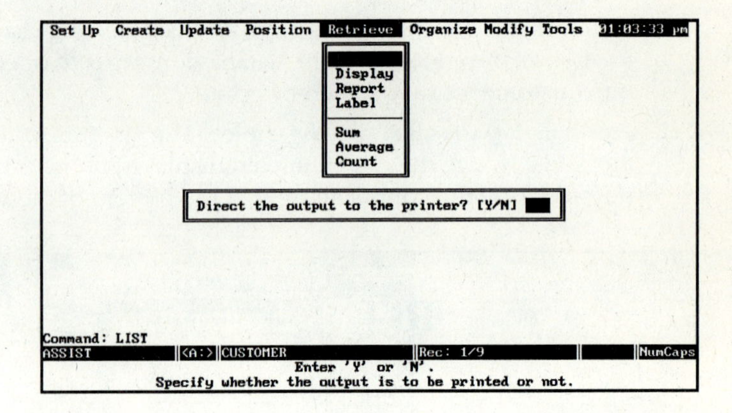

Fig. 3.12 To obtain a screen listing only, answer No.

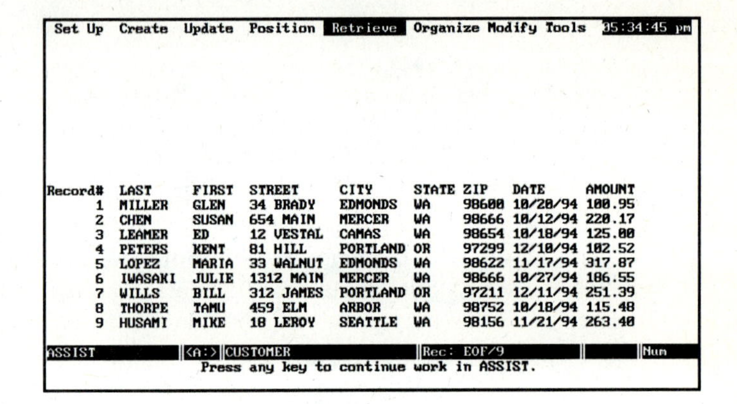

Fig. 3.13 The on-screen listing of the records.

Exercise 3.2: Listing Your Open Database File On-Screen and on the Printer

Before you begin printing, check with your instructor for any special procedures for printing.

To obtain a printout of your records, take these steps:

1. Move the selection bar highlight to the Retrieve menu.
2. Press ↵Enter to select List. The List submenu appears. Notice the command displayed in the command line.
3. Press ↵Enter to select Execute the Command.
4. This time you want a printout. Press Y; *don't* press ↵Enter.
5. Press any key to clear the screen and return to the Assistant.

6. Your printer probably will not eject the page that you printed. You probably will need to go immediately to the printer before someone else begins printing on your printout.

When you pick up the printout, most printers require that you to press the On Line button once. Press the Form Feed button, which should eject the printout. Press the On Line button again.

Objective 4: To Edit Data by Using the Edit Command

To *edit* data means to change data already stored in a record's field in the database. dBASE provides two ways to accomplish editing; the Edit command is one of these ways. This section illustrates the use of the Edit command. The Edit command brings up records on-screen in the same format that you entered them when you used the Append command. You can move among the records by using PgUp and PgDn. The second editing method, the Browse command, is discussed in the next section. When you are editing a field by using either Edit or Browse, Del and ←Backspace work just as they do when you are using Append. In the following exercise, you use the Edit command to edit the contents of two fields in two records.

Exercise 4.1: Editing Data with the Edit Command

Note: The Customer database file must be in use (open) to do this exercise.

To edit the Customer database by using the Edit command, take these steps:

1. Move the selection bar to the Update menu.
2. Move the selection bar down to the Edit choice, and read the message line. Then press ↵Enter.

   Your screen now resembles figure 3.14—although the record displayed in the form may be different. Notice the word `EDIT` displayed in the status bar. Pressing PgUp moves you up to a previous record unless record number 1 is on-screen. Pressing PgDn moves you down one record unless the last record is on-screen. If you are on the first record in the file, pressing PgUp returns you to the Assistant. If you are on the last record, pressing PgDn also returns you to the Assistant. Note the uses of the various keystrokes that are displayed at the top of the screen.

3

Fig. 3.14
The Edit screen.

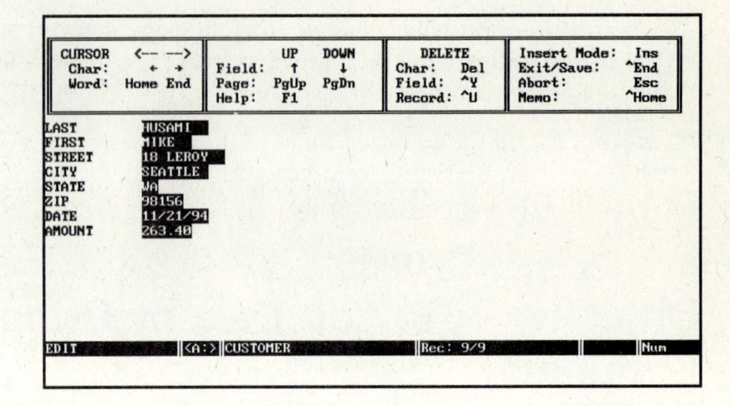

3. Using PgUp or PgDn as necessary, move to record number 5. The record numbers are shown in the Rec area of the status bar. As you press PgUp or PgDn, these record numbers tell you where you are in the database. After you make record 5 the active record, the Rec area will say 5/9. The screen should resemble figure 3.15. Note the black blinking dash (the cursor) at the far left of the LAST (name) field.

Fig. 3.15
Editing record number 5.

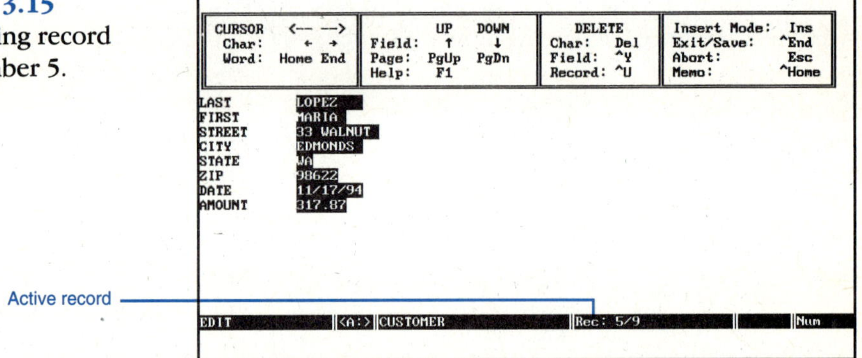

4. Press ↓ to move the cursor to the ZIP field. Type the new value, **98155**.

5. Press PgUp to move the cursor to record number 3. Move the cursor to the FIRST (name) field by using ↓. Type the new name **BETTY**, and press ↵Enter.

6. Use the Ctrl + End to save your editing changes.
7. Use the same steps you used in Exercise 3.1 to list the records in the Customer file on-screen and verify that the changes were made.

Objective 5: To View and Edit Data by Using the Browse Command

As mentioned previously, a second method is available when you are editing records—the Browse command. If you must look at other records before you know the editing change you need to make to a record's field, Browse is more efficient than the Edit command because Browse can display up to 17 records on-screen at a time. Browse is useful when you want to scan through data looking for an error and then make a correction immediately.

When a record has too many fields (is too wide) to fit on one line of the screen, Browse does a better job of displaying records than the List command. You learn about the List command in later chapters, when you use a database file that has more fields than the Customer file. Browse moves to fields that are *off the screen* if you press and hold down Ctrl and then press ← or →. This action is known as *panning* because you appear to move the screen to the left or right over a record just as a movie camara is panned over a movie set. Browse also lets you add a new record if you press ↓ when the cursor is on the last record.

The record that appears on-screen when you start to browse your database, as with the Edit command, depends on which record is the currently active record. The currently active record is the record whose number appears following `Rec:` in the status bar. For example, `7/30` means that the seventh record is the currently active record—the one that the dBASE pointer is on—and that 30 records exist in the file. If, however, the status bar says `Rec: EOF/9`, the record pointer is at the end of the database file on the 9th record.

When using Browse, you will notice a highlighted bar across all the fields of one record. This highlighted record is the current (active) record. Within this highlight, you see a black blinking dash like the one that you see while using the Edit command. To move the highlight up or down one record, use ↑ or ↓. To move the highlight over groups of 17 records (a screen), press PgUp or PgDn. To move the blinking dash, use ← and →. When you are editing a field using Browse, Del and ←Backspace work as they always do. In the following exercise, you use the Browse command to modify the Customer database.

3

Exercise 5.1: Editing Data Using the Browse Command

Note: The Customer database file must be in use (open) to do this exercise.

To use the Browse command to change data in the Customer file, take these steps:

1. Place the selection bar highlight on the Browse command in the Update menu. Notice the explanation in the message bar at the bottom of the screen.
2. Select the Browse command by pressing ↵Enter.

   The screen now should resemble figure 3.16. The word BROWSE should appear at the left side of the status bar. The record (or records) on-screen depend on which record is the current record. If you just completed Exercise 4.1, only the last record is displayed because when the List command is completed, the current record pointer is on the last record. Notice the keystroke information at the top of the screen. Many keys function in exactly the same way that they function when you use the Append and Edit commands.

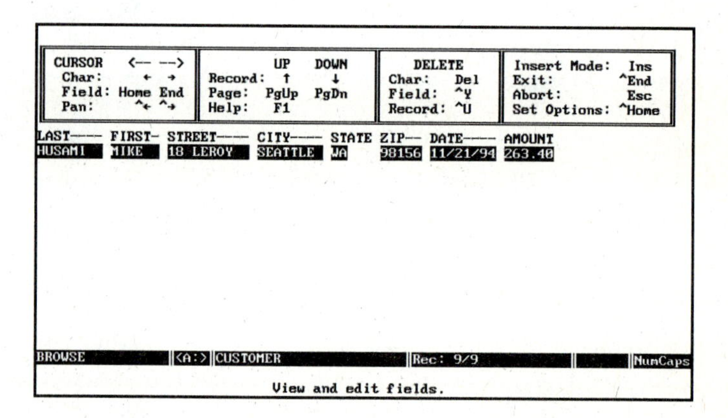

Fig. 3.16 The Browse screen with record 9 highlighted.

3. Move the highlight to record number 5 by pressing ↑ or ↓. You could also press End, which moves you across fields rapidly.
4. Use → to move the blinking black dash cursor to the CITY field. Change the CITY field to **ARBOR**.
5. Use ↑ to move the highlight to record 1. Change the LAST field to **MILLS**.

   Now your screen should look like figure 3.17.

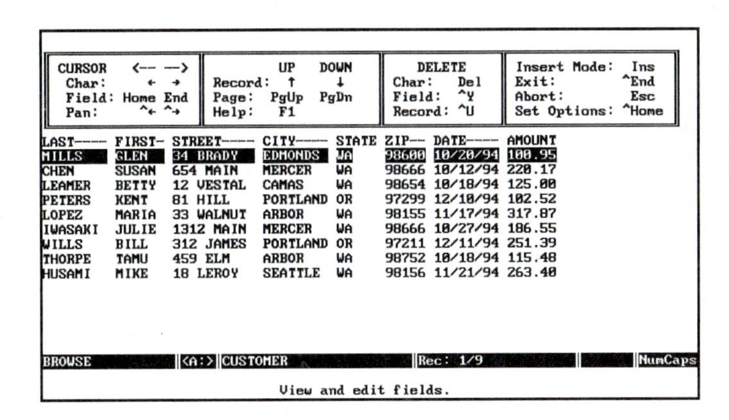

Fig. 3.17 The Browse screen with record 1 highlighted.

6. Press Ctrl + End to save the changes.
7. Use the List command to list the data on-screen and verify that the proper modifications were made to the Customer database file.

Objective 6: To Delete and Recall Records

Maintaining a database occasionally involves deleting records. For example, some customers may switch to another business, and you may choose to remove their records; or if you use a database to maintain a record of your retail store's inventory and decide to stop selling an item, the database must reflect this deletion from inventory. If you are not careful, however, you can accidentally delete one or more records that you really want to keep. Therefore, dBASE actually deletes records in a two-step process. This process is a safeguard for your data but often confuses students. The Delete command doesn't really delete records. Rather, the Delete command only *marks* records for deletion. The Pack command actually deletes records.

If you use the Delete command to mark records for deletion and then you list the records on-screen, you can see the *deletion mark*, which appears as an asterisk next to the record number. If you *do* want to delete all the marked records, you then use the Pack command. This command *does* delete all the marked records—even if hundreds of records are marked. The term *pack* is used because dBASE deletes records by copying all unmarked records (packing them) back into the database file. What do you do if you see that a record is marked for deletion but you don't want to delete the record? You can use the Recall command to *unmark* the record. If you then use the Pack command, the unmarked record is not deleted.

When you use the Assistant, the Delete, Recall, and Pack commands are grouped together at the bottom of the Update menu. Records, however, also can be marked for deletion when you are using the Append, Edit, and Browse commands, as you can see by looking at the list of keystrokes at the top of the Append, Edit, and Browse screens. To mark a record for deletion, you press Ctrl+U when the record that you want to delete is the active record (highlighted on-screen). An asterisk will *not* appear; you see the asterisk only if you use the List command to list the records. However, if you watch the status bar, the word `Del` (for Delete), appears at the right of the status bar (see fig. 3.18). When browsing or editing, to see whether a record is marked for deletion, make it the active record and check for the word `Del` in the status bar. In the Edit or Browse screen, to *unmark* a record, just press Ctrl+U again when the record is the active record. The word `Del` disappears from the status bar.

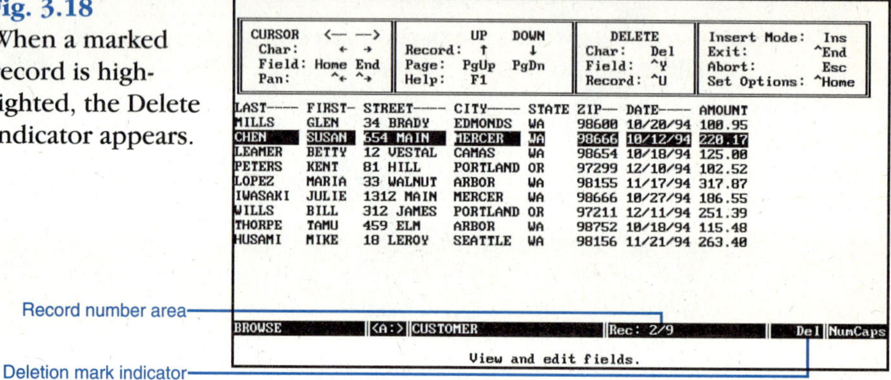

Fig. 3.18
When a marked record is highlighted, the Delete indicator appears.

No matter how you mark a record for deletion, always list your records to verify that only the records you want to delete are marked before you issue the Pack command. The following exercises illustrate these points.

Note: The Customer database file must be in use (open) to do the following exercises.

Exercise 6.1: Marking a Record for Deletion Using the Browse Command

To mark a record (record number 3) for deletion by using the Browse command, follow these steps:

1. From the Update menu, select Browse.
2. Move the active record highlight to record number 3.
3. To mark the active record (record 3) for deletion, press and hold down Ctrl and press U. The word Del should appear at the right of the status bar. Record 3 is now marked for deletion (see fig. 3.19).

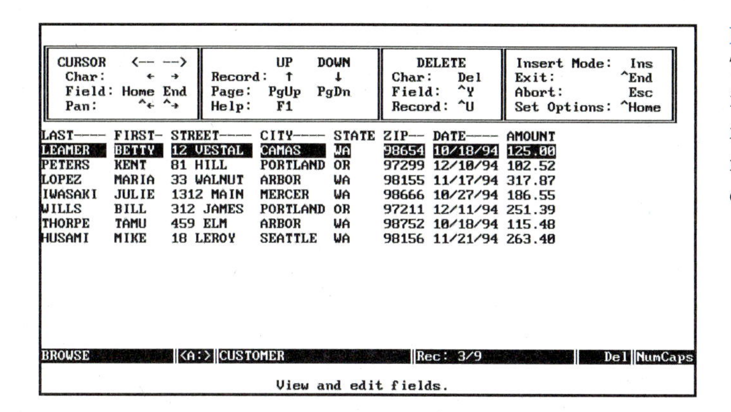

Fig. 3.19 The status bar indicates that record 3 is marked for deletion.

Remember that, in Append, Browse, or Edit, if a record is marked for deletion, the word `Del` appears in the status bar—but only when the marked record is the active record.

4. Press Ctrl+End to exit from Browse and save changes (in this case, the deletion mark).
5. Use the List command to verify that record number 3 is marked with an asterisk.

Exercise 6.2: Marking a Record for Deletion Using the Delete Command

To use the Delete command to mark a record (record number 5) for deletion, take these steps:

1. From the Update menu, highlight the Delete command, and press ↵Enter.
2. A submenu appears (see fig. 3.20).
3. From this submenu, highlight Specify Scope, and press ↵Enter.

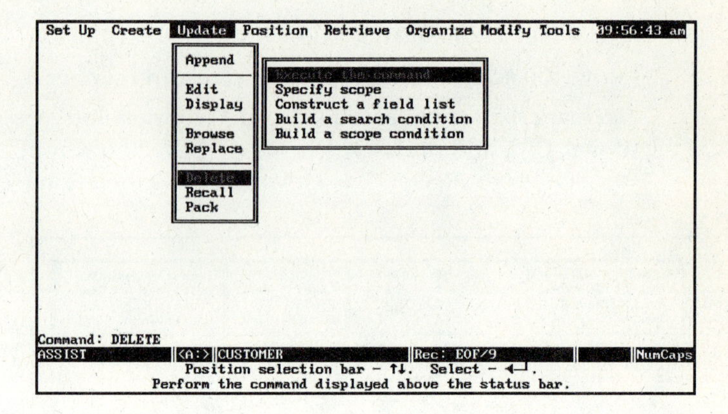

Fig. 3.20 The Delete submenu.

4. The Specify Scope submenu appears (see fig. 3.21). From this menu, highlight Record, and press ↵Enter.

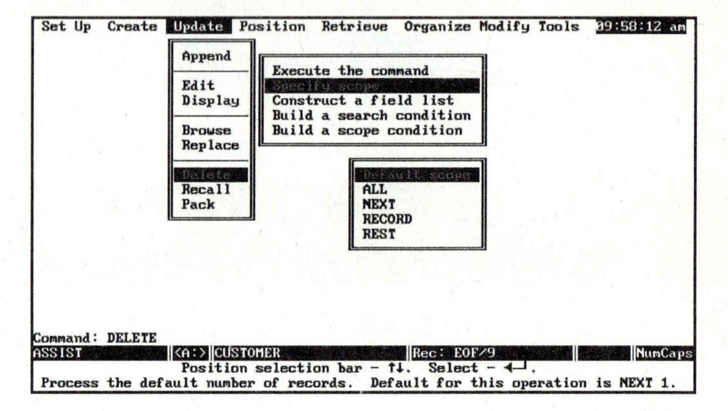

Fig. 3.21 The Delete Scope submenu.

5. Type the record number of the record that you want to mark for deletion. Type **5**, and press ↵Enter.

   Now the screen should resemble figure 3.22. Notice the command (in the action line) that you built by making selections from the various menus.

6. Use ↑ to highlight the Execute the Command choice, and then press ↵Enter.

   The `1 record deleted` message appears above the status bar.

7. Press ↵Enter again to return to the Assistant.

8. Use the List command to verify that record number 5 is marked with an asterisk.

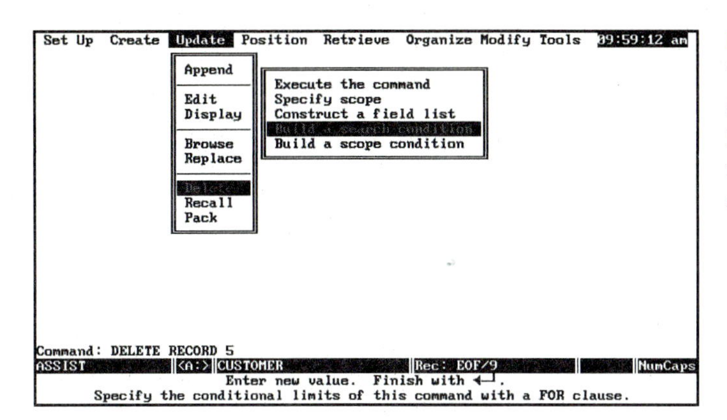

Fig. 3.22 The screen indicating that you have completed the Delete command.

Exercise 6.3: "Unmarking" a Record Using the Recall Command

To use the Recall command to unmark a record (record number 5) for deletion, take these steps:

1. From the Update menu, highlight the Recall command, and press ↵Enter.

   The Recall submenu appears (see fig. 3.23).

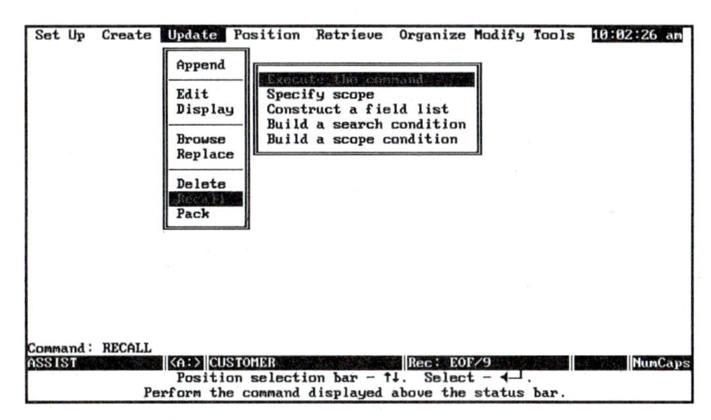

Fig. 3.23 The Recall submenu.

2. From this submenu, highlight the Specify Scope choice, and press ↵Enter.
3. The Specify Scope submenu appears (see fig. 3.24). From this menu, highlight the Record choice, and press ↵Enter.

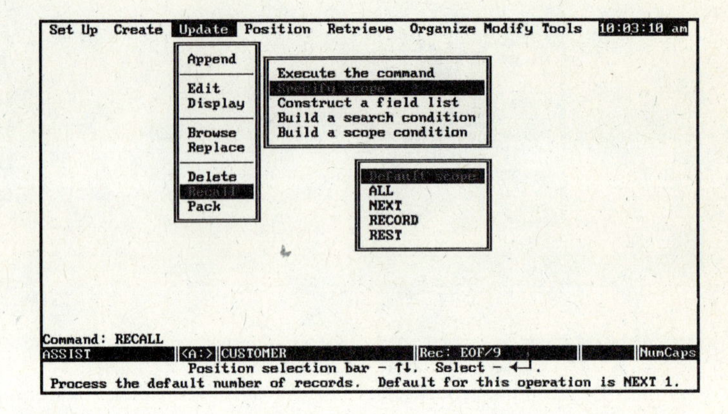

Fig. 3.24
The Recall Scope submenu.

4. Type the number of the record that you want to unmark for deletion. Here, type **5**, and press Enter.

   Now, the screen should resemble figure 3.25 . Notice the command (in the action line) that you have built by making selections from the various menus.

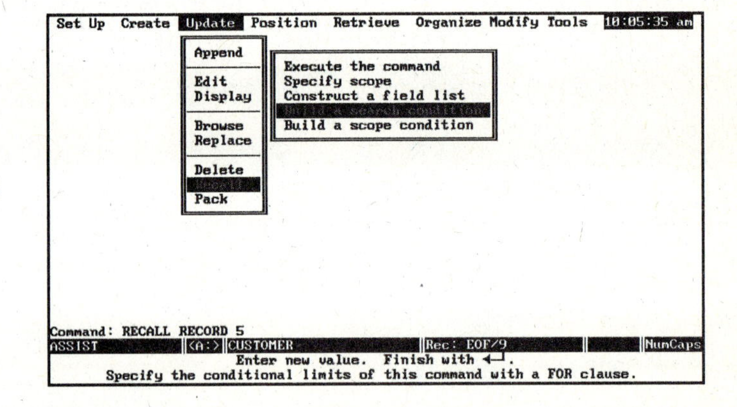

Fig. 3.25
The screen indicating that you are ready to execute the Recall command.

5. Use ↑ to highlight the Execute the Command choice, and then press Enter.
6. Press Enter again to return to the Assistant.
7. Use the List command to verify that record number 5 no longer is marked with an asterisk.

   Now, only record number 3 should be marked for deletion.

Exercise 6.4: Deleting by Using the Pack Command

To use the Pack command to remove all marked records—only one record (record number 3) in this exercise—take these steps:

1. From the Update menu, highlight the Pack command, and note the message (and warning) in the message line. Press ↵Enter.

   You should see the message `8 records copied` at the bottom of the screen. Old record number 3 now is removed from the database file.
2. Press ↵Enter again to return to the Assistant.
3. Use the List command to verify that the original record number 3 (LEAMER's record) no longer is in the database (see fig. 3.26).

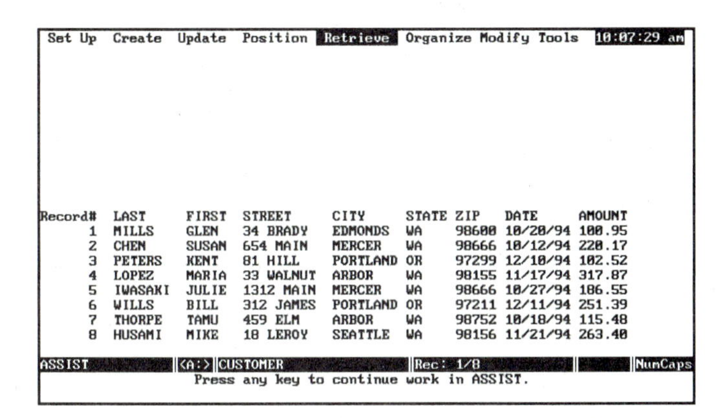

Fig. 3.26 The original record 3 has been deleted.

You now can exit from dBASE.

Chapter Summary

In this chapter, you have learned how to add data records to a database file. You have learned how to edit and delete records by using the Edit command and the Browse command. Finally, you learned how to list the records in a database file, both on-screen and at the printer.

In Chapter 4, you learn how to list selected records from the database, and you begin to learn how to use dot prompt commands.

Testing Your Knowledge

True/False Questions

1. The commands to edit database records are found in the Assistant's Modify menu.
2. To delete record number 5, you first mark the record with the Pack command.
3. You will know what records are in the database you are using because these records are always displayed on-screen.
4. The position indicator `Rec: EOF/30` indicates that record number 30 is the active record.
5. The Edit command enables you to change the width of a field in a database file.

Multiple-Choice Questions

1. To move to a previously entered record when you are using the Append command, press ________ .

   a. ↑

   b. F7

   c. Home

   d. none of these answers

2. When you use the List command to list records, records marked for deletion have _______ next to the record number.

   a. `-`

   b. `*`

   c. `Del`

   d. none of these answers

3. Which of the following commands can you use to add a new record to a database file?

   a. Append

   b. Browse

   c. Create

   d. a, b, and c

4. Which of the following commands can you use to mark a record for deletion from a database file?
   a. Append
   b. Browse
   c. Edit
   d. a, b, and c

5. Which menu contains the command that enables you to open (use) a database file stored on your disk?
   a. Retrieve
   b. Set Up
   c. Update
   d. none of these answers

Fill-in-the-Blank Questions

1. The command that you use to add new records to a database is the __________ command.
2. The command that you use to print database records is the __________ command.
3. The command that you use to *unmark* database records that you marked for deletion is the __________ command.
4. When using the Browse or Edit command, if the active record is marked for deletion, __________ is displayed in the status bar.
5. The keystroke combination used to *mark* or to *unmark* a record for deletion when using the Append, Browse, or Edit command is the __________ key combination.

Review: Short Projects

1. Creating and Printing a Database

   Create the Classes database shown in figure 3.27. Add the four records shown; then print the data records.

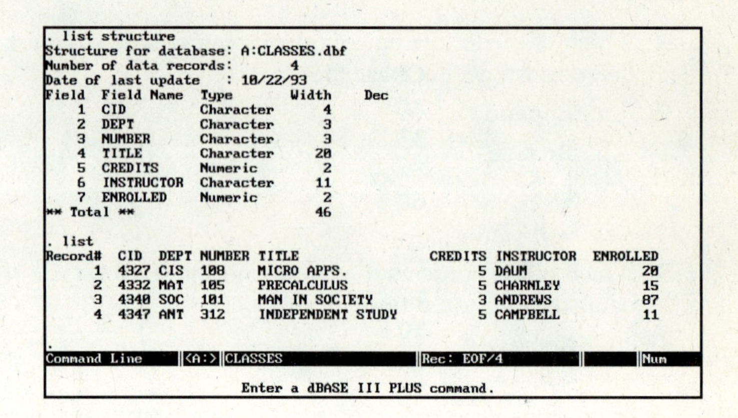

Fig. 3.27 The Classes database.

2. Editing a Database

   In the Classes database you set up in Short Project 1, use either Edit or Browse to change the instructors name from Campbell to **Harriet**. Change the Credits for ANT 312 to **2**. Change the Enrollment in Charnley's class to **7**. Print the data records.

3. Storing Data in the Courses Database File

   In this project, you enter five data records into the Courses database file that you created in Chapter 2 Short Project 2. Remember that you press ↵Enter to enter data in a field and move to the next field. After you add the records, perform the proper actions to save the data. Then print the contents of the database file.

Enter the following Courses data records:

ITEM:	**C001**	
DESCRIPT:	**African Civilizations**	
ROOM:	**33 Lynn Hall**	
TAUGHT_BY:	**Sands, Thomas, Wilcox**	
ENROLLMENT:	**60**	
ITEM:	**C002**	**C003**
DESCRIPT:	**Chinese Thought & Art**	**Philosophies of India**
ROOM:	**101 Angel Hall**	**17 Old Main Hall**
TAUGHT_BY:	**Hwang, Simmons, & Winters**	**Corbett, Merick, & Narwa**
ENROLLMENT:	**40**	**55**
ITEM:	**C004**	**C005**
DESCRIPT:	**Japanese Culture**	**Civilizations of Mexico**
ROOM:	**306 Parrington Hall**	**Social Sciences 247**
TAUGHT_BY:	**Ishii, Kimura, & Mikawa**	**Accursio, Corona, & Hernandez**
ENROLLMENT:	**60**	**60**

Review: Long Projects

1. Entering and Editing the Travel Agency Database Files

   This project uses the database file structures that you created in Chapter 2 Long Project 1.

   You enter 13 data records into the Tours database. Remember that you press ↵Enter to enter data into a field and move to the next field. After you add the records, perform the proper actions to save the data. Then print the contents of the database file.

   Enter the following data records to complete the Tours database:

Tour Code	*Destination*	*Depart from*	*Depart*	*Return*	*Cost*
A101	England	NYC	7/05/94	7/12/94	1255.00
A102	Ireland	Boston	7/19/94	7/26/94	1422.00
A103	Israel	NYC	8/11/94	8/20/94	1688.00
A104	Bermuda	NYC	11/05/94	11/08/94	657.00

continues

3

continued

Tour Code	*Destination*	*Depart from*	*Depart*	*Return*	*Cost*
A105	Kenya	NYC	11/15/94	11/28/94	3525.00
A106	Tanzania	NYC	12/06/94	12/19/94	3525.00
A107	Brazil	LA	1/08/95	1/12/95	1341.00
A108	Argentina	LA	3/09/95	3/13/95	1251.00
A109	Singapore	Portland	6/01/94	6/05/94	1375.00
A110	Hong Kong	Seattle	6/22/94	6/27/94	1379.00
C101	Cozumel	New Orleans	1/17/95	1/21/95	1995.00
C102	Jamaica	Miami	2/04/95	2/08/95	1755.00
C103	St. Thomas	Miami	2/21/95	2/25/95	1615.00

You now enter ten data records into the Clients database. Press Enter to enter data in a field and move to the next field. After you add the records, perform the proper actions to save the data. Then print the contents of the database file.

Enter the following data records to complete the Clients database:

Name	*Tour*	*Address*	*Phone*	*Interests*
Jean St Claire	C101	Carmel, WA	(206) 361-2315	Diving
Rashid Watts	A102	Vancouver, BC	(114) 225-1807	History, Fishing
Glen Henderson	A105	Portland, OR	(512) 527-3730	Photography
Maria Garcia	A103	Spokane, WA	(614) 108-1900	Art, Hiking
Hillary Smith	C101	Victoria, BC	(114) 981-0407	Archeology
Claudia Wong	A104	Seattle, WA	(206) 223-2512	Local Culture, Sun!
Roselea Mathews	A107	Pendleton, OR	(918) 625-3701	Music, Architecture

Name	*Tour*	*Address*	*Phone*	*Interests*
Tyrone Biggs	A104	Vista Lona, CA	(607) 331-9814	Diving, History
Wade Capron	A109	Lakeside, WA	(217) 825-4123	Shopping, Dining
Patti Mitchell	C102	Everett, CA	(704) 511-7742	Local sights

2. Setting Up a Climate Table

   This project uses the Climate database file structure that you created in Chapter 2 Long Project 2.

   You enter the following data records into the Climate database. Press Enter to enter data into a field and move to the next field. After you add the records, perform the proper actions to save the data. Then print the contents of the database file.

   Enter the following Data Records to complete the Climate database:

The Climate Table

Station	*Country*	*Jan. Max.*	*Jan. Min.*	*Annual Precip. (in inches)*	*Elevation (in feet)*
Addis Ababa	Ethiopia	75	43	49	8,038
Athens	Greece	54	42	16	351
Bombay	India	88	62	71	27
Buenos Aires	Argentina	85	63	37	89
Dublin	Ireland	47	35	30	155
Hong Kong	China	64	56	85	109
Istanbul	Turkey	45	36	32	59
Jerusalem	Israel	55	41	20	2,654
Nairobi	Kenya	77	54	38	5,971
Sao Paolo	Brazil	77	63	57	2,678
Sydney	Australia	78	65	47	62
Toronto	Canada	30	16	32	379

Print the new database file.

A. Use the Browse command to make the following changes:

- Sao Paolo's elevation should be **2570**.
- Hong Kong's Low temperature should be **49**.
- Athens' precipitation should be **20**.
- Mark Toronto's record for deletion.

Print the altered database file.

3. Storing Data in the Student Database File

In this project, you enter eight data records into the Student database that you created in Chapter 2 Short Project 3. Press ↵Enter to enter data into a field and move to the next field. After you add the records, perform the proper actions to save the data. Then print the contents of the database file.

A. Enter the following Student Data Records:

STUDENT#:	**068-56-8237**	**077-33-2535**
LAST_NAME:	**Becker**	**Whitman**
FIRST_NAME:	**Ken**	**Julia**
STREET:	**1700 N.E. 20th St.**	**47 East Flagler St.**
CITY:	**Miami**	**Hialea**
STATE:	**FL**	**FL**
ZIP:	**33155**	**33157**
PHONE:	**305-296-8864**	**305-331-7198**
ITEM:	**C003**	**C001**

STUDENT#:	**151-45-9427**	**101-73-5923**
LAST_NAME:	**Flores**	**Mariscos**
FIRST_NAME:	**Gloria**	**Julio**
STREET:	**17 Tamiami Trail**	**12500 West Dixie Hwy**
CITY:	**North Miami**	**Bal Harbour**
STATE:	**FL**	**FL**
ZIP:	**33145**	**33130**
PHONE:	**305-754-3485**	**305-198-1911**
ITEM:	**C005**	**C003**

STUDENT#:	**125-78-1256**	**133-07-1324**
LAST_NAME:	**Benoit**	**Spencer**
FIRST_NAME:	**Shaka**	**Allison**
STREET:	**4442 Collins Ave.**	**11000 S.W. 57th Ave.**
CITY:	**Miami Beach**	**Coconut Grove**
STATE:	**FL**	**FL**
ZIP:	**33140**	**33133**
PHONE:	**305-363-2416**	**305-211-3456**
ITEM:	**C004**	**C002**

STUDENT#:	**133-77-2636**	**527-88-3029**
LAST_NAME:	**Lopez**	**Wong**
FIRST_NAME:	**Lupe**	**Claudia**
STREET:	**7301 Crandon**	**37 Brickell Ave.**
CITY:	Key Biscayne	Opa-Locka
STATE:	**FL**	**FL**
ZIP:	**33149**	**33135**
PHONE:	**305-177-3602**	**305-835-9742**
ITEM:	**C002**	**C003**

B. Use the Edit command to make the following changes:

- Julia Whitman's first name should be **Ashante**.
- Allison Spencer's ZIP code should be **33103**.
- Claudia Wong's phone number should be **305-855-9742**.
- Mark Ashante Whitman's record for deletion.

After you finish the changes, print the new Student data.

Using Dot Prompt Commands to Display Your Database Records

4

The Assistant menu system is a good way to start to learn dBASE III Plus. The Assistant issues commands to dBASE by using the menu selections that you make. You will recall that these commands are displayed at the bottom of the Assistant screen. Once you become comfortable using dBASE and start to learn the commands you need, you will find it much more efficient
to enter these commands directly at the dot prompt. An additional benefit of using the dot prompt is that many useful commands are available only from the dot prompt. The Assistant does not have selections for these commands. In this chapter, you learn to use dot prompts, and you learn how to display records that are stored in your database.

Objectives

1. To Begin to Use Dot Prompt Commands
2. To Use the List Command
3. To Use the List For Command
4. To Print by Using the List Command
5. To Use the Set Commands
6. To Quit dBASE from the Dot Prompt

Key Terms in This Chapter	
Dot prompt	The dot or dot(DEMO) (the prompt from the student version of dBASE) displayed at the lower left of your screen.
Dot prompt commands	The command words that dBASE recognizes when they are entered at the dot prompt.

Objective 1: To Begin to Use Dot Prompt Commands

When you use the Assistant, you issue commands to dBASE by making selections from the Assistant menus. Previous chapters called your attention to the commands you were generating when using the Assistant. Recall that the last step in accomplishing an operation on the database often is selecting the Execute the Command choice from a menu. The command referred to is, of course, the one displayed in the action line. You can type this command at the dot prompt. When you press ↵Enter, the command is executed.

Commands are not executed until you press ↵Enter, so you can correct a command by using Del and ←Backspace and then retyping. You can work much more efficiently by entering commands directly at the dot prompt. As a further benefit, dBASE has a *history buffer* that stores your most recent commands—the default number is 20 commands—so that you can reuse or edit the commands. This buffer saves you typing and helps you learn because you can go back to check your commands to find an error if the command doesn't work the way you planned.

The exercises in this chapter require that you have in your default drive the disk with the Customer database stored on it and that the default drive be drive A. Press Caps Lock so that everything you type is in uppercase. You can use all lowercase letters or a mix of upper- and lowercase letters in the commands. For consistency between what you read in this text and what you see on your screen, however, type your commands in uppercase. This practice will eliminate a potential source of confusion. The next section describes the dot prompt commands that you previously practiced when you used the Assistant.

The Use Command

The Use command can open a database file. You type the command **USE** followed by a space and then the name of the database file you want to open. Then you press ↵Enter. When you press ↵Enter at the end of a Use command, if another database already is in use—is *in the computer*—all its data records are written out to disk and the file is closed. This process is completed before the second database file is opened. Some people close a database by typing just the word **USE** and then pressing ↵Enter. The database in use is closed, but no new database file is opened.

You don't have to save a database file before you begin work on another database provided you employ the Use command properly. Also remember that you don't have to save a database on which you are working if you quit dBASE properly.

Exercise 1.1: Opening a Database File

To open a database file for your use, follow these steps:

1. Start dBASE by using the method you were given by your instructor.
2. When the Assistant appears on-screen, press Esc.

   Your screen now should resemble figure 4.1.

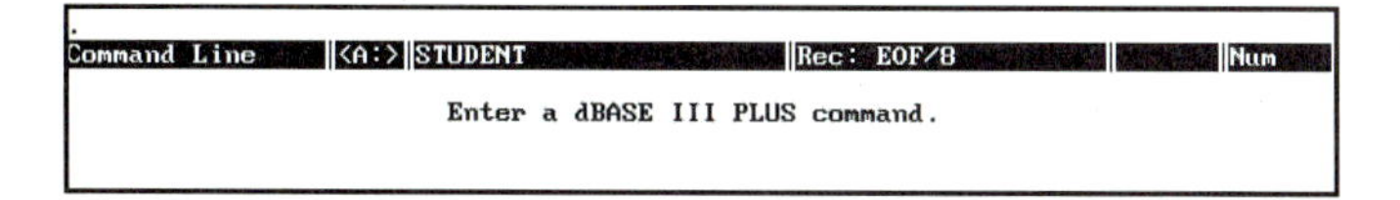

Fig. 4.1
The dot prompt command line screen.

3. Type **USE CUSTOMER**, and press Enter.

   The status bar, which functions exactly as it does when you use the Assistant, now should indicate that the Customer database is open. To verify that this database file is the same file with which you have been working, you can list the records.

The List Command

You can use the List command in the same way you issued the command from the Assistant.

Exercise 1.2: Listing the Database File in Use

If a database file is open (in use), you can list its records.

To list the records of the database file that is in use, take these steps:

1. At the dot prompt, type **LIST**.
2. Press Enter.

You can add records to the database in use by using the Append command. This command works in the same manner as it does when you issue the command by using the Assistant.

Exercise 1.3: Listing the Structure of the Database File in Use

To list on-screen the structure of the database file you are using, take these steps:

1. At the dot prompt, type the command **LIST STRUCTURE**.
2. Press Enter.

The Append Command

To add records to a database, you use the Append command. This command works the same way that it does when you access it from the Assistant.

Exercise 1.4: Adding Records to the Database File in Use

To add records by using the Append command, take these steps:

1. At the dot prompt, type **APPEND**, and press Enter.

   You now should see the familiar Append screen, with the data entry form displayed. Notice that the status bar signals that you are using the APPEND command.

2. Enter the following data records:

LAST	**PEREZ**	**NGUYEN**	**KING**
FIRST	**JUDY**	**MAI**	**MYFUME**
STREET	**6 PARK**	**10 JAMES**	**14 MAPLE**
CITY	**RENTON**	**MERCER**	**PORTLAND**
STATE	**WA**	**OR**	**OR**
ZIP	**98624**	**97054**	**97298**
DATE	**12/12/94**	**11/18/94**	**12/19/94**
AMOUNT	**200.97**	**105.27**	**212.00**

   Now, here is a shortcut to show you how confident the author is of you.

   You should begin with a completely blank data entry form on-screen.

3. Press Enter to signal dBASE that you have no more records to add and will not append an empty record to the bottom of the database. dBASE returns you to the dot prompt and saves your new entries.

4. At the dot prompt, type **LIST**, and press Enter.

The Edit Command

You can edit a database by using either the Browse or the Edit command. These commands work in the same way that they work when you use them when making selections from the Assistant menus.

Exercise 1.5: Editing Records in the Database File in Use

Mai Nguyen's ZIP code has changed. To modify her record, take these steps:

1. At the dot prompt, type **EDIT**, and press Enter.
2. Use PgUp to make Mai's record the active record and to place it in the data entry form.
3. Move the blinking dash cursor to the ZIP field, and type **97154**.
4. Press Ctrl and End to exit from EDIT and save changes.

The History Command

Now we want you to try using dBASE's capability of remembering a previous command that you entered at the dot prompt. The command you want to retrieve is an easy one just to type again, but in later chapters these commands become more complicated, and you can save time if you reuse a command. Also, as already mentioned, you can review your previous commands to see what you did right or wrong.

Exercise 1.6: Using History to Access a Previous Command

To access a previous command, take these steps:

1. You want to list your records. At the dot prompt, press ↑ twice so that the LIST command that you entered in step 4 of Exercise 1.4 appears after the dot prompt.

   If you go too far, just press ↓ until LIST appears.
2. Press Enter to execute the command.

You also can use the List History command to see a listing of the most recent commands you have executed. This command is useful because if a series of commands *work*, you want to be able to go back and review them. Unfortunately, these commands probably have scrolled off the screen by the time you see that they *did* work. The List History command also is useful for demonstrating to friends and instructors that you did in fact type what you were told to type but the computer *did not* do what it was supposed to do. Of course, this computer error is just a little facetious because, when a command doesn't seem to work, you made a mistake that you were not aware of. List History shows you what you actually typed.

Exercise 1.7: Using List History to Access a Previous Command

To see a listing of recent commands, take these steps:

1. At the dot prompt, type **LIST HISTORY**.
2. Press ↵Enter to execute the command.

The Clear Command

Sometimes the problem is not that a command has gone off-screen. Rather, the problem is that too many commands appear on-screen, and you want to clear the screen.

Exercise 1.8: Using the Clear Command

To clear the screen, take these steps:

1. At the dot prompt, type **CLEAR**.
2. Press ↵Enter.

The Delete, Recall, and Pack Commands

The Delete, Recall, and Pack commands function exactly as they function when you issue them from the dot prompt.

Exercise 1.9: Using the Delete Command to Mark a Record for Deletion

To delete a record, take these steps:

1. At the dot prompt, type the command **DELETE RECORD 3**, and press ↵Enter.
2. To see whether this command worked, at the dot prompt type **LIST**, and press ↵Enter.

   Record 3 should be marked for deletion. You now can delete this record by typing *PACK* and pressing ↵Enter but don't; you need to try the Recall command.

Exercise 1.10: Using the Recall Command to Unmark a Record

To unmark record number 3, take these steps:

1. At the dot prompt type **RECALL RECORD 3**. Press Enter.
2. To see whether this command worked, at the dot prompt, type **LIST**, and press Enter.

   Record 3's deletion mark should be removed.

Objective 2: To Use the List Command

You have already used the basic List command to list all the records in a database; you have also listed the history, and the structure of a database file. In this section and in the following section, you are introduced to some useful variations of the List command. The most common use of the List command is to view the contents of a database file. dBASE has another command that is similar to List: Display. In fact, for the purposes of this textbook, only one important difference remains between the two commands. If you display a database file with more than 20 records, you see that the Display command pauses after 20 lines are displayed on screen and prompts, `Press any key to continue ....`

The List command, on the other hand, just keeps displaying one record after another on the screen until it reaches the end of the file. You can *freeze* the listing of the records by pressing and holding down Ctrl and then pressing S. You have to be fast, however. To continue the display, press any key—pressing Ctrl+S again also starts the listing again. When you have more than 20 records in a file, use the Display command; you may prefer it. In this book, you use the List command. You don't have any databases with enough records to illustrate the difference between Display and List, so you see the difference when List Status is discussed in a following section of this chapter.

In the exercises in this section, you use the Student database that you created in Chapter 2 Short Project 3, and in which you stored data records in Chapter 3 Long Project 3. The reason for using this file is that each record in the Student database is too long to fit on one line of the screen or printer. I want to show you some ways of using the List command that are helpful with long records.

Exercise 2.1: Listing the Student Database

To list the records in the Student database file, follow these steps:

1. Open the Student file by typing **USE STUDENT** and pressing ↵Enter.
2. At the dot prompt, type **LIST**, and press ↵Enter.

   Your screen now should resemble figure 4.2.

```
. list
Record#  STUDENT_NO  LAST_NAME          FIRST_NAME STREET              CITY
      STATE ZIP    PHONE          ITEM
      1  068-56-8237 Becker             Ken        1700 N.E. 20th St.  Miami
      FL      33155 305-296-8864 C003
      2  077-33-2535 Whitman            Ashante    47 East Flagler St. Hialea
      FL      33157 305-331-7198 C001
      3  151-45-9427 Flores             Gloria     17 Tamiami Trail    North Miami
      FL      33145 305-754-3485 C005
      4  101-73-5923 Mariscos           Julio      12500 West Dixie Hwy Bal Harbour
      FL      33130 305-198-1911 C003
      5  125-78-1256 Benoit             Shaka      4442 Collins Ave.   Miami Beach
      FL      33140 305-363-2416 C004
      6  133-07-1324 Spencer            Allison    11000 S.W. 57th Ave. Coconut Gro
ve    FL      33103 305-211-3456 C002
      7  133-77-2636 Lopez              Lupe       7301 Crandon        Key Biscayn
e     FL      33149 305-177-3602 C002
      8  527-88-3029 Wong               Claudia    37 Brickell Ave.    Opa-Locka
      FL      33135 305-855-9742 C003

.
Command Line  <A:> STUDENT               Rec: EOF/8               Num

                    Enter a dBASE III PLUS command.
```

Fig. 4.2
Listing all the fields in Student.

4

This screen is not easy to read, and it would be even more difficult to read if each record had more fields. The situation would get worse if more than 20 records were added to the file because the field names then would disappear off the top of the listing. Printing the records does not help either because the printer just chops off lines longer than 80 characters. You would not be able to see the rightmost fields in the record.

When records have many fields, listing only some of the fields—the ones in which you are interested—with each List command is helpful. To do this, just type the names of the fields that you want to see, and separate the field names with commas. If you do not follow the word *LIST* with field names, dBASE's default is to list all the fields on a record.

Exercise 2.2: Using the List Command to List Specific Fields

To list only the first three fields of each record, take these steps:

1. At the dot prompt, type **LIST STUDENT_NO, LAST_NAME, FIRST_NAME**.
2. Press ↵Enter.

   The screen should resemble figure 4.3.

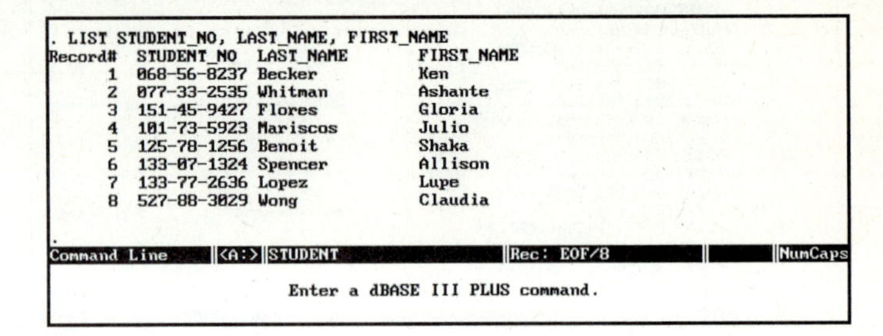

Fig. 4.3 Listing three fields.

3. At the dot prompt, type **CLEAR**, and press ↵Enter.
4. At the dot prompt, type **LIST FIRST_NAME, LAST_NAME, ITEM, PHONE**, and then press ↵Enter.

   The screen should resemble figure 4.4.

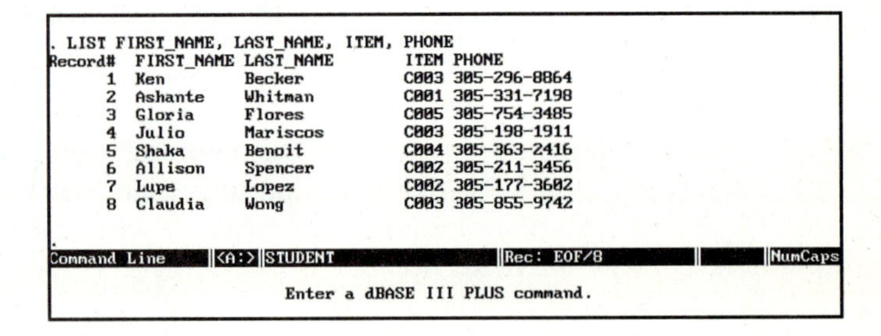

Fig. 4.4 Listing on a cleared screen.

Notice that by specifying the fields you want listed, you can view the fields in an order different from the order in which the fields are stored in a record.

You already saw that you can use the List Structure command to list the structure of the database file in use. Two more List commands are available that you should know: List Files and List Status.

The List Files Command

When you use the Assistant and you choose Database File from the Set Up menu, dBASE asks you for the disk drive. dBASE then displays all the database files you have stored on that drive. If you are working from the dot prompt, you need a command to show you the names of the database files on disk. The List Files command does this. You also are provided information on the number of records currently stored in the file and given the date on which you last made any changes to the file.

Exercise 2.3: Using the List Files Command

To see information on the database files on your default disk drive, take these steps:

1. At the dot prompt, type **LIST FILES**.
2. Press ↵Enter.

The information on any database files—files with a DBF file name extension—is displayed. If no database files exist, dBASE displays `None`.

The List Files command is useful, of course, when you are trying to find out which disk you stored a file on. You also can use the command before you create a new file to check to see whether a file of this name already exists on the disk. If you already have a database file of the same name on the disk, the new file completely blots out (*overwrites*) the old file—even though you desperately need to keep the 30,000 records you laboriously entered into the old file. Remember that database files in the same directory on a disk must have unique names.

The List Status Command

In dBASE, as in other programs, a great deal is going on behind the scenes that a beginning user doesn't know about—or want to know about. The List Status command pulls back the curtain that has concealed these complexities. List Status has nothing to do with social status. Rather, List Status displays the contents of important variables, such as which database file is in use, and shows all the default settings dBASE is using. List Status shows you what the settings are—in other words, the status of these settings. Don't worry; you don't need to know everything revealed by List Status until you become an advanced user. There are several useful pieces of information, however, of which you should be aware.

For example, you may want to turn off the bell that beeps every time you fill a field during an append or editing operation. dBASE starts out with many default settings—for example, the default drive setting and the bell setting—which you can change by using the Set command (which is explained in a following section of this chapter). However, you need a way to find out what these default settings are, and you need to verify that you have correctly changed them. This information is one product of List Status.

Another use of the List Status command is to list the uses of the function keys across the top of the keyboard. These keys provide a quick way to enter some standard commands without typing. Later sections in this chapter illustrate the use of some of these function keys. In a following chapter, you learn that you can have up to ten database files open at a time and that each of these files also can have multiple index files open. You can easily become confused about what files you are working with. By using the List Status command, you can avoid confusion because dBASE tells you exactly what database and index files are in use. The following exercises illustrate the use of both the List Status and the Display Status commands.

Exercise 2.4: Using the List Status Command

To use the List Status command, follow these steps:

1. At the dot, prompt type **LIST STATUS**.
2. Press Enter.

   The screen now looks like figure 4.5.

Fig. 4.5 The List Status screen.

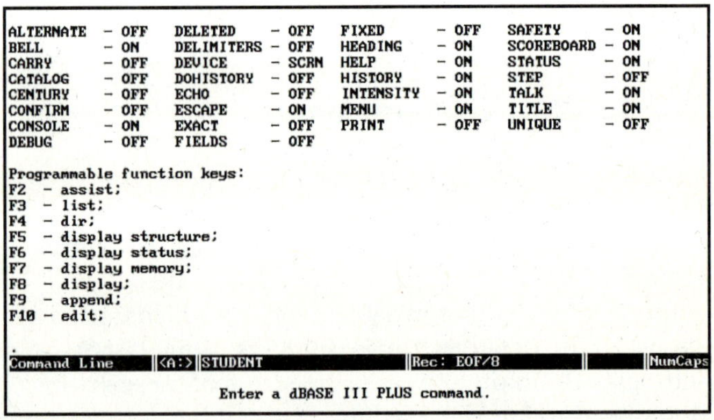

```
ALTERNATE   - OFF   DELETED    - OFF   FIXED      - OFF   SAFETY     - ON
BELL        - ON    DELIMITERS - OFF   HEADING    - ON    SCOREBOARD - ON
CARRY       - OFF   DEVICE     - SCRN  HELP       - ON    STATUS     - ON
CATALOG     - OFF   DOHISTORY  - OFF   HISTORY    - ON    STEP       - OFF
CENTURY     - OFF   ECHO       - OFF   INTENSITY  - ON    TALK       - ON
CONFIRM     - OFF   ESCAPE     - ON    MENU       - ON    TITLE      - ON
CONSOLE     - ON    EXACT      - OFF   PRINT      - OFF   UNIQUE     - OFF
DEBUG       - OFF   FIELDS     - OFF

Programmable function keys:
F2  - assist;
F3  - list;
F4  - dir;
F5  - display structure;
F6  - display status;
F7  - display memory;
F8  - display;
F9  - append;
F10 - edit;

.
Command Line   |<A:>|STUDENT          |Rec: EOF/8      |     |NumCaps
                    Enter a dBASE III PLUS command.
```

If you watched closely, some of the first information that was listed disappeared off the top of the screen because dBASE listed more information than can fit on one screen. As mentioned earlier, when this scrolling occurs, use the Display command. Use the Display command now so you can see the information you missed on the screen.

Exercise 2.5: Using the Display Status Command

To use the Display Status command, follow these steps:

1. At the dot prompt, type **DISPLAY STATUS**, and press ↵Enter.
2. After you read the first screen of information (see fig. 4.6), press ↵Enter to see the second screen (refer to fig. 4.5).

```
F2  - assist;
F3  - list;
F4  - dir;
F5  - display structure;
F6  - display status;
F7  - display memory;
F8  - display;
F9  - append;
F10 - edit;

. DISPLAY STATUS

Currently Selected Database:
Select area:  1, Database in Use: A:STUDENT.dbf    Alias: STUDENT

File search path:
Default disk drive: A:
Print destination:  PRN:
Margin =      0
Current work area =    1

Press any key to continue...
Command Line    <A:> STUDENT          Rec: EOF/8              NumCaps

                   Enter a dBASE III PLUS command.
```

Fig. 4.6
The Display Status screen.

When you use only one database, the first screen provides little information that you don't already know. The information reminds you of the default drive and the name of the database in use. This screen assumes more importance as you begin to work with multiple database files and indexes. The second screen shows the status of a variety of settings. Notice that the bell is set on. You will turn it off later.

The bottom half of the screen lists the uses of the function keys across the top of the keyboard. F2, as you already know, brings up the Assistant. F3 through F10 are designed to save you typing time. F4 lists the names of the database files on the default drive. Notice that pressing F6 is shorthand for typing *DISPLAY STATUS*. F1 is not shown. F1 accesses dBASE's Help system. Although this system is more of a reminder system than a help system, it can help you remember a command you previously used. You will not use the Help system in this text, but feel free to try it on your own.

Objective 3: To Use the List For Command

You have seen how the List command enables you to specify which *fields* you want to list from the database records. The List For command enables you to specify which *records* you want to see. You also can specify a selection criterion by using the contents of one or more of the fields in the database.

Establishing Conditions That Must Be Met before a Record Is Listed

A dBASE database file is a list of information about customers, students, classes, orders, inventory, sales figures, or any other data you may need to keep. Why do you ever need to set conditions for listing your data? After all, your data is already stored in the database, and you can easily see it and see which records meet your selection criterion. This situation certainly is true of the small databases shown in this text. A dBASE database file in a business, however, often contains many hundreds or thousands of records. To find information manually in a database of this size is incredibly time-consuming, and overlooked records are guaranteed.

With dBASE, you can establish a condition that must be met before records are listed. Stating the condition(s) for inclusion in the list is the purpose of the List For command. Depending on which database is in use, you can use a conditional List command to find all customers who live in Washington state. If you have a database of employees, for example, you can list the records of all employees who earn greater than a certain salary and who have been with the company for more than a certain number of years.

The List For command enables you to express clearly a selection criterion for the records you want to see. When dBASE lists these records, you can be sure that no records are overlooked and that no records that do not meet the selection criteria are included. The List For command expresses a request from you to dBASE asking for information that meets the criteria you express in your List For command. Of course, you can request only information that is stored in the database, and you can use as criteria only the fields that are actually contained in the database.

Before you use the List For command, you may find that writing down your statement of the records you want to see is beneficial. You then can refer to this written statement as you construct the List For command in dBASE.

A written query can help you clarify the List For statement and help you remember the exact information for which you are looking. You must be precise when entering your selection conditions. For example, because you have entered the database data in uppercase letters only, remember that you must use uppercase letters in the criteria. dBASE is case sensitive; *WA* is not the same as *Wa* or *wa*.

Note: In this section, the exercises use the Customer database file. At the dot prompt, enter the **USE CUSTOMER** command to close the Student database and open the Customer database file.

Exercise 3.1: Using the List For Command

To list the records of all the customers who live in Portland, take these steps:

1. At the dot prompt, type **LIST FOR CITY = "PORTLAND".**
2. Press ↵Enter.

   The screen now should resemble figure 4.7.

```
. LIST FOR CITY = "PORTLAND"
Record#  LAST      FIRST  STREET      CITY     STATE ZIP   DATE     AMOUNT
      3  PETERS    KENT   81 HILL     PORTLAND OR    97299 12/10/94 102.52
      6  WILLS     BILL   312 JAMES   PORTLAND OR    97211 12/11/94 251.39
     11  KING      MYFUME 14 MAPLE    PORTLAND OR    97298 12/19/94 212.00

.
Command Line  |<A:>|CUSTOMER         |Rec: EOF/11     |      |NumCaps

                    Enter a dBASE III PLUS command.
```

Fig. 4.7
The results of LIST FOR CITY = PORTLAND command.

You must Type the quotation marks around *PORTLAND* because dBASE requires you to place quotation marks around the data you are comparing with a Character type field.

Exercise 3.2: More Practice Using the List For Command

To list the records of all the customers who live in Washington, take these steps:

1. At the dot prompt, type **LIST FOR STATE = "WA"**.
2. Press ↵Enter.

   The screen now should resemble figure 4.8.

Fig. 4.8
The customers who live in Washington state.

```
. LIST FOR STATE = "WA"
Record#  LAST     FIRST  STREET     CITY     STATE ZIP   DATE     AMOUNT
      1  MILLS    GLEN   34 BRADY   EDMONDS  WA    98600 10/20/94 100.95
      2  CHEN     SUSAN  654 MAIN   MERCER   WA    98666 10/12/94 220.17
      4  LOPEZ    MARIA  33 WALNUT  ARBOR    WA    98155 11/17/94 317.87
      5  IWASAKI  JULIE  1312 MAIN  MERCER   WA    98666 10/27/94 186.55
      7  THORPE   TAMU   459 ELM    ARBOR    WA    98752 10/18/94 115.48
      8  HUSAMI   MIKE   18 LEROY   SEATTLE  WA    98156 11/21/94 263.40
      9  PEREZ    JUDY   6 PARK     RENTON   WA    98624 12/12/94 200.97

.
Command Line  |<A:>|CUSTOMER        |Rec: EOF/11     |    |NumCaps

                  Enter a dBASE III PLUS command.
```

4

The tricky part about setting up conditions is the problem of *data type mismatches*. This problem arises when the data type of the database field on the left side of the equal sign differs from the data type on the right side of the equal sign. The data type of a field and the field's contents are established when you create the structure of the database. When you type the criterion on the right side of the equal sign, if the field on the left side of the equal sign is a Character type field, the criterion *must be inside quotation marks*.

What about Numeric type fields? You see some examples of conditions that involve Numeric fields later in this section. The rule for conditions that involve Numeric fields is that comparisons that involve Numeric fields can have numbers only on the right side of the equal sign (or other comparison operator); therefore, you use no quotation marks in Numeric conditions.

Date type fields are tricky. Here is what you have to do:

1. You have to use a dBASE function on the Date field on the left side of the equal sign. The function is the DTOC function.
2. You have to put a valid date inside quotation marks on the right side of the equal sign.

What is the DTOC function? First, the DTOC function doesn't affect the data stored in the Date type field in the database; DTOC converts the data at the time of comparison in the List For statement. The DTOC function's name comes from *D*ate *T*o *C*haracter. At the time of comparison, the date is converted to character form so that you can specify a date inside quotation marks and not have a data type mismatch. An example may help you understand how this process works. The following command lists the records of customers who last made a purchase on October 30, 1994:

```
LIST FOR DTOC(DATE) = "10/30/94"
```

Notice that the name of the Date type field goes inside parentheses.

Exercise 3.3: Using Date Type Fields in the List For Command

To list the records of all the customers who last made a purchase on November 17, 1994, take these steps:

1. At the dot prompt, type **LIST FOR DTOC(DATE) = "11/17/94".**
2. Press ↵Enter.

   The screen now should resemble figure 4.9.

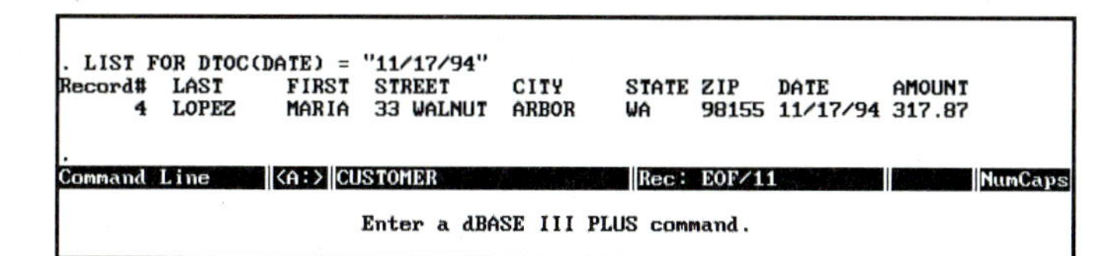

Fig. 4.9
The only customer purchasing on 11/17/94.

Multiple Selection Conditions in List For Commands

Occasionally, when you construct a List For criteria statement, your answer must meet several conditions, and your examples (selection criteria) must define these conditions. Creating a multiple-condition List For statement is not difficult but does take time and thought.

Multiple selection conditions can be in a logical AND relationship or in a logical OR relationship. When you use the .AND. condition you are saying to dBASE, "List a record if it has this *and* this *and* this." With criteria in an AND relationship, each record listed must meet *all* specifications of the criteria. You also can use the logical .OR. operator. With this operator, a record must meet *only one* of the criteria to be listed. The record does *not* need to meet all the criteria; you are telling dBASE, "List a record if it meets any one of the following conditions: this *or* this *or* this." dBASE also will list a record that meets all the selection criteria. An example of using an OR criteria is searching in the CITY field for either SEATTLE or PORTLAND.

Exercise 3.4: Using .AND. in a List For Command

To list the records of all the customers who live in Mercer, Washington, take these steps:

1. At the dot prompt, type:

   LIST FOR CITY = "MERCER" .AND. STATE = "WA".

2. Press Enter.

   The screen now should resemble figure 4.10. Notice that adding the additional condition STATE = "WA" is necessary because you also have customers in Mercer, Oregon.

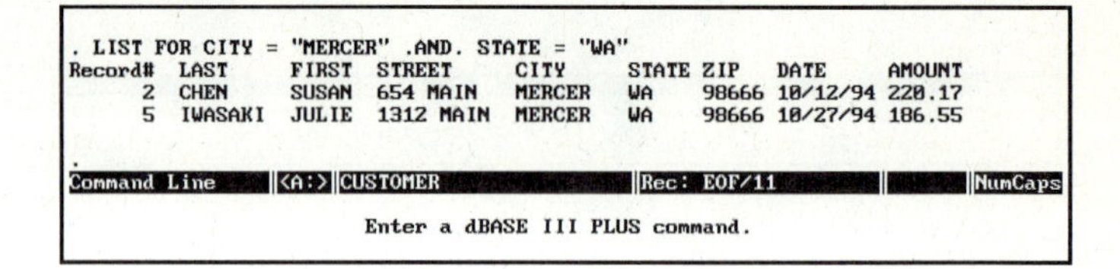

```
. LIST FOR CITY = "MERCER" .AND. STATE = "WA"
Record#  LAST     FIRST  STREET    CITY     STATE ZIP   DATE     AMOUNT
      2  CHEN     SUSAN  654 MAIN  MERCER   WA    98666 10/12/94 220.17
      5  IWASAKI  JULIE  1312 MAIN MERCER   WA    98666 10/27/94 186.55
.
Command Line  |<A:>|CUSTOMER        |Rec: EOF/11      |     |NumCaps
                    Enter a dBASE III PLUS command.
```

Fig. 4.10
The customers from Mercer, Washington.

Exercise 3.5: Using .OR. in a List For Command

To list the records of all the customers who live in Portland or Seattle, take these steps:

1. At the dot prompt, type

   LIST FOR CITY = "PORTLAND" .OR. CITY = "SEATTLE"

2. Press Enter.

   The screen now should resemble figure 4.11.

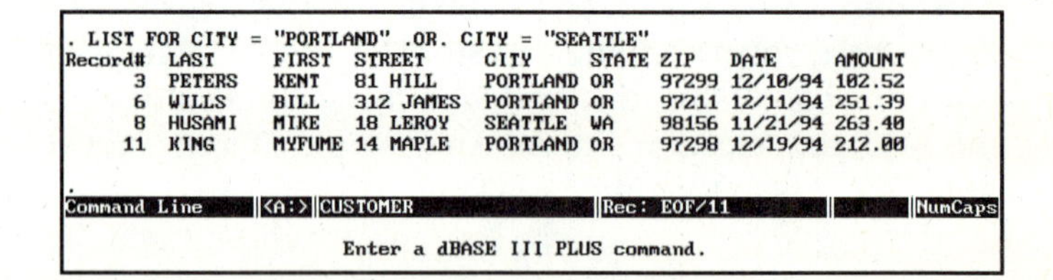

```
. LIST FOR CITY = "PORTLAND" .OR. CITY = "SEATTLE"
Record#  LAST     FIRST  STREET    CITY     STATE ZIP   DATE     AMOUNT
      3  PETERS   KENT   81 HILL   PORTLAND OR    97299 12/10/94 102.52
      6  WILLS    BILL   312 JAMES PORTLAND OR    97211 12/11/94 251.39
      8  HUSAMI   MIKE   18 LEROY  SEATTLE  WA    98156 11/21/94 263.40
     11  KING     MYFUME 14 MAPLE  PORTLAND OR    97298 12/19/94 212.00
.
Command Line  |<A:>|CUSTOMER        |Rec: EOF/11      |     |NumCaps
                    Enter a dBASE III PLUS command.
```

Fig. 4.11
The customers from Portland or Seattle.

A common mistake of people learning to use dBASE is not to repeat the name of the field. They want to type the command LIST FOR CITY = "PORTLAND" .OR. "SEATTLE", but this command cannot work because it is not proper dBASE command syntax.

Using the Comparison Operators in List For Commands

Comparison operators, or range operators, often are used to find values in numeric fields. You also can use these operators with Character fields. Often, the data you seek may be a range of information:

All the sales greater than $100

All the sales made between 1/1/94 and 1/31/94

All the customers whose last names start with the letter *K* up to and including the customers whose last names start with the letter *Q*

All the preceding queries are examples of looking for a range of records.

Table 4.1 lists the six types of dBASE comparison operators.

Table 4.1 Comparison (Range) Operators

Operator	*Definition*
=	Equal to a specific criteria
>	Greater than the specified criteria
<	Less than the specified criteria
>=	Greater than or equal to the criteria
<=	Less than or equal to the criteria
<>	Not equal to the criteria

Exercise 3.6: Using a Comparison Operator in a List For Command

In this exercise, you use the greater than operator to list the records of the customers who spent an amount greater than $200.00. Follow these steps:

1. At the dot prompt, type

   LIST FOR AMOUNT > 200.00

2. Press ↵Enter.

   The screen now should resemble figure 4.12.

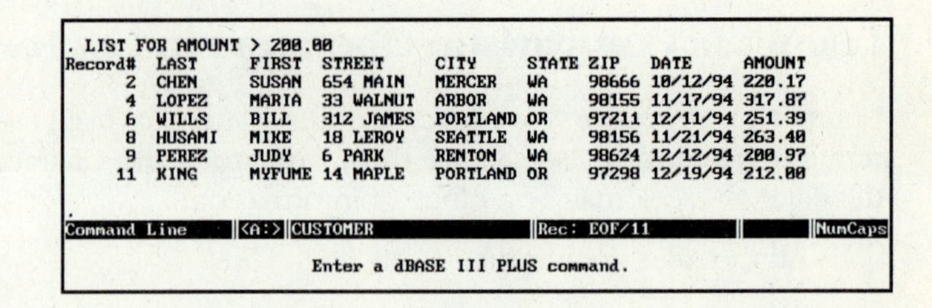

Fig. 4.12 The customers who spent more than $200.00.

4

Objective 4: To Print by Using the List Command

In the previous sections of this chapter, you listed all the fields of all the records in a database file. You also listed the structure and only one or two fields of all the records. In the last section, you listed only a selected group of records from the database. In this section, you perform the same listing that you did in the previous sections except that you now list the records on the printer rather than the screen. Luckily, this operation is easy. You can use exactly the same commands that you used in the previous sections. You need add only *TO PRINT* to the end of the command to cause the results of your List command to be sent to the printer.

The Eject command is useful when you are listing to print. Type the Eject command at the dot prompt after you finish listing to print. The Eject command, which causes the printer to eject one sheet of printer paper, is useful in a computer lab where several students share one printer, because you can eject the sheet on which you printed your work before anyone else can print on it.

Exercise 4.1: Using the List to Print Command

To list on the printer the records of all the customers who live in Washington, take these steps:

1. At the dot prompt, type **LIST FOR STATE = "WA" TO PRINT**.
2. Press ↵Enter.
3. At the dot prompt, type **EJECT**, and press ↵Enter.

   The results of the List command should print.

Exercise 4.2: Using the List to Print Command with Selection Criteria

In this exercise, you use the greater than operator to list on the printer the records of the customers who spent an amount greater than $200.00 by following these steps:

1. At the dot prompt, press ↑ until History places the following command after the dot prompt:

   ```
   LIST FOR AMOUNT > 200.00
   ```

2. Use → if necessary to place the cursor just to the right of `200.00`, and type **TO PRINT**.

   The command now should read `LIST FOR AMOUNT > 200.00 TO PRINT`.

   You also can just type the command, but this exercise is designed to remind you about History.

3. Press ↵Enter.
4. At the dot prompt, type **EJECT**, and press ↵Enter.

Exercise 4.3: Using the Full List to Print Command

In this exercise, you put everything together. You use the less than operator to list on the printer the FIRST and LAST fields in the records of the customers who have spent an amount less than $150.00. Follow these steps:

1. At the dot prompt, type **LIST FIRST, LAST FOR AMOUNT < 150.00 TO PRINT**.
2. Press ↵Enter.
3. At the dot prompt, type **EJECT**, and press ↵Enter.

Objective 5: To Use the Set Commands

When you used the List Status command, you saw a list of settings used by dBASE. dBASE starts with certain settings in effect, but you can alter these settings by using a Set command. Only two of these settings are important for readers of this text to understand and know how to alter with a Set command. The first command changes the default disk drive. The second command turns off the "bell" that some students find annoying when entering data.

The Set Default To Command

As you know, the default disk drive is the drive where all files are stored unless you specify otherwise. The status bar shows the letter of the default drive. When you start dBASE, the default drive probably will be the drive on which dBASE is stored. Chapter 2 explains how to change the default drive by selecting the Set drive command from the Tools menu in the Assistant. You also can use the Set Default To dot prompt command.

You may not know the setting now for your default drive, but assume that it is drive A. If so, you change the setting to drive C from the dot prompt by typing **SET DEFAULT TO C:** and pressing ↵Enter.

To set the default drive back to A, type **SET DEFAULT TO A:**, and press ↵Enter.

The Set Bell Off Command

Usually in dBASE, when you enter data, a warning bell rings (beeps) when you enter invalid data in a field or reach the end of a field. If you want to change this setting, enter the Set Bell Off command. If you later decide that you want the bell to ring, enter the command Set Bell On. The List Status command shows you the current setting of the bell.

Exercise 5.1: Turning Off the Bell

To turn off the warning bell, take these steps:

1. At the dot prompt, type **SET BELL OFF**.
2. Press ↵Enter.
3. Press F6 to verify that the bell is turned off.

Objective 6: To Quit dBASE from the Dot Prompt

After you finish your work in dBASE, exit properly to make sure that all your data is saved. To exit dBASE from the dot prompt, use the Quit command, which is the same as choosing Quit dBASE III Plus from the Assistant's Set Up menu.

Exercise 6.1: Using the Quit Command

To end the session with dBASE, take these steps:

1. At the dot prompt, type **QUIT**.
2. Press Enter.

You now can remove your disk from the disk drive. Your data has been saved.

Chapter Summary

In this chapter, you have learned how to issue commands at the dot prompt. You have learned the various forms of the List command. You have also learned how to list several fields from a record rather than the whole record. You learned how to express selection conditions in a List For command so that dBASE only lists the records that you request. Finally, you learned the uses of the function keys, and you learned how to use two of the most important Set commands.

In the following chapter, you learn how to restructure a database file. You use the Modify Structure command to change the name, size, and type of a field. You also learn how to add and delete fields. You learn how to use the Logical and Memo data types. You also learn the potential effects of restructuring on the data stored in a database.

Testing Your Knowledge

True/False Questions

1. The command LIST TO PRINT LAST_NAME FOR CITY = SEATTLE causes the last names of customers from Seattle to print.
2. To turn off the bell, you type **SET BELL OFF**.
3. To leave dBASE, you type **Exit** at the dot prompt, and press Enter.
4. The comparison operator that means less than or equal is >=.
5. To list the records with an AMOUNT (a numeric field) of exactly 150.00, you enter: **LIST AMOUNT = "150.00"**.

Multiple-Choice Questions

1. To exit from the Assistant and work from the dot prompt, press ______.
   a. End
   b. Exit
   c. Esc
   d. F1

2. When the dot prompt is on-screen, to use the Assistant, press ______.
   a. ↵Enter
   b. Esc
   c. F1
   d. F2
3. When using the List command to list several fields in a database, the fields must be separated by ________.
   a. a space
   b. a comma
   c. either a or b
   d. none of these answers
4. The command that closes a database file without opening another database file is the ______ command.
   a. Close
   b. Clear
   c. Open
   d. Use
5. The function key that displays the structure of the active database file is ______.
   a. F1
   b. F3
   c. F4
   d. F5

Fill-in-the-Blank Questions

1. The command to change the default drive to C is ____________________.
2. The command to list the records for customers from Oregon (OR) or Washington (WA) is ____________________.
3. To access a previously entered dot prompt command, you ____________________.
4. Only a few of the many dBASE commands are available from ____________________.
5. The ____________________ command pauses after listing about 17 data records.

Review: Short Projects

1. Using the List Command to List Individual Fields

   Use the Customer database file to perform the following tasks:

   a. List only the last names of customers and the amount the customers spent.

   b. List only the customer's first and last name and their city and state.

2. Using the List Command to List Records Meeting a Condition

   Use the Customer database file to perform the following tasks:

   a. List only the records of customers from Oregon.

   b. List only the records of customers from Edmonds or Arbor.

   c. List only the records of customers who live in the 97211 ZIP Code area of Portland.

3. Using the List Command to Print Fields from Records Meeting a Condition

   Use the Customer database file to perform the following tasks:

   a. Print the first and last names of all customers from Oregon who spent $200.00 or more. Eject the page.

   b. Print the Date field and the Amount field for all customers from Washington who spent less than $220.00. Eject the page.

Review: Long Projects

1. Using Dot Prompt Commands and the Student Database

   From Chapter 3 Long Project 3, use the proper dot prompt commands to perform these tasks:

   a. Open the Student database file.

   b. List at the printer all the fields in all the records.

   c. List at the printer only the LAST_NAME, STREET, and CITY fields.

   d. List at the printer only the FIRST_NAME, LAST_NAME, STREET, and PHONE fields.

   e. List at the printer the first and last names of all students from Miami.

   f. List at the printer the phone number of all students from the following cities: Coconut Grove, Key Biscayne, and Bal Harbour.

   g. List at the printer the first and last names of all students from Bal Harbour enrolled in item C003.

   h. List the first and last names of all students from Bal Harbour enrolled in item C002.

   i. Use the proper dot prompt command to exit from dBASE.

2. Using Dot Prompt Commands and the Tours Database

   From Chapter 3 Long Project 1, use the proper dot prompt commands to perform these tasks:

   a. Open the Tours database file.

   b. List at the printer all the fields in all the records.

   c. List at the printer only the tours that cost $1,300.00 or less.

   d. Turn off the bell.

   e. Use the Append command to add two new records. (You supply the data for these new records.)

   f. Mark the two new records and record 4 for deletion. List the database at the printer.

   g. Unmark record 4.

   h. Delete the two new records.

   i. List at the printer all the fields in the records of tours that depart on December 6, 1994.

   j. Use the proper dot prompt command to exit from dBASE.

Restructuring a Database File

5

A certain amount of trial and error is involved in the creation of a good database. When you use a database file, you may realize that it needs improvements; you often don't know the best design for a database file structure until you use the database. Some fields in a new database file may not be the right size or type. Or you may be asked for information you do not currently keep, and, as a result, you must add new fields to the database file's structure.

In this chapter, you learn to modify a database file's structure, retaining when possible the data that you have already entered in the database file. You learn the general rules that dBASE follows when it restructures a database file, and you learn how these rules may affect your old database file's data. In addition, because incorrect restructuring can cause you to lose data, this chapter gives guidelines for protecting your database even if you make a mistake as you restructure. In this chapter, you also learn about two new field types: Logical and Memo.

Objectives

1. To Understand dBASE's Rules for Restructuring a File
2. To Copy a Database File
3. To Change a Database File's Structure

4. To Use Logical and Memo Fields
5. To Rename a Database File
6. To Delete a Database File

Key Terms in This Chapter	
Restructuring	The process of modifying a database file structure by changing a field's name, type, or size or by moving, adding, or deleting fields. You restructure by using the Modify Structure command.
Backup	An extra copy of your database file. Often stored on a disk different from your working directory. Making a backup before beginning to restructure a database file is advised. Keeping a backup of a database file is a good practice even if you are not restructuring.
Use	A dot prompt command that, when typed without being followed by a file name, closes the active database and saves its records. No other database file is opened.

Objective 1: To Understand dBASE's Rules for Restructuring a File

Thus far in this text, the changes you have made to a database file have involved changing the data in the database file. To change the database file itself, not just the data contained in it, you must restructure—modify the structure of—the database file. Restructuring is easy; it involves many of the same steps that you followed when you first created your database.

If a database file contains no data, you can make any changes to the structure. If your old database file already contains data, however, the possibility of data loss exists. dBASE tries to ensure that the restructuring does not cause the loss of all your data. dBASE follows some restructuring rules and procedures that you should understand.

Some of the most important considerations are shown in the following list; you may want to keep these in mind when you are restructuring a database file that contains data you don't want to lose.

- Saving a copy of the original database file and its records on a different disk or with another name before you restructure a database file is wise. You then have a backup of your data if the restructuring produces unforeseen consequences.
- You should make multiple modifications to the structure one step at a time. Change field names only, for example, and then leave Modify Structure. Check the result by listing your data. If your data is all right, get back into Modify Structure, change field types or widths, and then leave Modify Structure to check your data. If your data is still all right, get back into Modify Structure, add or delete fields, and so on. You spend a little more time this way, but you can save much data reentry time by avoiding problems.
- When you delete a field from a structure, you delete all the data contained in that field in all the database file's records.
- If you shorten a Character field, data longer than the new field length is lost.
- If you shorten a Numeric field, data longer than the new field length is lost, and the field is filled with asterisks.
- If you change a field's type from Character to Numeric, you lose the data in that field in any record in which the field has alphabetic characters or special characters like *(* or *$*. You do not lose the data in that field in any record where the field contains only numbers or the decimal point.
- If you change a field's type from Date to Numeric, you lose the data in that field in all records.
- If you change a field's type from Character to Date, you do not lose the data in that field in any record in which the field contains valid dates in the mm/dd/yy form.
- If you change a field's type from Numeric or Date to Character, you do not lose the data in that field unless you make the width of the Character field too small for the data.
- If you change a field's name, you do not lose the data in that field unless dBASE displays the message `Database records will be APPENDED from backup fields of same name only` when you press Ctrl+End.
- When you are in the Modify Structure screen, you have not yet made changes to the actual database. If you see a potential problem or receive a warning message from dBASE, do not continue with the restructuring. Changes are applied to the database only after you

5

press Ctrl+End and indicate that the restructuring should be applied.

- When you first issue the Modify Structure command, dBASE makes a copy of your current database (DBF) file in a backup (BAK) file with the same file name as the DBF file. If you again issue a Modify Structure command for the same database file, dBASE's original backup file is overwritten. The BAK file provides some protection against data loss but does not substitute for your own backup of the original database. Your own backup always gets you back to where you were before you started modifying; dBASE's backup might not.

Objective 2: To Copy a Database File

A backup (extra) copy of a database file is like an insurance policy for your data. Computers are reliable, disks are reliable, you are reliable, and dBASE is certainly reliable. But accidents can happen. With a backup copy, all your eggs are not in one basket. Even if you are not restructuring your database or editing your data, having a backup is a good idea. You can easily create a backup by using the Copy To command. This command duplicates the active (open) database file in a new file. You must supply the drive on which the new file should be stored if you do not want to use the default drive. You also need to give the file a name; dBASE supplies the DBF extension.

In the next section of this chapter, you restructure the Student database. Therefore, you should make a backup copy of this database before you begin the restructuring. In this exercise, you store the copy on your default drive; keep in mind, however, that having the backup on a different drive from the original is the best practice. So that the name of the file reminds you of what is in the file, you name the file Stubak, which is an abbreviation of Student Backup.

Exercise 2.1: Making a Backup Copy of the Student Database File

To make a backup of your database file, follow these steps:

1. You must first make Student the active database file. Type **USE STUDENT**, and press Enter.

   Your status bar should indicate that Student is now the active database file.

2. Type **COPY TO STUBAK**, and press ↵Enter. dBASE copies the structure and contents of Student to Stubak.

When you restructure Student, Stubak is not affected, and you can use its data to recover from a restructuring disaster. Notice how quickly and easily you can make a backup; you have no reason not to make one.

Objective 3: To Change a Database File's Structure

Altering an existing database file's structure involves some of the same processes you used when you first created the structure. In fact, the screen displayed when you use the Modify Structure command is the same screen that you first used to create the structure. When you modify a database file structure, you can add or delete fields. You can move fields around in the structure. You can change the name, size, and type of fields. But remember the rules for restructuring discussed in the preceding section.

You change a database file's structure by using the Modify Structure command. Before a database file can be restructured, it must be the active database (in use); its name must appear in the status bar. In the following exercises, you restructure the Student database file. Although the step is not required, first make sure that you don't accidentally create a disaster for yourself during the restructuring. You can protect yourself by making an additional copy of your database file.

Before you begin, here is the procedure that you should follow whenever you restructure. Some of the steps are not required, but they protect you from frustration.

Following the Recommended Procedure When You Restructure

When you are restructuring a database file, follow this general procedure:

1. Use the Copy command to make a backup copy of your database file before you start the restructure. Give the copy a different name from the original database file name. The name should be meaningful. If the database file is the Tours database file, for example, name the backup

copy Toursbak. Then you can glance at the name of the copy and know what database file it is backing up.

2. If you are restructuring and intend to shorten a Character field, make sure that the data already stored in the field fits within the new shorter field size. Otherwise, you lose the characters of data too long to fit into the new field width.
3. If you are changing a field's type during a restructuring, check the rules in the "Objective 1" section so that you are aware of any potential problems.
4. If you need to change a field's name, do only that operation; do not also change sizes or types or add or delete fields. Change the name, and then immediately exit and save the change (press Ctrl+End).

If you follow these procedures, you will have fewer worries as you restructure. The most important guideline is the first one. If you completely destroy the original database file, delete it—as described at the end of this chapter—and then use the Copy command to copy the backup file into a database file with the original DBF file name. If you ruin the Tours database file, for example, first delete the remnants of that database file. Then copy Toursbak, and name the copy Tours. Do not restructure or delete your backup copy (Toursbak) until you are sure that the restructure of Tours caused no problem.

You already created a backup in the Stubak file, so you are ready to begin restructuring Student. In the following exercises, you add GPA, a Numeric type field, to the Student database file. Then you continue with exercises that illustrate all aspects of restructuring.

Exercise 3.1: Beginning the Restructuring of Student

You should have the dot prompt displayed. Your status bar should indicate that Student is the active database file. To start the process of restructuring, follow these steps:

1. Type **MODIFY STRUCTURE**.
2. Press ↵Enter.

   The Modify Structure screen appears (see fig. 5.1). As you can see, this screen is like the Create screen that you originally used to create the structure for Student. You use this screen the same way you use the Create screen.

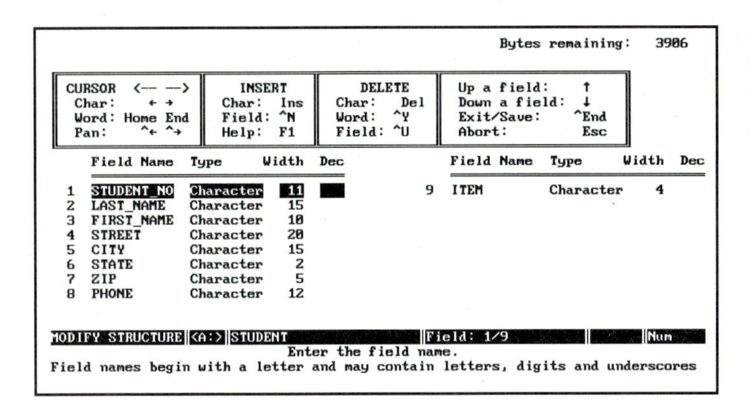

Fig. 5.1 The Modify Structure screen.

Adding Fields

Adding a new field to a database file during the restructuring process is easy. Depending on your requirements, you can insert a field between existing fields or add the new field at the end of the database file. To insert a field, move the cursor to the field where you want the new field to appear, and press Ctrl+N. A new line for the field then appears. In the next exercise, you add a field for the student's grade point average.

Exercise 3.2: Adding a New Field to the Database File

To add a field to the end of the structure, follow these steps:

1. Use ↓ to move the highlight to the ITEM field. Then press ↓ again to indicate that you want to add a new field.
2. Type the field name **GPA**. This field should be a Numeric field with a width of 4 and 2 decimal places.
3. Press ↵Enter.

The screen now should resemble figure 5.2. Don't exit from Modify Structure yet; you have more changes to make.

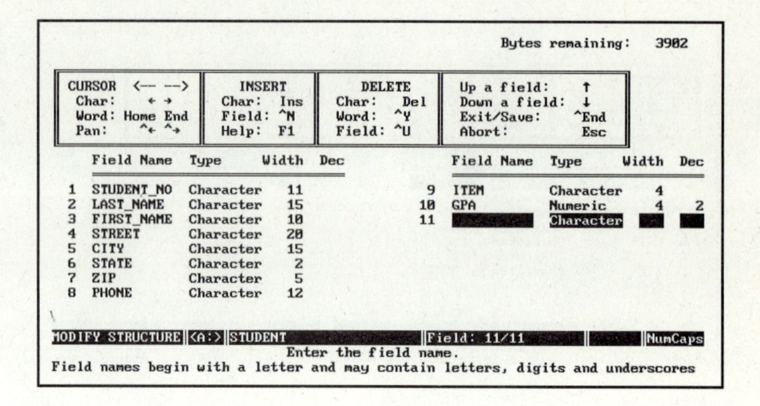

Fig. 5.2
The new field GPA.

Deleting Fields

You can remove unnecessary fields from a database file structure. You may decide to remove a field because the data in the field is not used, or you can keep the data in another database file. Try to keep your database files simple and not duplicate unnecessary information in the database files.

When you erase a field, remember that deleting a field specification from the database file structure also deletes all the database file data contained in that field. You cannot recover the data later unless you keep a backup copy of the database file.

Exercise 3.3: Deleting a Field from the Structure

Suppose that all your students are from Florida, so you can delete the STATE field. To delete the STATE field from the structure, follow these steps:

1. Use the arrow keys to move the highlight to the field you want to delete.
2. Press Ctrl+U. dBASE erases the field specification (see fig. 5.3).

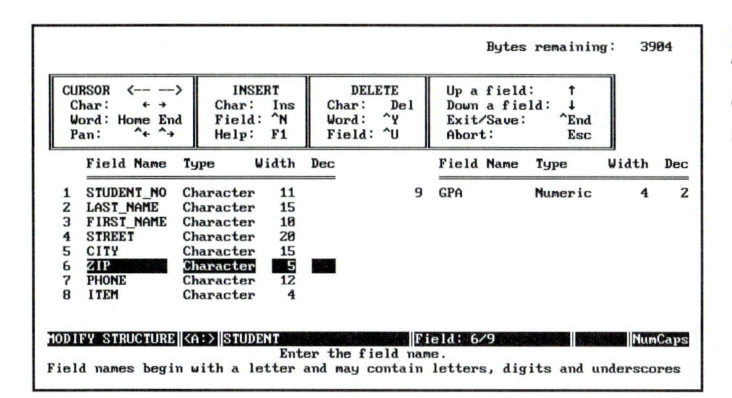

Fig. 5.3 The revised database file structure.

Moving Fields

In dBASE, you can move a field from one location to another in the structure. You first must delete the field you want to move. Then you insert the field at the new location. If you try to insert the field first, dBASE objects because you are trying to create two fields with the same name, and this situation is not allowed in a database file.

Exercise 3.4: Moving a Field in the Structure

To move the ITEM field specification to the second position, follow these steps:

1. Using the arrow keys, move the highlight onto the ITEM field.
2. Delete the ITEM field specification by pressing Ctrl+U.
3. Move the highlight over field 2 (LAST_NAME).
4. Press Ctrl+N to insert a field in position 2.

   The screen now should resemble figure 5.4.

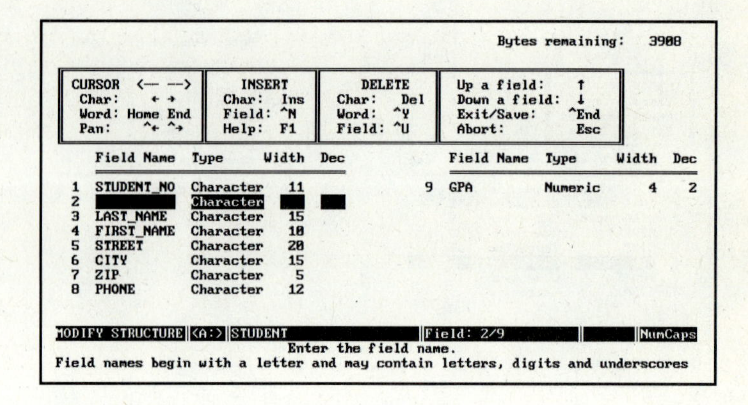

Fig. 5.4 The Modify Structure screen.

5

5. For Field Name type **ITEM**; for Type, select Character; and for Width, type **4**.
6. Press Enter.

The ITEM field now is in the second position, and the other fields have moved down in the roster. The screen now should look like figure 5.5.

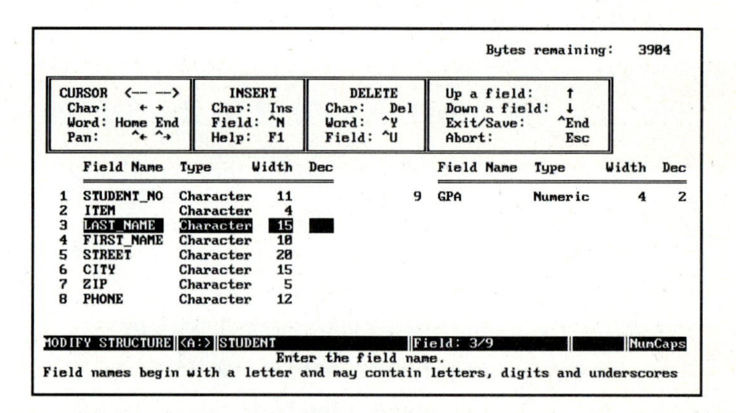

Fig. 5.5 The ITEM field in its new position.

Changing the Size of a Field

You can change a Character field's length. Increasing the length of a Character field never causes a loss of data, but this change may affect any reports used with the database file (for more information on reports, see Chapter 8).

Shortening a Character field, however, can cause loss of data. If a data value is too long to fit into the new field, the data is trimmed from the right until the data value is short enough. Trimmed data from the old database file is lost. As a rule, don't decrease the width of a Character field unless you know that this field in the old database file does not contain any data that is too long for the new field width.

Exercise 3.5: Changing the Width of a Character Field

To increase the width of a Character field to 25, follow these steps:

1. To increase the size of the STREET field, move the cursor to the Width column of the STREET field.
2. Type **25**, and press ↵Enter. Your structure should look like figure 5.6.

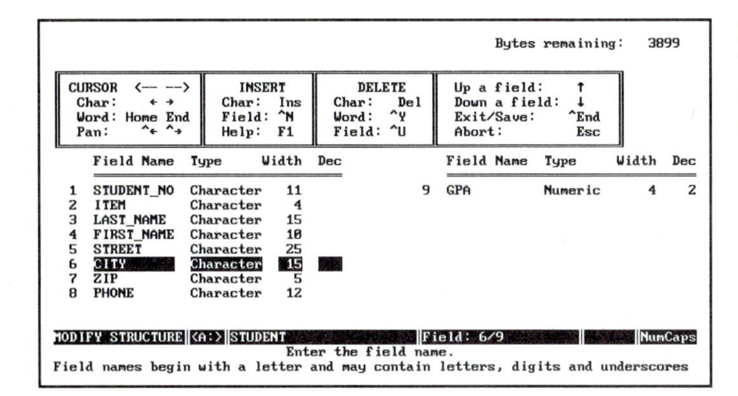

Fig. 5.6
The new width of the STREET field.

5

Changing a Field Type

To change the field type, first use the arrow keys to move the cursor to the item to change. Then enter the new field type and size. Changing a field's type, however, can cause various problems. Earlier in this chapter, you read an overview of what can happen when you change different field types. In the following exercise, you change the type of the ZIP field to Numeric. This exercise is to give you practice, not to suggest that ZIP *should* be changed to numeric. In fact, because you never perform arithmetic operations with a ZIP code, Character type is the appropriate type for a ZIP code field.

Exercise 3.6: Changing the Type of a Field

To change the type of the ZIP field to Numeric, take these steps:

1. Move the highlight to the ZIP field.
2. Move the cursor to the Type column by pressing →.
3. Press N to make the type Numeric.
4. Press ↵Enter to keep a width of 5.
5. Type **0** for the number of decimal places.
6. Press ↵Enter.

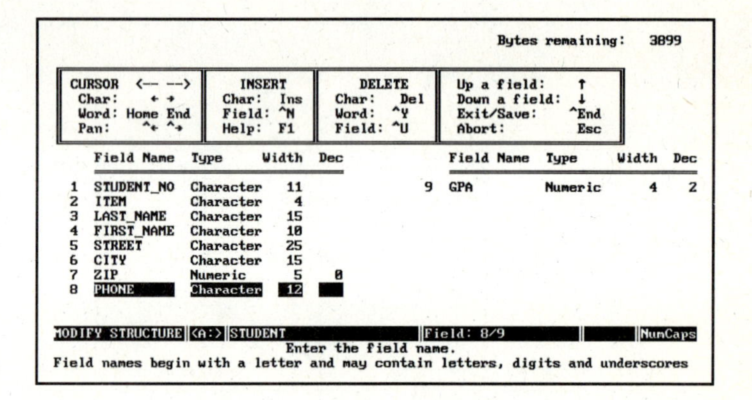

Fig. 5.7
The ZIP field is now Numeric.

Now your Modify Structure screen should look like figure 5.7.

Remember that you have not yet actually done anything to the structure of your database file. You still can just press ↵Enter, and your Student database remains absolutely unchanged. Changes do not occur until you leave Modify Structure.

When you are just learning to use dBASE, restructuring a database file can have disastrous and surprising effects. You might think, "Oh no, why did I do that!" Remember always to create a backup of your database file *before* you restructure it. Then, if you make a mistake or encounter a problem during a restructuring, you can just use the Copy To command to copy Stubak to Student. The "messed up" Student database is replaced (overwritten) by a duplicate of the original Student database. Later, you can delete the backup after you satisfactorily complete the restructuring.

You have made a number of changes to the structure of Student, but you still haven't changed a field name. If you want to change a field name, this change should be the only one you make. Remember the caution against changing field names at the same time you change sizes and types. Restructure now, see whether everything goes according to plan, and then change the field name.

Exercise 3.7: Restructuring the Student Database File

So far, you have changed the structure in the Modify Structure screen only, not in the database file. You still can press Esc if you do not want dBASE to restructure your database file. To restructure the database file, follow these steps:

1. Press Ctrl+End.

   Notice the message `Database Records will be APPENDED from backup fields of the same name only!!` (see fig. 5.8).

```
                                                   Bytes remaining:   3899

 CURSOR  <-- -->    INSERT         DELETE        Up a field:    ↑
  Char:    ← →      Char:   Ins    Char:   Del   Down a field:  ↓
  Word: Home End    Field:  ^N     Word:   ^Y    Exit/Save:   ^End
  Pan:    ^← ^→     Help:   F1     Field:  ^U    Abort:        Esc

     Field Name  Type       Width  Dec            Field Name  Type      Width  Dec

   1 STUDENT_NO  Character    11              9   GPA         Numeric      4    2
   2 ITEM        Character     4
   3 LAST_NAME   Character    15
   4 FIRST_NAME  Character    10
   5 STREET      Character    25
   6 CITY        Character    15
   7 ZIP         Numeric       5    0
   8 PHONE       Character    12

MODIFY STRUCTURE |<A:>|STUDENT            |Field: 8/9        |Ins  |NumCaps
              Press ENTER to confirm.  Any other key to resume.
  Database records will be APPENDED from backup fields of the same name only!!
```

Fig. 5.8
The warning message.

   This warning is dBASE's way of saying, "If you changed any field names, I'm not going to keep the data you stored in them if you restructure now." For this reason, you should change just the field names and then restructure immediately. You haven't changed any field names yet, so you have nothing to worry about.

2. Press ↵Enter.

The restructuring is complete.

Exercise 3.8: Viewing the Restructured Student Database File

To see what you have done so far to the structure of the database file, press F5. The structure should look like figure 5.9.

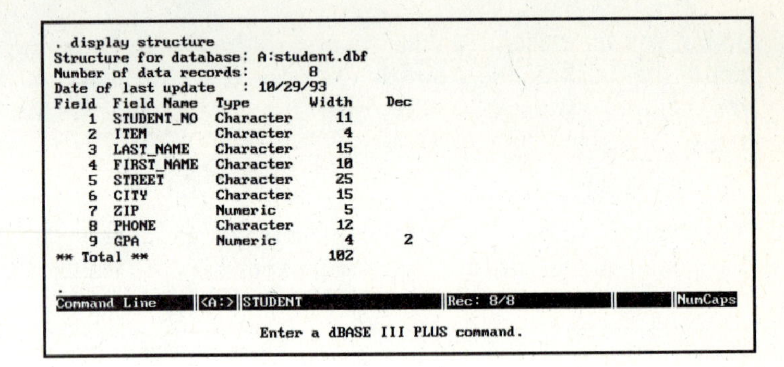

```
. display structure
Structure for database: A:student.dbf
Number of data records:       8
Date of last update   : 10/29/93
Field  Field Name  Type       Width    Dec
    1  STUDENT_NO  Character     11
    2  ITEM        Character      4
    3  LAST_NAME   Character     15
    4  FIRST_NAME  Character     10
    5  STREET      Character     25
    6  CITY        Character     15
    7  ZIP         Numeric        5
    8  PHONE       Character     12
    9  GPA         Numeric        4      2
** Total **                     102

Command Line  <A:> STUDENT  Rec: 8/8  NumCaps
                Enter a dBASE III PLUS command.
```

Fig. 5.9 The new structure.

Notice that the field order has changed, STATE no longer is in the database file, STREET is now 25 characters wide, and ZIP is a Numeric field. Now you will finish your restructuring by changing only a field name.

Changing the Name of a Field

Changing an existing field name is like creating a new specification. You can change the field name by erasing or adding text for the new field names. To change the field name, use the arrow keys to move the cursor to the item to change; then enter the new field name.

In the following exercise, you change the field name of the ZIP field.

Exercise 3.9: Changing a Field Name

In this exercise, you use a short form of the Modify Structure command. To change the field name of the ZIP field, follow these steps:

1. Type **MODI STRU**, and press Enter.
2. Move the cursor to the Field Name column of the ZIP field by using the arrow keys.
3. Type **ZIP_CODE**, and press Enter.

   Your structure should now look like figure 5.10.

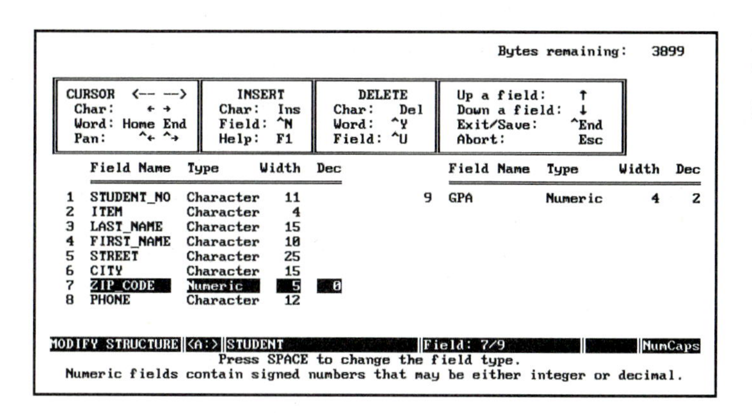

Fig. 5.10 The new field name.

4. Press Ctrl + End.

   The screen now should resemble figure 5.11.

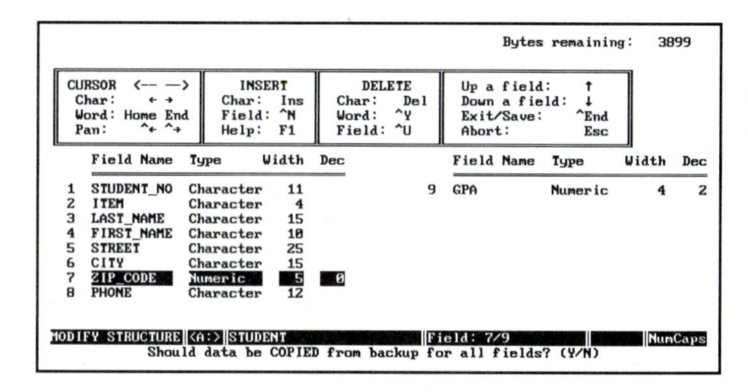

Fig. 5.11 The message that indicates dBASE understands the name change.

The message at the bottom of the screen is dBASE's way of saying "You used a different field name, but I can see what you want me to do; you won't lose data." Contrast this message with the warning in figure 5.8.

If you change only the name of a field in a database file and the field contains data, dBASE copies the data in the field with the new name. You don't lose data.

5. Press Y and then ↵Enter.

6. Press F5 to check the structure and verify the name change (see fig. 5.12).

Fig. 5.12
The new database structure.

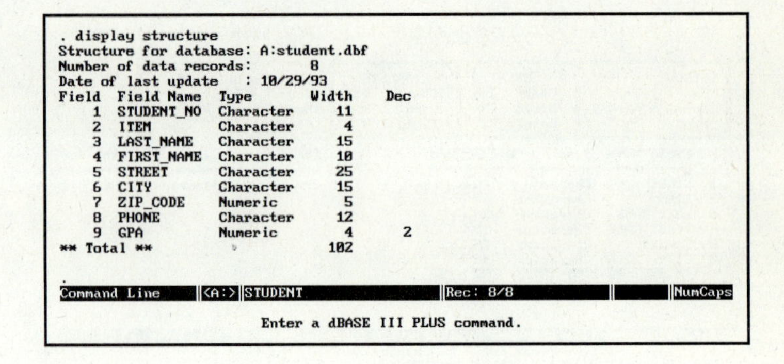

```
. display structure
Structure for database: A:student.dbf
Number of data records:       8
Date of last update   : 10/29/93
Field  Field Name  Type       Width    Dec
    1  STUDENT_NO  Character     11
    2  ITEM        Character      4
    3  LAST_NAME   Character     15
    4  FIRST_NAME  Character     10
    5  STREET      Character     25
    6  CITY        Character     15
    7  ZIP_CODE    Numeric        5
    8  PHONE       Character     12
    9  GPA         Numeric        4      2
** Total **                     102

Command Line      <A:> STUDENT          Rec: 8/8          NumCaps
                  Enter a dBASE III PLUS command.
```

5

7. To check to see whether you have lost any data, press F3.

Objective 4: To Use Logical and Memo Fields

Two types of dBASE fields that you have not yet used are the Logical and the Memo fields. These fields are not used as often as the Character, Numeric, and Date fields.

Understanding the Logical Data Type

The Logical data type is always one character wide and can contain one of two possible conditions: True (.T.) or False (.F.). When entering data into a Logical field, you can type—in either upper- or lowercase—*Y* or *T*, or N or *F*. Obviously, a Logical type field can hold only Yes or No type data.

Understanding the Memo Data Type

The Memo data type is similar to the Character type field. The Character field can hold a maximum of 254 characters, but the Memo field can hold at least 5,000 characters. Now, 254 is a larger number of characters, and Character type fields are useful, but sometimes Character fields are not wide enough for the large blocks of text that you need to store. Another problem is listing the fields of a database file with one or more large Character type fields. Reading a listing of such a file is difficult. Rather than seeing distinct records, you see what looks like one big "data fruit salad." Memo fields solve this problem.

Perhaps an example of a *real world* application where a Memo field was required can help you judge where Memo fields can be useful.

The first time I needed to use a Memo type field was while I was consulting for a university that received the donation of a collection of approximately 3,000 photographs. These photographs had been taken during the latter half of the 19th century. Most were in the form of fragile, easily scratched, and irreplaceable glass negatives.

So that researchers could browse through a dBASE database and decide which photographs they wanted to request from the university, the content of the photographs had to be clearly and completely described by historians at the university. Try getting professors to do that in 254 characters or fewer. And the university wanted the researchers to be able to have any new verifiable facts about the photographs added to the stored data on the photograph. Clearly, this requirement could be handled only by the Memo type field.

Understanding Memo Files

To store the paragraphs of text that are entered into a Memo field, dBASE creates a new file. This file has the same name as the database file with which it is associated, but the file has the extension DBT.

Using Memo Fields

You enter data into a Memo type field and list the data in a Memo field differently than you enter or list any of the other field types. The contents of a Memo field when displayed with the List command and the width of a Memo type field when displayed in a database file's structure also need some explaining.

When you are creating the structure of a database file, you make a field the Memo type just as you make a field a Date or a Character type. dBASE then automatically makes the width of the field 10 characters. How can 5,000 characters be stored in a field that is only 10 characters wide? They can't; as explained previously, the content of a record's Memo field (the block of text) is stored in the separate Memo (DBT) file. The Memo field in a database file record contains 10 characters of information that link that particular record to its associated text block in the Memo file. The difference in the way that Memo fields are stored and the fact that you need a word processing program to enter large amounts of text efficiently leads to two unique aspects of Memo fields: how you enter them and how you list them.

In the following exercise, you add a Logical type field and a Memo type field to the Student database file.

Exercise 4.1: Adding Logical and Memo Type Fields to a Database File Structure

You should have the dot prompt displayed, and your status bar should indicate that Student is the active database file. To add the fields to the database structure, follow these steps:

1. Type **MODIFY STRUCTURE** (or **MODI STRU** if you prefer), and press ↵Enter.
2. Move the highlight to the GPA field.
3. Press ↓ to signal that you want to add a field.
4. Type the field name and type for the following fields:

ADVISED	**Logical**
NOTES	**Memo**

   The screen now should resemble figure 5.13.

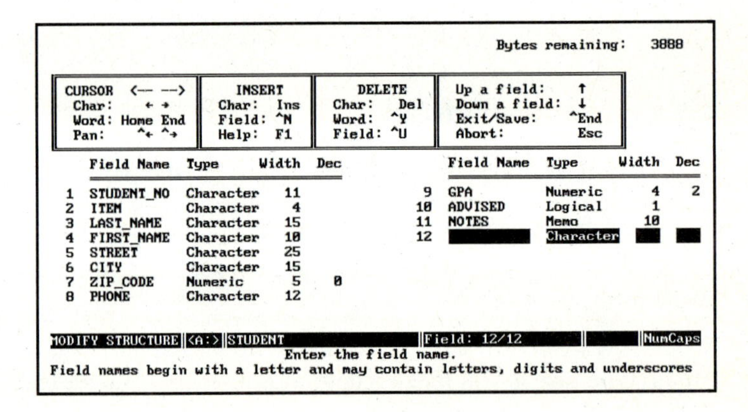

Fig. 5.13 The new database structure with added fields.

5. Press Ctrl+End.
6. Type **LIST LAST_NAME, ADVISED, NOTES**, and press ↵Enter.

Notice that all the ADVISED fields are initially set to `.F.`; this setting is always the case with Logical type fields. The Memo field is empty for all records (see fig. 5.14).

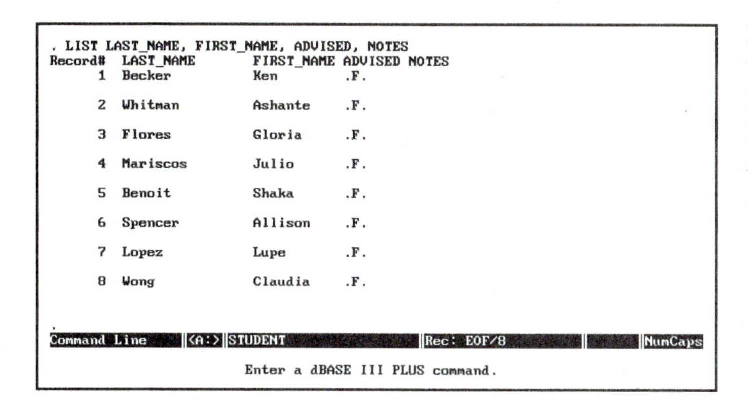

Fig. 5.14 The LAST_NAME, FIRST_NAME, ADVISED, and NOTES fields.

Entering Text into a Memo Field

You can enter text into a memo field by using either the Append command or the Edit command. The Browse command doesn't allow you to enter text into a Memo field. To enter text into a Memo field when using either Append or Edit, you first place the blinking dash cursor in the Memo field and then press Ctrl+End. This action places you in dBASE's word processor (see fig. 5.15). The text that you enter is placed in the Memo field of the record number you were editing or appending. The record number will be placed in the memo file so that when you list the Memo field, you will see the record number followed by the text that is associated with that record number.

```
Edit: NOTES                                      Num
CURSOR:  <-- -->    UP  DOWN         DELETE      Insert Mode:     Ins
Char:     ← →      Line:    ↑   ↓    Char:  Del   Insert line:     ^N
Word:  Home End    Page: PgUp PgDn   Word:   ^T   Save: ^W  Abort:Esc
Line:    ^← ^→     Find:    ^KF      Line:   ^Y   Read file:       ^KR
Reformat: ^KB      Refind: ^KL                    Write file:      ^KW
```

Fig. 5.15 Part of the screen for entering data into a Memo field.

You can use the Memo field word processor to insert text into an empty Memo field. You can also add to existing text in the field, edit and update text, or delete text. As shown in figure 5.15, the keys that you use for editing and cursor movement are displayed in a menu at the top of the screen. In the blank area of the screen, you type text just as you type in a word processing program. One keystroke combination that isn't shown in the menu is the standard Ctrl+End combination, used to signal dBASE to "save this work" and return to the dot prompt or to the Assistant. You also can use this command to exit from the Memo field word processor. When you press Ctrl+End, you are returned to the Edit or Append screen.

Exercise 4.2: Adding Data to Logical and Memo Type Fields

Assume that Ken Becker and Allison Spencer were seen by their advisor, and the advisor made some notes on the advising session. To update the database to reflect this session, take these steps:

1. At the dot prompt, type **EDIT**, and press Enter.
2. Move up to Ken Becker's record by pressing PgUp.
3. Move the cursor to the ADVISED field and type **Y**.

   The cursor moves to the NOTES field.

4. Press Ctrl+PgDn to switch to the word processor so that you can enter the memo text.
5. Press Ins to place the word processor in Insert mode (Typeover mode is the default).
6. Enter the following text:

   I spoke with Mr. Becker on 10/29/93. I explained that we wondered whether there was any way that we might advise him because we felt that if he could raise his GPA, he would have a better chance of competing successfully in our competitive job market.

   Mr. Becker said that he felt that he was doing just fine. He said that he was working full time at night and that the computer labs were too crowded during the day hours for him to have adequate time on the computer.

7. Press Ctrl+End to return to the Edit screen.

   Your screen should look like figure 5.16.

8. Press PgDn to move the highlight to Allison Spencer's record.
9. Move the cursor to the ADVISED field, and type **Y**.

   The cursor moves to the NOTES field.

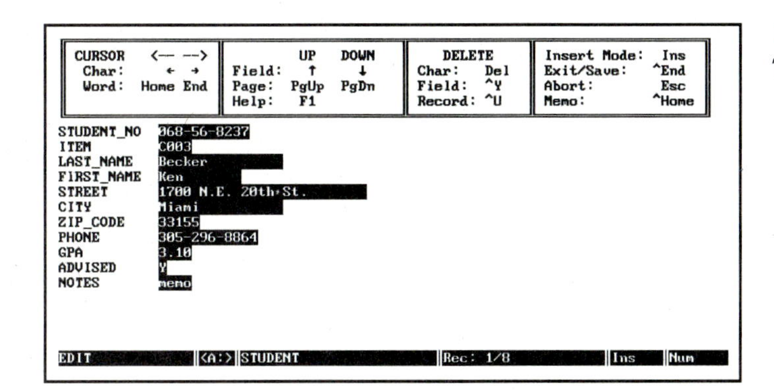

Fig. 5.16
The Edit screen.

10. Press Ctrl + PgDn to switch to the word processor so that you can enter the memo text.
11. Type any advice you feel is appropriate for Allison. After you finish, press Ctrl + End to return to the Edit screen.
12. Press Ctrl + End to leave the Edit screen and save the data that you entered.

Listing the Contents of Memo Fields

Just as you use a unique technique to place data in Memo fields, when you list Memo fields, you also use a special method. If you simply type *LIST* and press ↵Enter, you see the contents of all the fields except the Memo field. Only the word *Memo* will appear in the list, regardless of whether the Memo field in a record is empty or contains data. To actually see the contents of a Memo field, you must follow the List command with the name of the Memo field. For example, if the database in use contains a Memo type field named NOTES, you type *LIST NOTES* to see the contents of the NOTES field. You also can use the names of other fields in the list command. For example, you can enter *LIST FIRST_NAME, LAST_NAME, NOTES*.

If when you are listing Memo fields, you find the record numbers at the left of the screen distracting, use the List Off option of the List command. This version of the List command does not display record numbers. You can list any type of dBASE field with the List Off command; this command is not just for Memo fields.

Exercise 4.3: Listing Logical and Memo Type Fields

To list the contents of the Logical and Memo type fields, take these steps:

1. At the dot prompt, type

   LIST OFF LAST_NAME, ADVISED, NOTES TO PRINT

2. Press ↵Enter.
3. Type **EJECT**, and press ↵Enter.

   Notice that the ADVISED fields for Ken and Allison now contain .T. (see fig. 5.17).

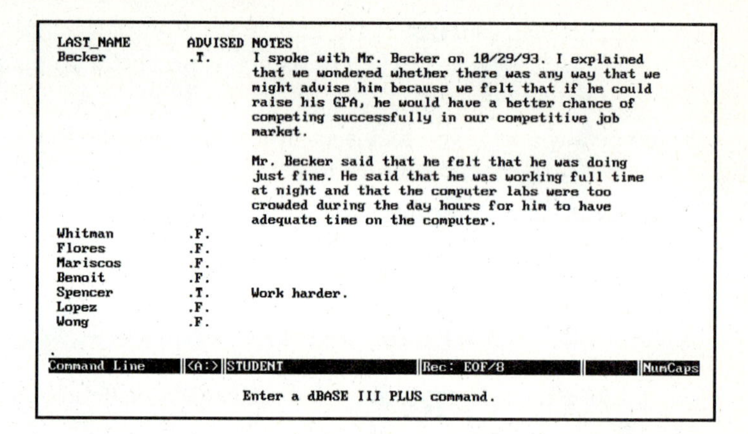

Fig. 5.17
The Logical and Memo fields displayed.

Objective 5: To Rename a Database File

Although renaming files is not a necessary part of restructuring, you will find that knowing how to rename a file is useful. Now is a good time to learn. When you rename a file, you don't create a new file; you just change the name of an existing file. Now that you have completed the restructuring of Student, you can safely delete the Stubak file (dBASE has kept Student.bak for you); and although Student now has the two new fields, ADVISED and NOTES, Stubak does not. You are going to delete this old file in the following section, so you can practice the Rename command now.

There are several points that you must remember when you use this command:

- The file that you rename cannot be in use (active). If it is active, type **USE**, and press ↵Enter to close the file.

- Both the old file name and the new file name must include file extensions (such as DBF or BAK).
- If the files are not on the default drive, precede the file names with the proper drive designators (such as A: or C:).
- If the database file contains a Memo field, the file has a memo file (DBT file) with the same name as the database file. This file's name does *not* also change when you rename the database file. If you rename a database file with an associated memo file, you also must rename the corresponding memo file to match the database file.

Exercise 5.1: Renaming the Stubak Database File

To do this exercise, you cannot be using Stubak. If Stubak is active, type **USE**, and press ↵Enter to close the file.

To rename Stubak, take these steps:

1. Type **RENAME STUBAK.DBF TO STUDENT2.DBF**.
2. Press ↵Enter.
3. Press F4 to verify that Stubak was renamed.

Objective 6: To Delete a Database File

When a database file is no longer necessary or if information is duplicated across database files, you want to delete the database file. In dBASE, deleting a database file is a simple task. You should conduct this kind of housecleaning task routinely. If you don't use certain database files, delete them from your disk. Be cautious when you delete database files; make sure that you really don't need a database file and its data records before you permanently delete it.

Two commands are available for deleting files. The commands are the Erase command and the Delete File command. No real difference exists in their effect. Just as you cannot rename an open file, you cannot delete an open file. The name of the file you are deleting must include the file extension. If the file is not on the default drive, you must include the drive designator (A: or C:) when you type the command. Remember that these delete commands delete only the file that you specify. If you delete a database file (a DBF file) that contains a Memo type field, this step does *not* delete the associated memo (DBT) file. The memo file must be deleted separately.

Exercise 6.1: Deleting a Database File

To delete Student2, make sure that this file is not in use. If it is active, type **USE**, and press ↵Enter to close the file Student2.

To delete the Student2 database file, follow these steps:

1. Type **DELETE FILE STUDENT2.DBF**.
2. Press ↵Enter.

   You should see the message `File has been deleted` at the bottom of the screen.
3. Press F4 to verify that the file was deleted.

Chapter Summary

In this chapter, you have learned how to adjust the structure of a database file either to improve the old database file or to accommodate additional fields. You have learned that dBASE creates a backup database file with the extension BAK to avoid losing any of your data if a problem occurs during restructuring. You have learned how to rename, copy, and delete database files. You have also learned how to use Logical and Memo fields. Finally, you learned both the importance of backing up your database files and the way to create a backup.

In Chapter 6, you learn how to sort the data in a database file by using the Sort command and by using indexes. You also learn when these two techniques are appropriate, and you learn the advantages and disadvantages of the two approaches.

Testing Your Knowledge

True/False Questions

1. You cannot copy a database file that is in use.
2. When you rename a database file, dBASE automatically supplies the DBF extension.
3. To add data to a Memo type field, you first must place the cursor in the field.

4. You can use the Browse command to add data to a Memo type field.
5. If you decrease the size of a Character type field, you lose all data that does not fit into the new smaller field.

Multiple-Choice Questions

1. Which of the following function keys displays the structure of the active database file?
   a. F3
   b. F4
   c. F5
   d. none of these answers
2. Which command enables you to close a database file without opening another database file?
   a. Use
   b. Close
   c. Select
   d. none of these answers
3. Which type of field has its width automatically set by dBASE?
   a. Date
   b. Logical
   c. Memo
   d. all these answers
4. If you are using the Modify Structure command and you decide *not* to restructure, press ________.
   a. F1
   b. F6
   c. ↵Enter
   d. none of these answers
5. You can switch dBASE out of Typeover mode by pressing ________.
   a. Ins
   b. ↵Enter
   c. Ctrl+T
   d. none of these answers

Fill-in-the-Blank Questions

1. To delete a database file, you use the ________ command.
2. To change the structure of a database file, you use the ________ command.
3. To move into the dBASE word processor, you press the ________ keys.
4. To move out of the dBASE word processor, you press the ________ keys.
5. To create a backup of your database file, you use the ________ command.

Review: Short Projects

For these short projects, first copy the Student database to a database named Practice, and then enter the command **USE PRACTICE**.

1. Changing a Field's Name

   Use the Restructure command to change the name of one of the fields. Print the altered database structure.
2. Using the Restructure Command to Change a Field Length

   Change the width of the STREET field to 10. Print the altered database file.
3. Deleting a Field from a Structure

   Delete a field, and then print the structure of the database.

Review: Long Projects

1. Restructuring the Climate Database File

   Create a backup of the Climate database file; name the copy Climateb. Restructure Climateb in the following ways:
   - Make STATION a field with a width of **25**.
   - Delete the JAN. MAX. field.
   - Add a new field, **JUNE_MIN**.
   - Rename JAN. MIN as **JANUARY**.
   - Change the length of the COUNTRY field to **6**.
   - Restructure Climateb.
   - Print the structure and the records of the Climateb database file.

2. Restructuring the Courses Database File

   Create a backup of the Courses database file; name the copy Coursesb. Restructure Coursesb in the following ways:

   - Make the ITEM field have a width of **6**.
   - Shorten the DESCRIPT field to the width **10**.
   - Delete the TAUGHT_BY field.
   - Change the name of the ENROLLMENT field to **ENROLLED**.
   - Move the ITEM field to the end of the record.
   - Add a Memo field named **REPUTATION**. Enter text in this field in at least 3 records.
   - Print the structure and the records of the Coursesb database file.

Sorting and Indexing Database Files

6

In previous chapters, you entered records into your databases in the order that you received them. Usually, the records were not in a meaningful order—that is, they were not in alphabetical order by student name or grouped by city or ZIP code. But for people who actually work with the data in a database, to be able to see the data in a special order is often important. The real estate agents, for example, who consult the database of their listings need to see the records grouped by location (neighborhood). For each location, agents may want the records in order from lowest to highest price. In a large database of homes, agents may want to see the records grouped by location and within location sorted by increasing price and within a given price from smallest to largest number of square feet.

With dBASE, you can sort data in any order you require. Two techniques are available—sorting and indexing. The only real restrictions are that you can sort only on a database field (obviously) and that you cannot sort on Logical or Memo type fields. You can use sorting or indexing to display data in any useful order. You can also use sorting or indexing to see trends in the data or to group the data by categories.

This chapter shows you how to sort and index dBASE database files. When dBASE sorts your records, it sorts them just as you sort records on sheets of paper. An exception is in the manner in which numbers stored in Character fields are sorted; you learn about this exception later in the chapter. Remember that although the databases used in this chapter have only a few records, databases that contain thousands of records are very common. If you practice the techniques of sorting and indexing by using these small databases, you then can confidently apply your skills to larger databases and discover how useful sorting and indexing are.

Objectives

1. To Understand How dBASE Sorts Character, Date, and Numeric Fields
2. To Sort a Database File Using One Sort Field
3. To Sort a Database File Using Multiple Sort Fields
4. To Sort a Database File in Descending Order
5. To Understand the Problems Created by Sorting
6. To Understand What Indexing a File Does
7. To Index a File on One Field
8. To Use Index Files
9. To Index a File Using Multiple Fields

Key Terms in This Chapter	
Sort	To order records in a database file based on selected fields; records can be arranged in ascending or descending order.
ASCII	An acronym for American Standard Code for Information Interchange; dBASE's sorting order follows this standard.
Ascending	Sorting records in order from lowest to highest value of a field.
Descending	Sorting records in order from highest to lowest value of a field.
Index file	A file that contains a list of record numbers from a database file. The record numbers cause dBASE to display the records in a sorted order.
Key field	The database field used to create an index.

Objective 1: To Understand How dBASE Sorts Character, Date, and Numeric Fields

Records in an unsorted database file are displayed in the order the records were entered (unless you inserted some records in the middle of the file rather than adding them at the bottom of the database file). By default, the first record you added is number 1, the second record is number 2, and so on. If you want to see the records in chronological order—the record of your first customer first, and so on—this order is satisfactory, but most people who work with data find this order limiting.

Sorting enables you to change the actual order of the records in a file, but you must create an additional duplicate file for each sorted order you need. Indexing changes the order in which records are displayed and leaves the records in their original order in a single database file. Indexing is useful because you have only one database to update, but you can work with it in many orders.

Sorting on a Character Type Field

When comparing records to place them in sorted order based on a Character field, dBASE is case sensitive (upper- and lowercase letters do not sort together). dBASE sorts everything stored in a Character type field by moving from left to right and "looking at" the characters one at a time. Suppose that dBASE is sorting first names and finds a record with *Sam* in the FIRST NAME field and another record with *Dan* in the FIRST NAME field. To sort the records, dBASE has to look at only the first character (letter) of the name. *D* comes before *S*, so Dan's record is placed before Sam's.

Now, suppose that one record has a FIRST NAME of *Dawn* and the other has the FIRST NAME of *Dave*. The first two characters are the same in both names, so dBASE must keep moving to the right comparing characters until it finds one character that differs. In this example, *v* comes before *w*, so dBASE immediately stops comparing characters. dBASE knows that *Dav* comes before *Daw*, regardless of what characters are to the right of the third character in the name. "Of course!" you say. "This order is the way names appear in a phone book, words appear in a dictionary, or anything else alphabetic; that's exactly what we expect dBASE to do."

The only strange result you may notice occurs when you sort *numbers* stored in a Character type field. The number 100 sorts as "less than" 90. Why? And why store numbers in a Character type field anyway?

Think about a number like a ZIP code, a Social Security number, an account number, or an insurance policy number. You store these numbers in a Character type field because leading zeros are significant, the values don't have decimal places, and the numbers are not going to be used in a calculation. These numbers are sorted just as the characters in any Character type field are sorted. dBASE looks at the first character. If the first characters are different, the larger (or later alphabetically or numerically) character is moved down. If the first characters are the same, dBASE compares the second characters, and so on until a difference is found and the records can be placed in order.

Now can you see why a Character type policy number of 100 comes before 99? Which number is less—1 or 9? In a Character type sort, comparing 1 and 9 is just like comparing A with Z. In a Character type sort, *any* number that starts with 1 is grouped with all the other numbers that start with 1. This grouping is followed by all the numbers that start with 2 and so on. For example, a typical sort of Character type numbers in ascending order may look like this:

10

11345

21

278

300

4

432

517

53 ...and so on

Sorting Numeric and Date Type Fields

You should be pleased to learn that Numeric type fields sort just as you expect, from smallest to largest number—nothing unexpected here. Date type fields also sort just as you probably sort them by hand. Remember that Logical and Memo fields cannot be sorted or indexed.

Objective 2: To Sort a Database File Using One Sort Field

If you want to sort a database, you must first make it the active database file. Then you tell dBASE what field to sort on and where to place the sorted records. You cannot sort a database into itself. You have to create a new database file whenever you sort. The new database file is sorted, not the file that is in use.

Sorting Database Files

If you are sorting a database file by using the Sort command, you must supply dBASE with the name of the new database file in which you want the sorted records placed. After the sort is completed, you have two database files: the old database file in the original order and the new, sorted database file that dBASE automatically creates and saves on disk. When you sort, you also must supply the name of the field dBASE should use in the sort.

All the fields in a record are moved as a unit during the sort. Specifying field names in the Sort command doesn't indicate that only these fields in the record should be moved during the sort. Instead, listing one or more fields in the command tells dBASE that these fields control the sort order and the placement of a record in the sorted database file.

Exercise 2.1: Sorting the Student Database File by Using the CITY Field

To sort or index a database file, the index or file must be in use (active). The Student database file should be active—the file name should appear in the status bar. When you sort, you must specify both the field that determines the sorted order and the name of the file you create to store the sorted database.

To perform a sort operation by using the CITY field and Student2 as the new database file in which the records are placed in sorted order, follow these steps:

1. Type **SORT ON CITY TO STUDENT2**, and press Enter.

   dBASE displays a message at the bottom of the screen:

   ```
   100% Sorted  8 records sorted ...  copying text file.
   ```

   The text file is the file that contains the Memo type field.

2. Type the command **LIST STUDENT_NO, LAST_NAME, CITY**, and press Enter.

   These records are *not* sorted on CITY because the database in use is Student. The sorted records are in the Student2 file.

3. To see the records in Student2, type **USE STUDENT2**, and press Enter.

4. Type **LIST**, and press Enter.

The records now appear sorted in alphabetic order on CITY (see fig. 6.1).

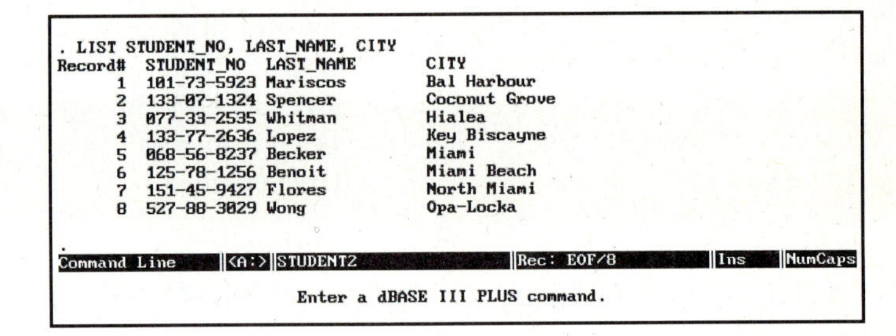

Fig. 6.1
The records in the database file sorted in ascending alphabetic order on CITY.

5. Press F5. You see that the structure of Student2 is the same as that of Student.

Objective 3: To Sort a Database File Using Multiple Sort Fields

Often sorting on a single field is not sufficient to put a database file in the order you need because you have duplicate values in that field. Records with the same value in a sort field (or fields) are called *ties* for a position in the database file. To break ties when you have duplicate values in one field, you can use additional sort fields. The records in the database file can be sorted based on either a single field or several fields.

To sort a database file by the contents of a field (with any ties broken by sorting with a second field) and, if necessary, by a third field, you must specify all the fields to be used by dBASE in determining the sort order. This kind of sorting is sometimes referred to as a *three-level sort* or a "sort inside a sort."

The Major Sort Field

The first field you specify is the *major* (most important) sort field. The major sort field determines the overall order of the sorted database file's data. Only if duplicate values exist in the major sort field does dBASE check the other fields you specified as it sorts the records. If ties (duplicates) occur in the major sort field, dBASE sorts within the value of the major sort field by using the second sort field in the list. If dBASE still finds ties in the combined first two sort fields, dBASE resolves the order of these tied records by referring to the field you have placed third in the list. If you sort student records alphabetically by name, LAST NAME is the major field, FIRST NAME is the next field in the list, and INITIAL is the third field in the list.

Now sort the Student2 database file by using two of the database's fields. Before you do this, create some records with ties on the LAST_NAME field. LAST_NAME is the first—major—sort field. Only if ties exist in the major field do you see the effect of the second sort field.

Exercise 3.1: Setting Up Ties in the Student2 Database File

Using the Edit command and Student2, create two ties in the LAST_NAME field by doing the following:

1. Change Allison Spencer's last name to **Benoit**.
2. Change Ashante Whitman's last name to **Mariscos**.
3. List the LAST_NAME field to verify that two records have the last name of Benoit and two records have the last name of Mariscos. These are the pairs of records to be tied.

Exercise 3.2: Sorting Using Two Fields

To sort the database file Student2 using two sort fields and create a new database file, Student3, follow these steps:

1. Make sure that Student2 is in use.
2. Type **SORT ON LAST_NAME, FIRST_NAME TO STUDENT3**, and press [↵Enter].
3. Type **USE STUDENT3**, and press [↵Enter].
4. Type **LIST**, and press [↵Enter].

Your records now should be in order of LAST_NAME, the major sort field. Those records with duplicate last names should be in order by first name (see fig. 6.2).

6

Fig. 6.2
The sorted database file.

```
. USE STUDENT3
. LIST
Record#  STUDENT_NO  ITEM LAST_NAME       FIRST_NAME STREET                  C
ITY             ZIP_CODE PHONE        GPA ADVISED NOTES
      1  068-56-8237 C003 Becker          Ken        1700 N.E. 20th St.      M
iami            33155 305-296-8864 3.10 .T.     Memo
      2  133-07-1324 C002 Benoit          Allison    11000 S.W. 57th Ave.    C
oconut Grove    33103 305-211-3456 2.00 .T.     Memo
      3  125-78-1256 C004 Benoit          Shaka      4442 Collins Ave.       M
iami Beach      33140 305-363-2416 4.00 .F.     Memo
      4  151-45-9427 C005 Flores          Gloria     17 Tamiami Trail        N
orth Miami      33145 305-754-3485 3.97 .F.     Memo
      5  133-77-2636 C002 Lopez           Lupe       7301 Crandon            K
ey Biscayne     33149 305-177-3602 3.85 .F.     Memo
      6  077-33-2535 C001 Mariscos        Ashante    47 East Flagler St.     H
ialea           33157 305-331-7198 3.98 .F.     Memo
      7  101-73-5923 C003 Mariscos        Julio      12500 West Dixie Hwy    B
al Harbour      33130 305-198-1911 3.89 .F.     Memo
      8  527-88-3029 C003 Wong            Claudia    37 Brickell Ave.        O
pa-Locka        33135 305-855-9742 3.95 .F.     Memo

.
Command Line   |<A:>|STUDENT3          |Rec: EOF/8    |      |NumCaps

                     Enter a dBASE III PLUS command.
```

Objective 4: To Sort a Database File in Descending Order

Usually, you sort a database file as you have sorted in the preceding examples. You choose the fields to use as the sort fields and then let dBASE perform the sort operation. This sort places the records in ascending order based on the selected sort field(s).

Ascending and Descending Order

When sorting (but not indexing), you can tell dBASE not only the fields to use for sorting a database file but also the order in which to sort the fields.

The default sorted order is *ascending* order—from smallest (or first in the alphabet) to largest (or last in the alphabet). You also can use a descending sort order when sorting a database file. *Descending* order is from largest (or last in the alphabet) to smallest (or first in the alphabet). Specify descending order by either typing *Descending* after the sort field name or, as a short cut, typing */D* after the sort field name.

Exercise 4.1: Sorting a Database File in Descending Order

To sort the Student3 records in descending order on the ZIP_CODE field, follow these steps:

1. Make sure that Student3 is in use.
2. Type **SORT ON ZIP_CODE /D TO STUDENT4**, and press Enter.
3. Type **USE STUDENT4**, and press Enter.
4. Type **LIST**, and press Enter.

Your Student4 database file should look like figure 6.3.

```
. USE STUDENT4
. LIST
Record#  STUDENT_NO  ITEM LAST_NAME       FIRST_NAME STREET                    C
ITY           ZIP_CODE PHONE        GPA ADVISED NOTES
      1  077-33-2535 C001 Mariscos        Ashante     47 East Flagler St.       H
ialea          33157 305-331-7198 3.98 .F.     Memo
      2  068-56-8237 C003 Becker          Ken         1700 N.E. 20th St.        M
iami           33155 305-296-8864 3.10 .T.     Memo
      3  133-77-2636 C002 Lopez           Lupe        7301 Crandon              K
ey Biscayne    33149 305-177-3602 3.85 .F.     Memo
      4  151-45-9427 C005 Flores          Gloria      17 Tamiami Trail          N
orth Miami     33145 305-754-3485 3.97 .F.     Memo
      5  125-78-1256 C004 Benoit          Shaka       4442 Collins Ave.         M
iami Beach     33140 305-363-2416 4.00 .F.     Memo
      6  527-88-3029 C003 Wong            Claudia     37 Brickell Ave.          O
pa-Locka       33135 305-855-9742 3.95 .F.     Memo
      7  101-73-5923 C003 Mariscos        Julio       12500 West Dixie Hwy      B
al Harbour     33130 305-198-1911 3.89 .F.     Memo
      8  133-07-1324 C002 Benoit          Allison     11000 S.W. 57th Ave.      C
oconut Grove   33103 305-211-3456 2.00 .T.     Memo

.
Command Line      |<A:>|STUDENT4            |Rec: EOF/8        |      |NumCaps

                     Enter a dBASE III PLUS command.
```

Fig. 6.3 The database file sorted in descending order by ZIP code.

Saving the Sorted Database Files

When you exit from dBASE, all the new database files you created during your sorting operations are saved. All database files you re-sorted are saved by using the last order in which you sorted them. You now can safely exit from dBASE.

Objective 5: To Understand the Problems Created by Sorting

As you have seen, sorting a file is an easy procedure, and you can use sorting to place a file in virtually any order you want. Sorting does have some downsides, however.

Problems Created by Sorting Database Files

Consider the following problems, which may occur when you sort a database file:

- Each time you sort, you create a new file. These files waste a great deal of disk space if the database is large. Moreover, you can easily lose track of all the files and forget which files are sorted on field. You should perform disk "housekeeping" frequently.
- The original and all the files that were *cloned* when you sorted on different fields initially contain the same data. If you add, delete, or modify records, you have to perform all the sorts again to make sure that the records in each file are updated and in the proper order.
- Sorting a large database by a computer takes a surprisingly long time.
- A "law" that applies to data files used in businesses and other organizations can be stated the following way: *If more than one file of your data exists, the records in the different data files—initially the same—come to differ over time as they are used in an organization. Soon, no file contains completely accurate data*. This fact may not seem like a big problem, but it is. Organizations depend on the reliability of the data on their computers; the data must be correct. Orders must be taken, invoices sent, accounts updated, mailings sent, and so on.

Trying to reconcile differences among files that are supposed to contain the same data is time-consuming and often impossible. That this problem occurs is not a database problem but rather a human problem. An employee makes a change in one database file and forgets to update the other copies. Different employees make the same error but with different files. Eventually, somebody notices a discrepancy between the information in the different files. The boss then asks, "Which file is right?" Unfortunately, the answer is "None of them."

You can see the problems that result from the multiple databases created when you use the Sort command to satisfy your organization's data requirements. In the best of all possible worlds, you have a single database file that appears to a user in the sorted order that user needs. Each problem is solved—everyone uses and updates one database file. If you know how to *index* a database, you can have a single database file that can display in many sorted orders.

Index Files

This apparent impossibility—the single database file displayed in many orders—is accomplished through the use of *index files*. An index file alone is useless. It does *not* contain the database records; only database (DBF) files contain database records. You cannot even list the contents of an index file to see what it contains. When used with the database file from which the file was created, however, an index file acts as a filter. The index file causes the records in the database to be presented in ascending order on one or more database fields. If you use a different index file with the database, the records display in a different order. You give the index file a name, and dBASE adds the file name extension NDX.

Objective 6: To Understand What Indexing a File Does

Do you recall that when you opened a database file using the Assistant, it asked whether the file was indexed? You were told at that time always to answer no because none of your databases was indexed. Now you are going to use dBASE to produce and save some indexes in index files. Any index (in an index file) is based on the records in a specific database. To understand what dBASE does when you index a file, therefore, you will create an index by using a database file. The example indexes in the exercises for this section are based on the Customer database file. In the following exercise, you open and then print the records in the Customer database so that you can use these records to create some indexes.

Exercise 6.1: Printing the Customer Database File

To print the Customer database file, take these steps:

1. Type **USE CUSTOMER**, and press Enter.
2. Type **LIST TO PRINT**, and press Enter.
3. When the printer stops printing, type **EJECT**, and press Enter.

Your listing should resemble figure 6.4.

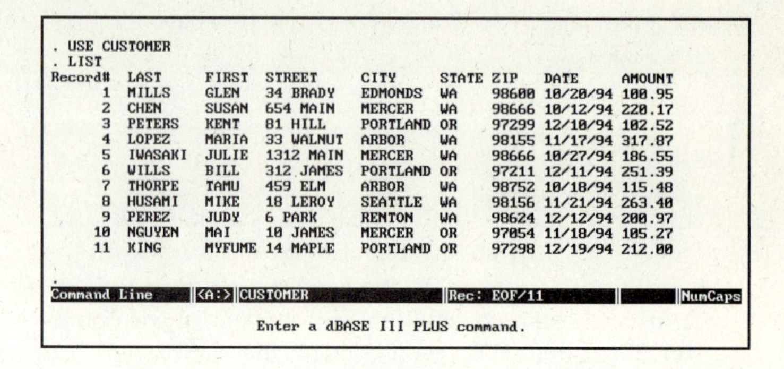

```
. USE CUSTOMER
. LIST
Record#  LAST     FIRST  STREET      CITY     STATE ZIP   DATE     AMOUNT
      1  MILLS    GLEN   34 BRADY    EDMONDS  WA    98600 10/20/94 100.95
      2  CHEN     SUSAN  654 MAIN    MERCER   WA    98666 10/12/94 220.17
      3  PETERS   KENT   81 HILL     PORTLAND OR    97299 12/10/94 102.52
      4  LOPEZ    MARIA  33 WALNUT   ARBOR    WA    98155 11/17/94 317.87
      5  IWASAKI  JULIE  1312 MAIN   MERCER   WA    98666 10/27/94 186.55
      6  WILLS    BILL   312 JAMES   PORTLAND OR    97211 12/11/94 251.39
      7  THORPE   TAMU   459 ELM     ARBOR    WA    98752 10/18/94 115.48
      8  HUSAMI   MIKE   18 LEROY    SEATTLE  WA    98156 11/21/94 263.40
      9  PEREZ    JUDY   6 PARK      RENTON   WA    98624 12/12/94 200.97
     10  NGUYEN   MAI    10 JAMES    MERCER   OR    97054 11/18/94 105.27
     11  KING     MYFUME 14 MAPLE    PORTLAND OR    97298 12/19/94 212.00

.
Command Line     |<A:>|CUSTOMER          |Rec: EOF/11     |      |NumCaps

                    Enter a dBASE III PLUS command.
```

Fig. 6.4
The Customer database file.

6

In the next two exercises, you create two different indexes for the Customer database file. You create these indexes on paper. The two indexes show how to display the Customer database in two sorted orders.

Exercise 6.2: Manually Indexing the Customer Database File on the LAST Field

To manually index the Customer database file to display the database records in last name order, take these steps:

1. At the top of the paper, write the index name **Lastindx**.
2. Next, on your paper, write the record number (**2**) of the record that should be first alphabetically using the LAST field.
3. Then write the contents of the LAST field in the record **(CHEN)**.
4. Continue this process alphabetically (in a row or in a column) until you have written the record number and contents of the LAST field for the last record alphabetically.

   Your paper should look something like this:

   2 CHEN   8 HUSAMI   5 IWASAKI   11 KING

   and so on until record 6, the last record.

Exercise 6.3: Manually Indexing the Customer Database File on the CITY Field

To manually index the Customer database file to display the database records in order on the CITY field, take these steps:

1. At the top of the paper, write the index name, **Cityindx**.
2. Next, on your paper, write the record number (either **4** or **7**) of the record that should be first alphabetically, using the CITY field.
3. Then write the contents of the CITY field in that record (**ARBOR**).
4. Continue this process alphabetically (in a row or in a column) until you have written the record number and contents of the LAST field for the last record alphabetically.

   Your paper should look something like this:

   4 ARBOR 7 ARBOR 1 EDMONDS 2 MERCER

   and so on until record 8, the last record. Notice that this list contains ties.

You did these two exercises to imitate exactly what dBASE does when you ask it to create an index. The only real difference is that you saved your index on a sheet of paper and dBASE saves the index on disk in an index file.

You can list the database records in the file in their natural order if you ignore the indexes. If you look at the records in the record number order in Lastindx, you access the records in alphabetical order. If you look at the records in the record number order in Cityindx, the records appear to be sorted on the CITY field. In this manner, the data can be used in three different orders.

This important point bears repeating. If the list of record numbers in Lastindx controls your access to the data, you see the records as sorted alphabetically by last name. If the list of record numbers in Cityindx controls your access to the data, you see the records as sorted by city. If no index is active, you see the records in numeric order from record 1 through record 11. This example shows you exactly how index files work: they *control the order* in which you see the records in a database file. Index files don't contain database records. Rather, the index file *points to* the *database file's* record numbers in a particular order. The record number in the index points to a record in the database file and tells dBASE to retrieve that record. If you don't tell dBASE to use a database file with an active index file, you see the records in their natural order.

Maintaining Index Files

Index files are useful only because they control the order in which database records are displayed. If you add or delete records in the database, therefore, the index file must be updated to reflect the changes. Otherwise, the record numbers in the index point to records no longer in the file if you deleted records. If you added new records, the index does not contain the new record numbers. Then if you use the index to control access to the database records, you never see the new records.

If you modify the contents of a field that has been used to create an index, you have to update that index to reflect that change. For example, if Maria Lopez moves from Arbor to Tacoma, the record number order in Cityindx also has to be changed. If you don't update the index, the index still points to Maria's record as one of the first two records rather than as the last record.

This fact leads to the following warning: *If you add, delete, or modify records in an active database file, the index files associated with that database also have to be active.* The reason for this warning is that if the index files are active, dBASE can update the indexes as you make changes to the data. If an index file is not active, dBASE does not automatically update the index. If you make changes to a database that affect an index but you forget to make the index active before you make changes, you can use the Reindex command to update the index.

Now that you have a background on indexes, in the following sections, you learn exactly how to use indexes with dBASE.

Objective 7: To Index a File on One Field

Now that you understand what an index is and how it works, use dBASE to build the two indexes you created manually—Lastindx and Cityindx. *indx* in the file name indicates that these files are index files, but dBASE does not require this convention. dBASE identifies its indexes by using the extension NDX for index files.

To create the indexes, first make sure that your Customer database is open. You should also have at hand the paper on which you wrote the indexes in the earlier exercises.

Exercise 7.1: Creating an Index Using the LAST Field

To create an index to use with the Customer database, take these steps:

1. Press F6 to verify that Customer is the database in use and that no index files (NDX files) are active. Then press ↵Enter to complete displaying the status.
2. Name this index file Lastindx. At the dot prompt, type the command

   INDEX ON LAST TO LASTINDX

   and press ↵Enter. You should see the message

   `100% indexed      11 Records indexed.`

3. Press F6. The first screen should look like figure 6.5. Notice that the Lastindx is active and the Master index file. The *key* field is the field used to create the index.

   Press ↵Enter to complete displaying the status.

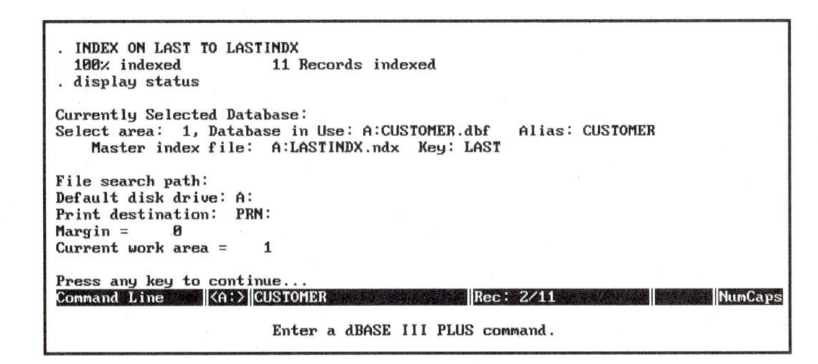

Fig. 6.5
The first Display Status screen when creating an index on LAST.

4. Type **LIST**, and press ↵Enter. Your screen should look like figure 6.6.

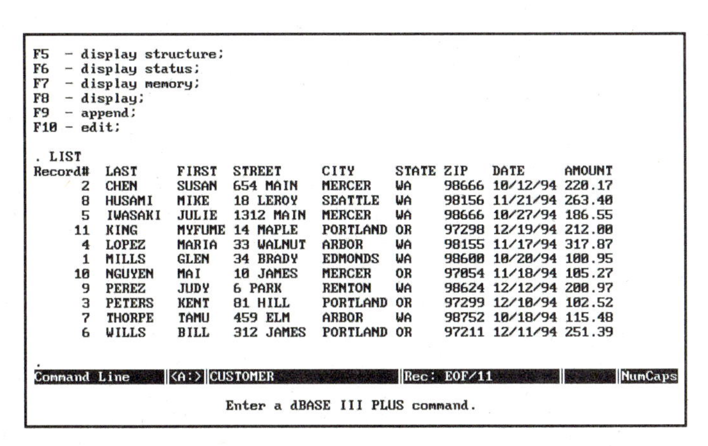

Fig. 6.6
The Customer database file in order controlled by Lastindx.

Notice that the order of the record numbers displayed at the left of the screen is exactly the same as the record number order you came up with when you created Lastindx on paper. This fact is a tip-off to you that an index file must be active; otherwise, the records would be displayed in 1,2,3... order. Lastindx does not contain the database records; it only controls the record order in which dBASE displays the database file.

In the next exercise, you create a new index on the CITY field. Before dBASE creates the new index, Cityindx, dBASE saves Lastindx in a file named LASTINDX.NDX. And after creating the Cityindx, dBASE makes this index active.

Exercise 7.2: Creating an Index Using the CITY Field

To create a second index to use with the Customer database, take these steps:

1. Press F6 to verify that Customer is the database in use. Then press ↵Enter to complete displaying the status.
2. Name this index file Cityindx. Type the command **INDEX ON CITY TO CITYINDX**, and press ↵Enter.

   You should see the message

   ```
   100% indexed     11 Records indexed.
   ```

3. Press F6. The first screen should look like figure 6.7. Notice that Cityindx is active.

   Press ↵Enter to complete displaying the status.

Fig. 6.7
The first Display Status screen when creating an index on CITY.

```
      1  MILLS    GLEN   34 BRADY   EDMONDS  WA    98600 10/20/94 100.95
     10  NGUYEN   MAI    10 JAMES   MERCER   OR    97054 11/18/94 105.27
      9  PEREZ    JUDY   6 PARK     RENTON   WA    98624 12/12/94 200.97
      3  PETERS   KENT   81 HILL    PORTLAND OR    97299 12/10/94 102.52
      7  THORPE   TAMU   459 ELM    ARBOR    WA    98752 10/18/94 115.48
      6  WILLS    BILL   312 JAMES  PORTLAND OR    97211 12/11/94 251.39

. INDEX ON CITY TO CITYINDX
  100% indexed          11 Records indexed
. display status

Currently Selected Database:
Select area:  1, Database in Use: A:CUSTOMER.dbf   Alias: CUSTOMER
    Master index file:  A:CITYINDX.ndx  Key: CITY

File search path:
Default disk drive: A:
Print destination:  PRN:
Margin =     0
Current work area =    1

Press any key to continue...
Command Line     |<A:>|CUSTOMER           |Rec: 4/11       |      |NumCaps

                         Enter a dBASE III PLUS command.
```

4. Type **LIST**, and press Enter. Your screen should look like figure 6.8.

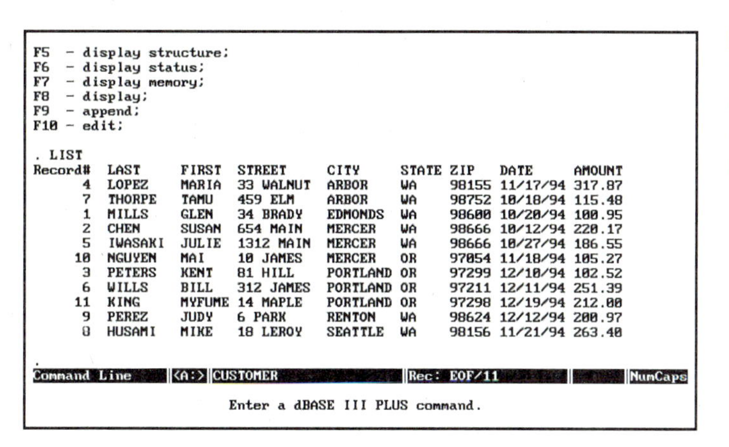

```
F5  - display structure;
F6  - display status;
F7  - display memory;
F8  - display;
F9  - append;
F10 - edit;

. LIST
Record#  LAST     FIRST  STREET     CITY     STATE ZIP   DATE     AMOUNT
      4  LOPEZ    MARIA  33 WALNUT  ARBOR    WA    98155 11/17/94 317.87
      7  THORPE   TAMU   459 ELM    ARBOR    WA    98752 10/18/94 115.48
      1  MILLS    GLEN   34 BRADY   EDMONDS  WA    98600 10/20/94 100.95
      2  CHEN     SUSAN  654 MAIN   MERCER   WA    98666 10/12/94 220.17
      5  IWASAKI  JULIE  1312 MAIN  MERCER   WA    98666 10/27/94 186.55
     10  NGUYEN   MAI    10 JAMES   MERCER   OR    97054 11/18/94 105.27
      3  PETERS   KENT   81 HILL    PORTLAND OR    97299 12/10/94 102.52
      6  WILLS    BILL   312 JAMES  PORTLAND OR    97211 12/11/94 251.39
     11  KING     MYFUME 14 MAPLE   PORTLAND OR    97298 12/19/94 212.00
      9  PEREZ    JUDY   6 PARK     RENTON   WA    98624 12/12/94 200.97
      8  HUSAMI   MIKE   18 LEROY   SEATTLE  WA    98156 11/21/94 263.40

.
Command Line  |<A:>|CUSTOMER  |Rec: EOF/11  |  |NumCaps

              Enter a dBASE III PLUS command.
```

Fig. 6.8
The Customer database file in order controlled by Cityindx.

Notice that the order of the record numbers displayed at the left of the screen is exactly the same as the record number order that you came up with when you created Cityindx on paper. Cityindx contains the same information that you wrote on your paper. You can never actually list the contents of an index file, but now you know what is in the index file because you created one yourself.

5. Type the command **CLEAR ALL**, and press Enter. This command saves and then closes all active database and index files. In this case, you could also have typed **USE** and pressed Enter.

6. Press F6 to verify that no database file is in use and that all indexes are inactive. Now your screen should look like figure 6.9. Press Enter to complete displaying the status.

```
      4  LOPEZ    MARIA  33 WALNUT  ARBOR    WA    98155 11/17/94 317.87
      7  THORPE   TAMU   459 ELM    ARBOR    WA    98752 10/18/94 115.48
      1  MILLS    GLEN   34 BRADY   EDMONDS  WA    98600 10/20/94 100.95
      2  CHEN     SUSAN  654 MAIN   MERCER   WA    98666 10/12/94 220.17
      5  IWASAKI  JULIE  1312 MAIN  MERCER   WA    98666 10/27/94 186.55
     10  NGUYEN   MAI    10 JAMES   MERCER   OR    97054 11/18/94 105.27
      3  PETERS   KENT   81 HILL    PORTLAND OR    97299 12/10/94 102.52
      6  WILLS    BILL   312 JAMES  PORTLAND OR    97211 12/11/94 251.39
     11  KING     MYFUME 14 MAPLE   PORTLAND OR    97298 12/19/94 212.00
      9  PEREZ    JUDY   6 PARK     RENTON   WA    98624 12/12/94 200.97
      8  HUSAMI   MIKE   18 LEROY   SEATTLE  WA    98156 11/21/94 263.40

. CLEAR ALL
. display status

File search path:
Default disk drive: A:
Print destination:  PRN:
Margin =      0
Current work area =     1

Press any key to continue...
Command Line  |<A:>|  |  |  |NumCaps

              Enter a dBASE III PLUS command.
```

Fig. 6.9
The Display Status screen after clearing the screen.

Objective 8: To Use Index Files

Once you have created an index, it is stored on your disk. You can use the index file with the database file you used to create the index. Remember that you cannot *use* an index file; you can only make it active while a database file is *in use*. Having created the Lastindx and Cityindx files, you now have four alternatives available when you want to work with the data in the Customer database. These alternatives are

- Use the Customer database without activating either index.
- Use the Customer database with the index based on the LAST field (Lastindx). Do this if you want to work with the database as if it were in order by last name.
- Use the Customer database with the index based on the CITY field (Cityindx). Do this if you want to work with the database as if it were in order by city.
- Use the Customer database with both indexes active. Do this if you are going to add, delete, or modify Customer database records. Then dBASE updates both indexes to reflect modifications made to the database; otherwise, the indexes don't work correctly. Of course, only one of the indexes controls the order in which records are displayed. You learn about this alternative in detail later.

Exercise 8.1: Working with Indexes

To learn how to use indexes, take these steps:

1. Press F6 to execute the Display Status command. Your screen should look like figure 6.10. Then press ↵Enter to complete displaying the status.
2. At the dot prompt, type the command **USE CUSTOMER INDEX LASTINDX**, and press ↵Enter.

   This command opens the database and makes the Lastindx active.

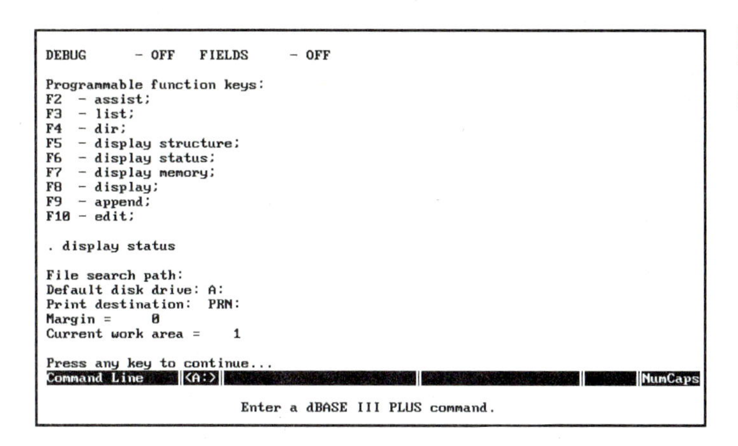

```
DEBUG       - OFF   FIELDS      - OFF

Programmable function keys:
F2  - assist;
F3  - list;
F4  - dir;
F5  - display structure;
F6  - display status;
F7  - display memory;
F8  - display;
F9  - append;
F10 - edit;

. display status

File search path:
Default disk drive: A:
Print destination:  PRN:
Margin =      0
Current work area =     1

Press any key to continue...
Command Line     |<A:>|                              |NumCaps
                 Enter a dBASE III PLUS command.
```

Fig. 6.10
The first Display Status screen.

3. Type **LIST**, and press Enter.

   Now your screen should look like figure 6.11.

```
F6  - display status;
F7  - display memory;
F8  - display;
F9  - append;
F10 - edit;

. USE CUSTOMER INDEX LASTINDX
. LIST
Record#  LAST     FIRST  STREET     CITY     STATE ZIP   DATE     AMOUNT
      2  CHEN     SUSAN  654 MAIN   MERCER   WA    98666 10/12/94 220.17
      8  HUSAMI   MIKE   18 LEROY   SEATTLE  WA    98156 11/21/94 263.40
      5  IWASAKI  JULIE  1312 MAIN  MERCER   WA    98666 10/27/94 186.55
     11  KING     MYFUME 14 MAPLE   PORTLAND OR    97298 12/19/94 212.00
      4  LOPEZ    MARIA  33 WALNUT  ARBOR    WA    98155 11/17/94 317.87
      1  MILLS    GLEN   34 BRADY   EDMONDS  WA    98600 10/20/94 100.95
     10  NGUYEN   MAI    10 JAMES   MERCER   OR    97054 11/18/94 105.27
      9  PEREZ    JUDY   6 PARK     RENTON   WA    98624 12/12/94 200.97
      3  PETERS   KENT   81 HILL    PORTLAND OR    97299 12/10/94 102.52
      7  THORPE   TAMU   459 ELM    ARBOR    WA    98752 10/10/94 115.40
      6  WILLS    BILL   312 JAMES  PORTLAND OR    97211 12/11/94 251.39

.
Command Line     |<A:>|CUSTOMER         |Rec: EOF/11        |NumCaps
                 Enter a dBASE III PLUS command.
```

Fig. 6.11
The Customer database opened with Lastindx active.

To close the Lastindx and use Customer with Cityindx active, take these steps:

1. At the dot prompt, type the command **USE CUSTOMER INDEX CITYINDX**, and press Enter.
2. Type **LIST**, and press Enter.

Now your screen should look like figure 6.12.

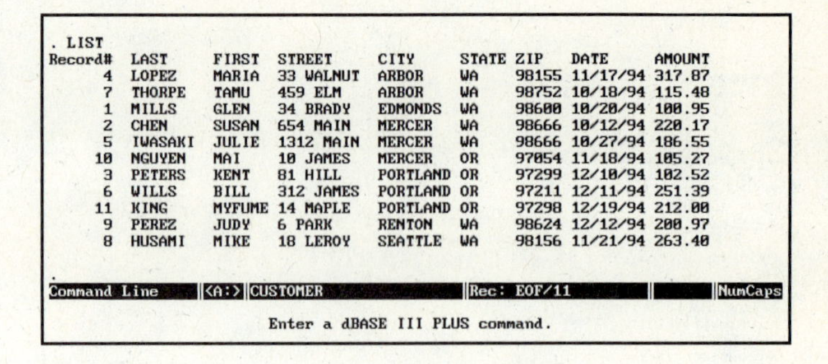

. LIST

Record#	LAST	FIRST	STREET	CITY	STATE	ZIP	DATE	AMOUNT
4	LOPEZ	MARIA	33 WALNUT	ARBOR	WA	98155	11/17/94	317.87
7	THORPE	TAMU	459 ELM	ARBOR	WA	98752	10/18/94	115.40
1	MILLS	GLEN	34 BRADY	EDMONDS	WA	98600	10/20/94	100.95
2	CHEN	SUSAN	654 MAIN	MERCER	WA	98666	10/12/94	220.17
5	IWASAKI	JULIE	1312 MAIN	MERCER	WA	98666	10/27/94	186.55
10	NGUYEN	MAI	10 JAMES	MERCER	OR	97054	11/18/94	105.27
3	PETERS	KENT	81 HILL	PORTLAND	OR	97299	12/10/94	102.52
6	WILLS	BILL	312 JAMES	PORTLAND	OR	97211	12/11/94	251.39
11	KING	MYFUME	14 MAPLE	PORTLAND	OR	97298	12/19/94	212.00
9	PEREZ	JUDY	6 PARK	RENTON	WA	98624	12/12/94	200.97
8	HUSAMI	MIKE	10 LEROY	SEATTLE	WA	98156	11/21/94	263.40

Command Line <A:> CUSTOMER Rec: EOF/11 NumCaps

Enter a dBASE III PLUS command.

Fig. 6.12 The Customer database opened with Cityindx active.

Exercise 8.2: Activating Multiple Indexes When You Are Going to Modify a Database

To open the Customer database with two indexes active, take these steps:

1. At the dot prompt, type the command **USE CUSTOMER INDEX CITYINDX, LASTINDX**, and press Enter.

   This command opens the database and makes both Lastindx and Cityindx active.

   You can make up to seven indexes active at the same time. The index that is first in the list of indexes (Cityindx in this example) controls the order of the database records. However, all the listed indexes are updated. Indexes that are not in the list are not updated.

2. To see the order of the database records, type **LIST**, and press Enter.

   Now your screen should look like figure 6.13.

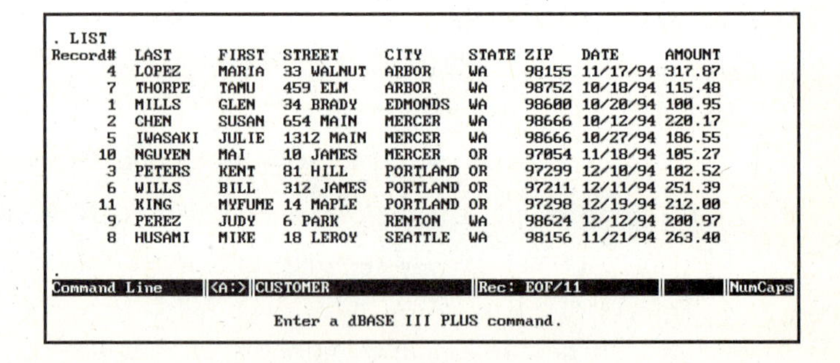

. LIST

Record#	LAST	FIRST	STREET	CITY	STATE	ZIP	DATE	AMOUNT
4	LOPEZ	MARIA	33 WALNUT	ARBOR	WA	98155	11/17/94	317.87
7	THORPE	TAMU	459 ELM	ARBOR	WA	98752	10/18/94	115.40
1	MILLS	GLEN	34 BRADY	EDMONDS	WA	98600	10/20/94	100.95
2	CHEN	SUSAN	654 MAIN	MERCER	WA	98666	10/12/94	220.17
5	IWASAKI	JULIE	1312 MAIN	MERCER	WA	98666	10/27/94	186.55
10	NGUYEN	MAI	10 JAMES	MERCER	OR	97054	11/18/94	105.27
3	PETERS	KENT	81 HILL	PORTLAND	OR	97299	12/10/94	102.52
6	WILLS	BILL	312 JAMES	PORTLAND	OR	97211	12/11/94	251.39
11	KING	MYFUME	14 MAPLE	PORTLAND	OR	97298	12/19/94	212.00
9	PEREZ	JUDY	6 PARK	RENTON	WA	98624	12/12/94	200.97
8	HUSAMI	MIKE	10 LEROY	SEATTLE	WA	98156	11/21/94	263.40

Command Line <A:> CUSTOMER Rec: EOF/11 NumCaps

Enter a dBASE III PLUS command.

Fig. 6.13 The Customer database file controlled in Cityindx.

3. Press F6 to execute the Display Status command. Your screen should look like figure 6.14. Notice that the indexes are both active, but the first index you listed in the command in step 1 is the Master index.

The Master index controls the order in which the records are displayed.

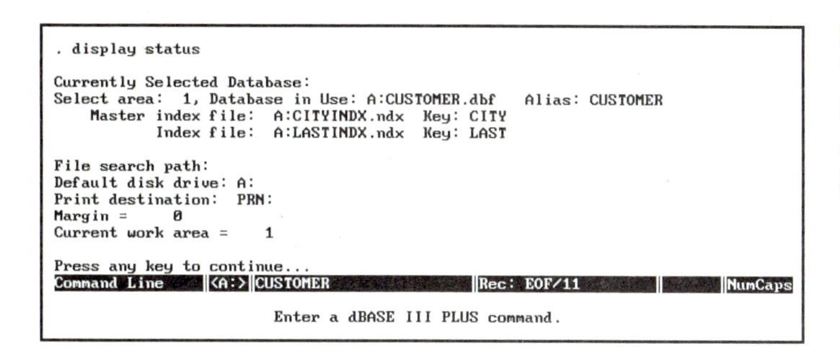

```
. display status

Currently Selected Database:
Select area:  1, Database in Use: A:CUSTOMER.dbf   Alias: CUSTOMER
    Master index file:  A:CITYINDX.ndx  Key: CITY
           Index file:  A:LASTINDX.ndx  Key: LAST

File search path:
Default disk drive: A:
Print destination:  PRN:
Margin =     0
Current work area =    1

Press any key to continue...
Command Line     |<A:>|CUSTOMER          |Rec: EOF/11        |     |NumCaps

                 Enter a dBASE III PLUS command.
```

Fig. 6.14 The Display Status screen showing active indexes.

4. Press ↵Enter to complete displaying the status.
5. At the dot prompt, type the command **USE CUSTOMER INDEX LASTINDX, CITYINDX**, and press ↵Enter.
6. To see the order of the database records, type **LIST**, and press ↵Enter.

   Now your screen should look like figure 6.15.

```
. LIST
Record#  LAST     FIRST  STREET     CITY     STATE ZIP   DATE     AMOUNT
      2  CHEN     SUSAN  654 MAIN   MERCER   WA    98666 10/12/94 220.17
      8  HUSAMI   MIKE   18 LEROY   SEATTLE  WA    98156 11/21/94 263.40
      5  IWASAKI  JULIE  1312 MAIN  MERCER   WA    98666 10/27/94 186.55
     11  KING     MYFUME 14 MAPLE   PORTLAND OR    97298 12/19/94 212.00
      4  LOPEZ    MARIA  33 WALNUT  ARBOR    WA    98155 11/17/94 317.87
      1  MILLS    GLEN   34 BRADY   EDMONDS  WA    98600 10/20/94 100.95
     10  NGUYEN   MAI    10 JAMES   MERCER   OR    97054 11/18/94 105.27
      9  PEREZ    JUDY   6 PARK     RENTON   WA    98624 12/12/94 200.97
      3  PETERS   KENT   81 HILL    PORTLAND OR    97299 12/10/94 102.52
      7  THORPE   TAMU   459 ELM    ARBOR    WA    98752 10/18/94 115.48
      6  WILLS    BILL   312 JAMES  PORTLAND OR    97211 12/11/94 251.39

.
Command Line     |<A:>|CUSTOMER          |Rec: EOF/11        |     |NumCaps

                 Enter a dBASE III PLUS command.
```

Fig. 6.15 The Customer database with Lastindx as the Master index.

7. Press F6 to execute the Display Status command. Your screen should look like figure 6.16. Notice that the indexes are both active, but the first index you listed in the command in step 5 is the Master index, which controls the order of the records.
8. Press ↵Enter to finish displaying the status.
9. At the dot prompt, type **CLEAR ALL**, and press ↵Enter. All open files are closed.

6

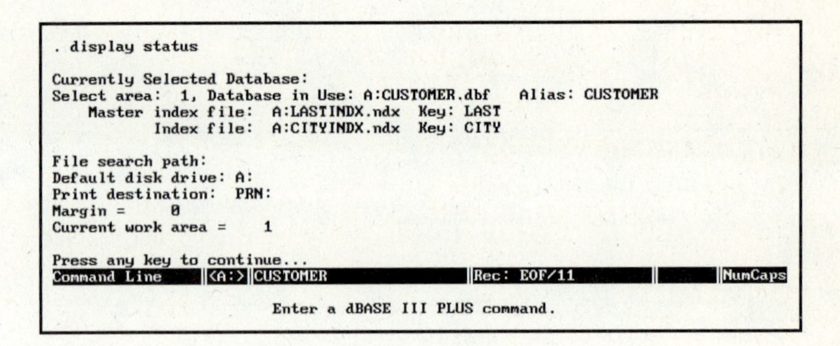

Fig. 6.16 The Display Status screen showing active indexes and the Master index.

Objective 9: To Index a File Using Multiple Fields

At times, indexing a file on one field does not give you the record order you want. Remember the issue of ties in the discussion of sorting and the necessity of breaking ties by using a second or even a third sort field. This same capability exists when you index a file instead of sorting the file. Notice that in your Customer file, you have three records with a CITY value of MERCER; therefore, these records are ties on the CITY field. One record has a STATE value of OR. The other two records are WA records. If you want to distinguish between the MERCER, OR, records and the MERCER, WA, records, you have to create an index on the combination of the two fields. In the following exercise, you create an index using the combination of the CITY and STATE fields.

Exercise 9.1: Creating a Multiple-Field Index

To learn how to create a multiple-field index, follow these steps:

1. At the dot prompt, type the command **USE CUSTOMER**, and press ↵Enter.

   This command opens the database.

2. At the dot prompt, type the command **INDEX ON CITY + STATE TO C_S_INDX**, and press ↵Enter.

3. Press F6. Your screen should look like figure 6.17. Notice the information you are given on the active indexes.

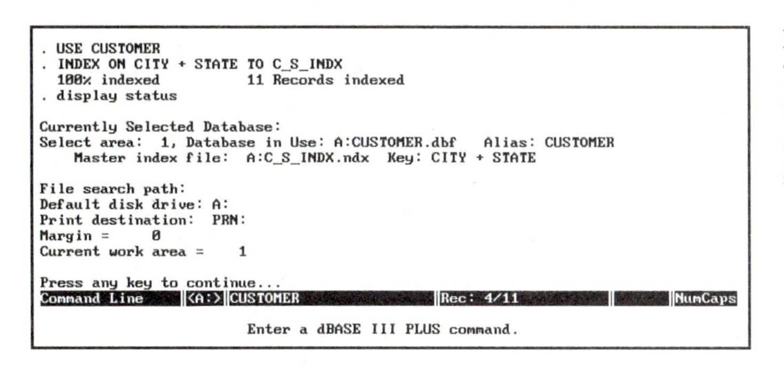

```
. USE CUSTOMER
. INDEX ON CITY + STATE TO C_S_INDX
  100% indexed          11 Records indexed
. display status

Currently Selected Database:
Select area:  1, Database in Use: A:CUSTOMER.dbf   Alias: CUSTOMER
    Master index file:  A:C_S_INDX.ndx  Key: CITY + STATE

File search path:
Default disk drive: A:
Print destination:  PRN:
Margin =      0
Current work area =     1

Press any key to continue...
Command Line     |<A:>|CUSTOMER            |Rec: 4/11     |     |NumCaps

                  Enter a dBASE III PLUS command.
```

Fig. 6.17
The Display Status screen for an index on two fields.

4. Type **LIST**, and press Enter.

   Now your screen should look like figure 6.18. Notice that the MERCER, WA, records are grouped together.

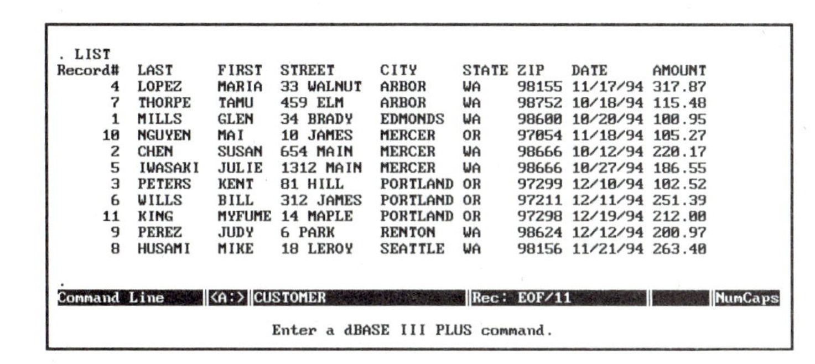

```
. LIST
Record#  LAST     FIRST   STREET     CITY     STATE ZIP   DATE     AMOUNT
      4  LOPEZ    MARIA   33 WALNUT  ARBOR    WA    98155 11/17/94 317.87
      7  THORPE   TAMU    459 ELM    ARBOR    WA    98752 10/18/94 115.48
      1  MILLS    GLEN    34 BRADY   EDMONDS  WA    98600 10/20/94 100.95
     10  NGUYEN   MAI     10 JAMES   MERCER   OR    97054 11/18/94 105.27
      2  CHEN     SUSAN   654 MAIN   MERCER   WA    98666 10/12/94 220.17
      5  IWASAKI  JULIE   1312 MAIN  MERCER   WA    98666 10/27/94 186.55
      3  PETERS   KENT    81 HILL    PORTLAND OR    97299 12/10/94 102.52
      6  WILLS    BILL    312 JAMES  PORTLAND OR    97211 12/11/94 251.39
     11  KING     MYFUME  14 MAPLE   PORTLAND OR    97298 12/19/94 212.00
      9  PEREZ    JUDY    6 PARK     RENTON   WA    98624 12/12/94 200.97
      8  HUSAMI   MIKE    18 LEROY   SEATTLE  WA    98156 11/21/94 263.40

.
Command Line     |<A:>|CUSTOMER            |Rec: EOF/11   |     |NumCaps

                  Enter a dBASE III PLUS command.
```

Fig. 6.18
The Customer database with C_S_Indx controlling the record order.

5. Type **CLEAR ALL**, and press Enter. All open files are closed.

You can now exit from dBASE.

Chapter Summary

In this chapter, you have learned how dBASE sorts records, and you have learned to use dBASE to sort a database file by using one or more fields. You know what an index is, and you know how to create and use indexes with dBASE. You have also learned the advantages of indexing in comparison to sorting.

In the next chapter, you learn a set of commands that are especially useful if you want to work efficiently with large databases. You also learn more about techniques for finding information in a database. Using the methods discussed in Chapter 7 enables you to extract from your database file the data that meets your requirements.

Testing Your Knowledge

True/False Questions

1. dBASE can sort on a maximum of two fields.
2. Only one index can be active at a time.
3. The default sort order in dBASE is descending order.
4. You can sort Numeric fields, but you cannot sort Character type fields.
5. Indexes can display a database in descending order on a field.

Multiple-Choice Questions

1. To find out which index file (if any) is active, press _______.
   a. F1
   b. F5
   c. F6
   d. F9
2. All index files are given the extension _______ by dBASE.
   a. IND
   b. INX
   c. INDX
   d. NDX
3. Every time you sort, you create a ________.
   a. file
   b. index
   c. both a and b
   d. none of these answers

4. If Statindx is an index file, you can see the data records stored in Statindx by typing the command __________ at the dot prompt.
    a. **OPEN STATINDX**
    b. **USE STATINDX**
    c. **INDEX STATINDX**
    d. none of these answers
5. You can have up to ______ index files active with a database file at one time.
    a. one
    b. two
    c. seven
    d. none. You cannot have an index file active when a database is in use.

Fill-in-the-Blank Questions

1. To sort a database file into a new file, you use the __________ command.
2. To __________ means to order records in a database file based on selected fields.
3. When more than one index file is open, the __________ index file controls the order in which records are displayed.
4. __________ means from the highest to the lowest value in a field.
5. __________ means from the lowest to the highest value of a field.

Review: Short Projects

1. Sorting a Database File on One Field

    Sort the Climate database file in order of increasing Elevation in Feet. Print the sorted database file.

2. Sorting a Database File on Two Fields

    Sort the Climate database file in order of increasing January Maximum temperature. Break ties using the January minimum. Place the sorted records into a database file Climate2. Print the Climate2 database file.

3. Sorting a Database File in Descending Order Using One Field

   Sort the Climate2 database file in order of decreasing annual inches of precipitation. Print the sorted database file.

Review: Long Projects

1. Sorting the Tours Database
   a. Sort the Tours database file to a new database file named Tours2. Perform the sort so that all the records of tours that depart from a particular city are grouped together. Print the new database file.
   b. Sort the Tours2 database file so that it is in alphabetical order by Destination. Print the database file.
   c. Sort the Tours2 database file in order of decreasing cost. Break ties using decreasing order of the RETURN field. Print the database file.

2. Sorting a Database Using Multiple Fields

   Assume that you are responsible for a database containing several thousand records. The fields in the database file are LAST_NAME, FIRST_NAME, INITIAL, SOCSECURIT, GENDER (F or M), ETHNICITY, AGE, STREET, CITY, STATE, Zip, and DEPARTMENT.

   You are asked to produce a listing of the database according to the following requirements:

   All the females should be listed, followed by all the males. Within each group, the records should be in order of ETHNICITY. Within each GENDER and ETHNICITY category, the records should be ordered by decreasing AGE. Where ties exist on this field combination, the records should be in order by name in the same way that entries occur in the phone book. If any records are duplicates on all these fields, order these records using ascending DEPARTMENT.

Write out the dBASE sort statement that will accomplish this task.

3. Sorting a Database by Using Indexes

   Use indexes—not the Sort command—in these exercises.

   a. Sort the Tours database file by using index files. Perform the sort so that all the records of tours that depart from a particular city are grouped together. Print the database file in order based on the index file.
   b. Sort the Tours database file so that it is in alphabetical order by destination. Print the database file.
   c. Sort the Tours database file in order of increasing cost. Break ties using increasing order of the RETURN field. Print the database file with your index active.
   d. Sort the Climate database file in order of increasing elevation in feet. Print the sorted database file.

7

Working Efficiently with Large Databases

The previous chapters in this book explain the basics of working with a dBASE database. This chapter introduces some commands that you will find especially useful when you work with a large database. First, you learn about the Goto command, which enables you to move around quickly in a database, and the Insert command, which enables you to add a new record anywhere in a file. Then, you learn about the Delete For command, with which you can quickly mark groups of records for deletion. Next, you work with the Replace command, which enables you quickly to change the contents of many records. This chapter also covers commands that perform arithmetic operations on Numeric type data so that you can efficiently obtain summary information—counts, sums, and averages—from a database.

In Chapter 4, you learned how to use the List and List For commands to display all or a special part of your data. This chapter introduces two new commands—Find and Seek. These commands are often more useful than the List command when you are using large indexed databases, because the commands go directly to a record so that Find and Seek display the record much more rapidly than the List command does. Finally, this chapter explains two commands, List Next and List While, that work together with the Find and Seek commands.

Objectives

1. To Use the Goto Command
2. To Use the Insert Command
3. To Use the Delete For Command
4. To Use the Recall Command
5. To Use the Replace Command
6. To Use the Count, Sum, and Average Commands
7. To Use the Find Command
8. To Use the Seek Command

Key Term in This Chapter	
Primary key field	A field containing a unique value for each record. You can use primary key fields to retrieve a particular record from a database. Social Security number, part number, account number, customer number, vehicle identification number, and patient number are all examples of fields that could be used as primary key fields. A specific value would be found in only one database record.

Objective 1: To Use the Goto Command

The Goto (or Go) command is used to position the record pointer to a particular record number in an active database file. You also can go to the Top or the Bottom of the file. If a file doesn't have an active index, Top is record 1, and Bottom is the last record in the file. If a file has an active index, Top is the first record number in the index, and Bottom is the last record number in the index.

Goto only positions the record pointer; this command doesn't show you the record. If you want to see the record, use the Display command. Goto frequently is used to go to and display a record before using the Edit command. Using this technique means that you don't have to use PgUp and PgDn to search through the database for the record that you need to change. In a large database, paging up and down to find a record is very inefficient. Usually, you go to the record; then you display it to verify that you have the right one. Next, you can edit the record. If you have a printed listing of the database with record numbers, you simply type *EDIT* followed by the record number (such as *EDIT 321*). Then, you can press ↵Enter.

Note: For the exercises in this chapter, use the Customer database file with no active indexes.

Exercise 1.1: Using the Goto Command

Make sure that the Customer database is used with no index active. Notice that the current record in the status bar is record number 1 (see fig. 7.1).

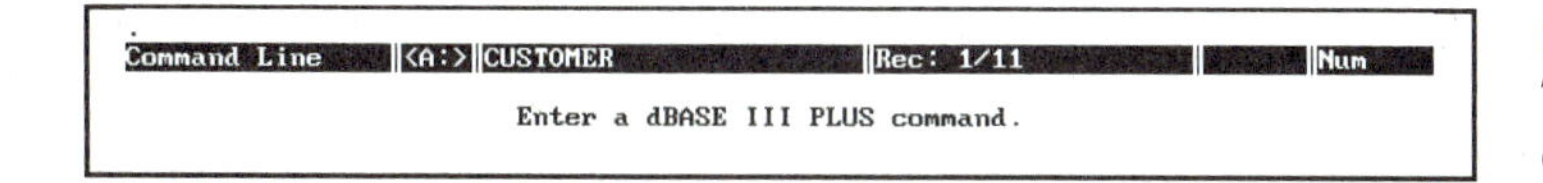

Fig. 7.1 The open Customer database file.

To use the Goto command to go directly to a record, take these steps:

1. At the dot prompt, type **GOTO 5**; then press ↵Enter.

   The current record indicator in the status bar should show that record number 5 is now the current record (see fig. 7.2).

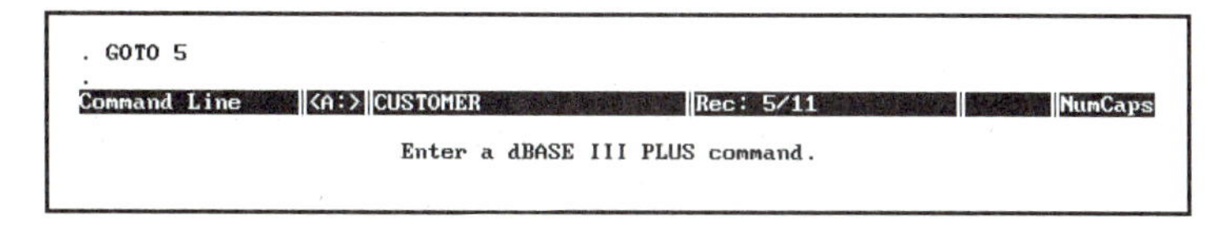

Fig. 7.2 The status bar indicates the current record.

2. Type **DISPLAY**; then press ↵Enter.

   Julie Iwasaki's record should display.

3. Type **GOTO TOP**; then press ↵Enter.
4. Type **DISPLAY**; then press ↵Enter.

   Glen Mills' record should display.

5. Type **GOTO BOTTOM**; then press Enter.
6. Type **DISPLAY**; then press Enter.

   Myfume King's record should appear on-screen.

Objective 2: To Use the Insert Command

Suppose that you are keeping a large database file in order by sorting the file. After sorting, you want to add several records in their proper (sorted) positions. You cannot use the Append command because it always adds records to the end of the file. To place a new record anywhere in a file that is not indexed, use the Insert command.

If a file is indexed and the index is active, using the Insert command is pointless. When an index is active, an inserted record is placed at the end of the file, just as if you had used the Append command. The index, however, displays the record in sorted order, unless you list the database without making the index active.

The Insert command is also useful if you are doing an exercise in a database class and you accidentally leave out a record as you are entering an example database. The instructor expects you to enter the records in the order shown in the example database. Usually, you cannot add the record to the end of the file and then sort it into its proper position. You can, however, use the Insert command to insert the record wherever you want.

Before you use the Insert command, you use the Goto command to move to the position in the file where you want the record inserted. The default with the Insert command is that the new record is inserted *after* the current record. The Insert Before command, however, inserts the new record into a position preceding the current record.

The following exercise demonstrates how you use the Insert command. Assume that you accidentally omitted a record from the Customer database file. The record should be placed between records 7 and 8.

Exercise 2.1: Using the Insert Command

To insert a new record between records 7 and 8, take these steps:

1. At the dot prompt, type **GOTO 7**, and press Enter.
2. Type **INSERT**, and press Enter.

   Now, your screen should resemble fig. 7.3.

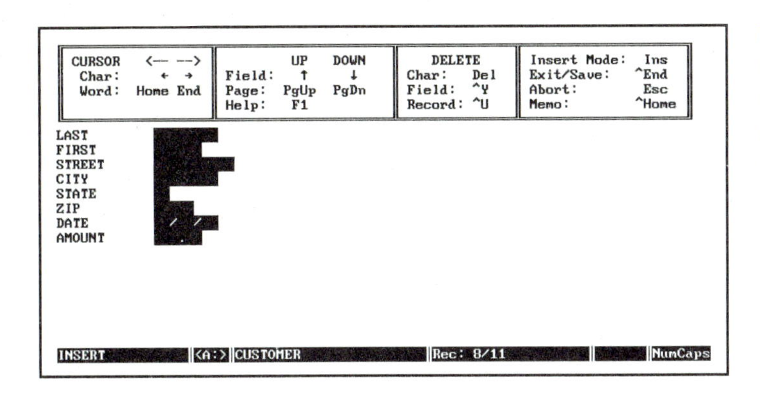

Fig. 7.3 Inserting a record by using the Insert command.

3. Enter the following data:

Field	*Data*
LAST:	**OWEN**
FIRST:	**CHRIS**
STREET:	**43 TAFT**
CITY:	**ENDWELL**
STATE:	**OR**
ZIP:	**97290**
DATE:	**11/10/94**
AMOUNT:	**324.95**

   As soon as you fill in the AMOUNT field, the completed record is inserted, and you return to the dot prompt.

4. At the dot prompt, type **LIST**, and then press Enter.

   Now, your screen should resemble fig. 7.4.

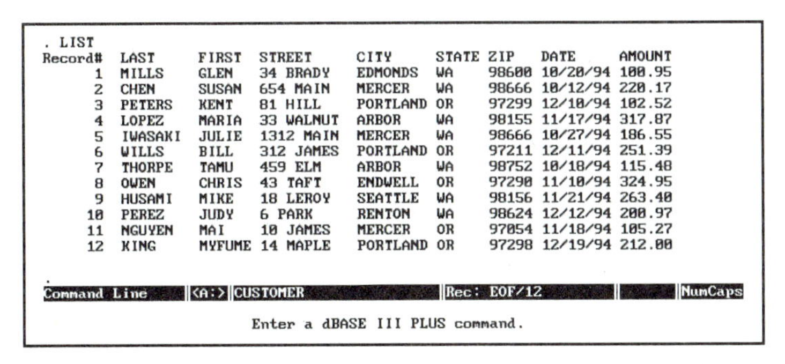
. LIST

Record#	LAST	FIRST	STREET	CITY	STATE	ZIP	DATE	AMOUNT
1	MILLS	GLEN	34 BRADY	EDMONDS	WA	98600	10/20/94	100.95
2	CHEN	SUSAN	654 MAIN	MERCER	WA	98666	10/12/94	220.17
3	PETERS	KENT	81 HILL	PORTLAND	OR	97299	12/10/94	102.52
4	LOPEZ	MARIA	33 WALNUT	ARBOR	WA	98155	11/17/94	317.87
5	IWASAKI	JULIE	1312 MAIN	MERCER	WA	98666	10/27/94	186.55
6	WILLS	BILL	312 JAMES	PORTLAND	OR	97211	12/11/94	251.39
7	THORPE	TAMU	459 ELM	ARBOR	WA	98752	10/18/94	115.40
8	OWEN	CHRIS	43 TAFT	ENDWELL	OR	97290	11/10/94	324.95
9	HUSAMI	MIKE	18 LEROY	SEATTLE	WA	98156	11/21/94	263.40
10	PEREZ	JUDY	6 PARK	RENTON	WA	98624	12/12/94	200.97
11	NGUYEN	MAI	10 JAMES	MERCER	OR	97054	11/18/94	105.27
12	KING	MYFUME	14 MAPLE	PORTLAND	OR	97298	12/19/94	212.00

Command Line | <A:> CUSTOMER | Rec: EOF/12 | NumCaps

Enter a dBASE III PLUS command.

Fig. 7.4 Record 8 inserted into the file.

Notice that the new record is inserted following record 7, Tamu Thorpe's. Also, note that all the old records after record 7 have been moved down and renumbered to make a space for the new one in the file.

Recall that no indexes were active as you added the record, so if you have indexes for this database, you have to reindex. The reason is that dBASE has not updated the indexes. The purpose of this exercise is to show you how the Insert command works when no indexes are active. Remember that if an index is active, the record cannot be *inserted* in the actual database file; it is *appended* to the end of the database file.

Objective 3: To Use the Delete For Command

You used the Delete command in a previous chapter to mark individual records for deletion. If you want to mark a group of records for deletion, the Delete For command is helpful. You might mark for deletion all records with an AMOUNT field of less than $200.00. You might also use the Delete For command to delete old records, if these records have a Date field that indicates how long they have been in the database.

The Delete For command works in a manner similar to the List For command. When you use the List For command, you specify a condition that you want any listed records to meet. For example, you might type:

```
LIST FOR CITY = "MERCER"
```

or

```
LIST FOR AMOUNT < 200
```

or

```
LIST FOR DTOC(DATE) < "10/15/94"
```

The Delete For command works in the same way. After the command, you state a deletion criterion (a deletion condition) following the word *for*. In fact, you can just substitute the word *DELETE* for the word *LIST* in the preceding commands. You then have marked for deletion all the records that meet the specified condition. In the following two exercises, you learn to use the Delete For command.

Exercise 3.1: To Use the Delete For Command

To use the Delete For command to mark all the records of customers from Portland, take these steps:

1. At the dot prompt, type **DELETE FOR CITY = "PORTLAND"**. Then press [↵Enter].
2. Type **LIST**, and press [↵Enter].

All the records with PORTLAND in the CITY field should be marked for deletion (see fig. 7.5).

```
. DELETE FOR CITY = "PORTLAND"
     3 records deleted
. LIST
Record#  LAST      FIRST  STREET      CITY     STATE ZIP   DATE     AMOUNT
      1  MILLS     GLEN   34 BRADY    EDMONDS  WA    98600 10/20/94 100.95
      2  CHEN      SUSAN  654 MAIN    MERCER   WA    98666 10/12/94 220.17
      3 *PETERS    KENT   81 HILL     PORTLAND OR    97299 12/10/94 102.52
      4  LOPEZ     MARIA  33 WALNUT   ARBOR    WA    98155 11/17/94 317.87
      5  IWASAKI   JULIE  1312 MAIN   MERCER   WA    98666 10/27/94 186.55
      6 *WILLS     BILL   312 JAMES   PORTLAND OR    97211 12/11/94 251.39
      7  THORPE    TAMU   459 ELM     ARBOR    WA    98752 10/18/94 115.48
      8  OWEN      CHRIS  43 TAFT     ENDWELL  OR    97290 11/10/94 324.95
      9  HUSAMI    MIKE   18 LEROY    SEATTLE  WA    98156 11/21/94 263.40
     10  PEREZ     JUDY   6 PARK      RENTON   WA    98624 12/12/94 200.97
     11  NGUYEN    MAI    10 JAMES    MERCER   OR    97054 11/18/94 105.27
     12 *KING      MYFUME 14 MAPLE    PORTLAND OR    97298 12/19/94 212.00

.
Command Line  <A:> CUSTOMER              Rec: EOF/12               NumCaps

                   Enter a dBASE III PLUS command.
```

Fig. 7.5
The PORTLAND records marked for deletion.

Exercise 3.2: Using the Delete For Command with Date Type Fields

Remember that you must convert Date type fields to Character type with the DTOC() function when you are stating selection criteria.

To mark records for deletion based on the contents of a Date type field, take these steps:

1. At the dot prompt, type **DELETE FOR DTOC(DATE) < "11/20/94"**. Then, press [↵Enter].
2. Type **LIST**, and press [↵Enter].

   All the records with a date before November 20, 1994, should be marked for deletion (see fig. 7.6). The PORTLAND records are also marked for deletion.

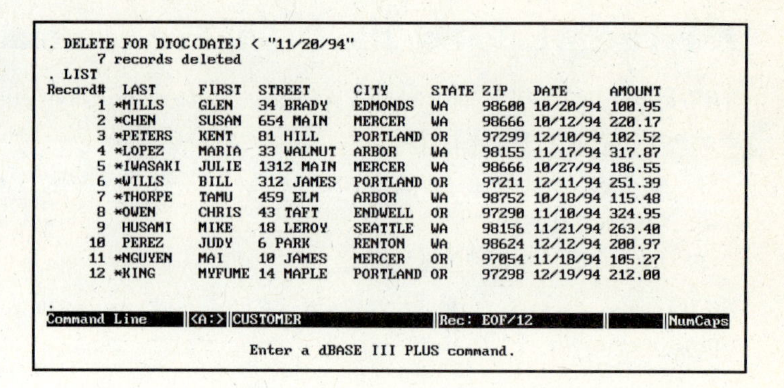

```
. DELETE FOR DTOC(DATE) < "11/20/94"
     7 records deleted
. LIST
Record#  LAST      FIRST   STREET      CITY      STATE ZIP   DATE     AMOUNT
      1 *MILLS     GLEN    34 BRADY    EDMONDS   WA    98600 10/20/94 100.95
      2 *CHEN      SUSAN   654 MAIN    MERCER    WA    98666 10/12/94 220.17
      3 *PETERS    KENT    81 HILL     PORTLAND  OR    97299 12/10/94 102.52
      4 *LOPEZ     MARIA   33 WALNUT   ARBOR     WA    98155 11/17/94 317.87
      5 *IWASAKI   JULIE   1312 MAIN   MERCER    WA    98666 10/27/94 186.55
      6 *WILLS     BILL    312 JAMES   PORTLAND  OR    97211 12/11/94 251.39
      7 *THORPE    TAMU    459 ELM     ARBOR     WA    98752 10/18/94 115.48
      8 *OWEN      CHRIS   43 TAFT     ENDWELL   OR    97290 11/10/94 324.95
      9  HUSAMI    MIKE    18 LEROY    SEATTLE   WA    98156 11/21/94 263.40
     10  PEREZ     JUDY    6 PARK      RENTON    WA    98624 12/12/94 200.97
     11 *NGUYEN    MAI     10 JAMES    MERCER    OR    97054 11/18/94 105.27
     12 *KING      MYFUME  14 MAPLE    PORTLAND  OR    97298 12/19/94 212.00

.
Command Line     <A:> CUSTOMER            Rec: EOF/12            NumCaps

                    Enter a dBASE III PLUS command.
```

Fig. 7.6
Records marked for deletion.

If you entered a Pack command (Don't do it now!), all the records marked for deletion would be removed from the database just as if you had marked the records individually. You could have marked the records individually. In a large database, however, individual marking is very time-consuming. You probably would miss some records that should be deleted or accidentally mark a record that should not be marked. The better method is to let dBASE search through the file and mark the records you have identified in your deletion criteria.

Some people mark groups of records—not to delete them, but rather to make them stand out on a screen listing or printout (although they run the risk of accidental deletion). The asterisk by the record number helps you pick out certain records as you scan through a listing. This capability means—especially in a large database of thousands of records—that you need an efficient way to unmark some of or all the marked records. In the following section, you learn how to perform these tasks by using the Recall For and Recall All commands.

Objective 4: To Use the Recall Command

When you used the Recall command to unmark records in Chapter 3, you learned that you can unmark a particular record (for example, record 5) by typing *RECALL RECORD 5*. You can use the Recall command in other ways, too. If you simply type *RECALL*, the command "unmarks" the current record. If you type *RECALL ALL*, the command unmarks all your marked records. If you specify a recall criterion (a recall condition) following the word *FOR*, only records that meet your condition are unmarked.

In the following exercises, you use both the Recall For and the Recall All commands. To do these exercises, a listing of your data should resemble figure 7.6.

Exercise 4.1: Using the Recall For Command

To unmark only the records of customers from Portland, take these steps:

1. At the dot prompt, type **RECALL FOR CITY = "PORTLAND"**, and press Enter.
2. Type **LIST**, and press Enter.

All the records with PORTLAND in the CITY field no longer should be marked for deletion (see fig. 7.7).

```
. RECALL FOR CITY = "PORTLAND"
      3 records recalled
. LIST
Record#  LAST     FIRST  STREET     CITY     STATE ZIP   DATE     AMOUNT
      1 *MILLS    GLEN   34 BRADY   EDMONDS  WA    98600 10/20/94 100.95
      2 *CHEN     SUSAN  654 MAIN   MERCER   WA    98666 10/12/94 220.17
      3  PETERS   KENT   81 HILL    PORTLAND OR    97299 12/10/94 102.52
      4 *LOPEZ    MARIA  33 WALNUT  ARBOR    WA    98155 11/17/94 317.87
      5 *IWASAKI  JULIE  1312 MAIN  MERCER   WA    98666 10/27/94 186.55
      6  WILLS    BILL   312 JAMES  PORTLAND OR    97211 12/11/94 251.39
      7 *THORPE   TAMU   459 ELM    ARBOR    WA    98752 10/18/94 115.48
      8 *OWEN     CHRIS  43 TAFT    ENDWELL  OR    97290 11/10/94 324.95
      9  HUSAMI   MIKE   18 LEROY   SEATTLE  WA    98156 11/21/94 263.40
     10  PEREZ    JUDY   6 PARK     RENTON   WA    98624 12/12/94 200.97
     11 *NGUYEN   MAI    10 JAMES   MERCER   OR    97054 11/18/94 105.27
     12  KING     MYFUME 14 MAPLE   PORTLAND OR    97298 12/19/94 212.00

.
Command Line  <A:> CUSTOMER          Rec: EOF/12           NumCaps

                 Enter a dBASE III PLUS command.
```

Fig. 7.7 The PORTLAND records are unmarked.

Exercise 4.2: Using the Recall All Command

To use the Recall All command, follow these steps:

1. At the dot prompt, type **RECALL ALL**, and press Enter.
2. Type **LIST**, and press Enter.

All the records that were marked should no longer be designated for deletion (see fig. 7.8).

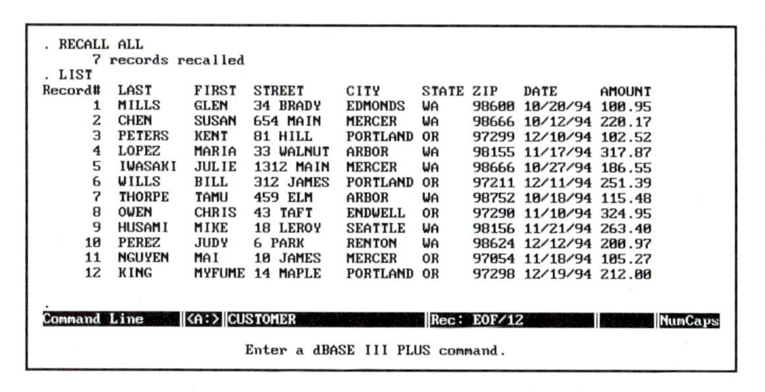

```
. RECALL ALL
      7 records recalled
. LIST
Record#  LAST     FIRST  STREET     CITY     STATE ZIP   DATE     AMOUNT
      1  MILLS    GLEN   34 BRADY   EDMONDS  WA    98600 10/20/94 100.95
      2  CHEN     SUSAN  654 MAIN   MERCER   WA    98666 10/12/94 220.17
      3  PETERS   KENT   81 HILL    PORTLAND OR    97299 12/10/94 102.52
      4  LOPEZ    MARIA  33 WALNUT  ARBOR    WA    98155 11/17/94 317.87
      5  IWASAKI  JULIE  1312 MAIN  MERCER   WA    98666 10/27/94 186.55
      6  WILLS    BILL   312 JAMES  PORTLAND OR    97211 12/11/94 251.39
      7  THORPE   TAMU   459 ELM    ARBOR    WA    98752 10/18/94 115.48
      8  OWEN     CHRIS  43 TAFT    ENDWELL  OR    97290 11/10/94 324.95
      9  HUSAMI   MIKE   18 LEROY   SEATTLE  WA    98156 11/21/94 263.40
     10  PEREZ    JUDY   6 PARK     RENTON   WA    98624 12/12/94 200.97
     11  NGUYEN   MAI    10 JAMES   MERCER   OR    97054 11/18/94 105.27
     12  KING     MYFUME 14 MAPLE   PORTLAND OR    97298 12/19/94 212.00

.
Command Line  <A:> CUSTOMER          Rec: EOF/12           NumCaps

                 Enter a dBASE III PLUS command.
```

Fig. 7.8 No records are marked for deletion.

If the only records marked were records with a date before 11/20/94, you could have accomplished the same unmarking by using RECALL FOR DTOC(DATE) < "11/20/94". In cases in which one condition statement does not describe all the records that should be unmarked, you may need to use several RECALL FOR statements or the Recall All command.

Objective 5: To Use the Replace Command

In earlier chapters, you have seen how you can use either the Edit or the Browse command to modify the contents of a data field in a record. When you use these commands, you alter the contents of your records one at a time. Sometimes, the same change has to be made to a field in all the records or in a group of records. You use the Replace command for this purpose. As you might expect, this command has two versions: Replace All and Replace For. One benefit of dBASE is the consistency in the way all the commands are set up. For example, after you have learned how to state a condition in the List For command, you can confidently use the same technique when you need to state a condition with another For command.

When you work with an indexed database and you have an active index, the results of the Replace All and Replace For commands may not be what you expect. Rather than try to learn some complicated rules, just remember one guideline: When you use the Replace For and the Replace All commands, the best method is to open the database with no active indexes, do the Replace, and then use the Reindex command to replace your index files. If you follow this procedure, your database is changed by your Replace command just as was previously described. Reindexing takes only a little extra time.

In the following exercises, you use the Replace command to make some changes to the Tours database file.

Exercise 5.1: Using the Replace Command

This exercise uses the Tours database file. Make sure that your disk with this file is in your computer. Open the Tours database so that the name *Tours* is displayed in the status bar.

To replace the contents of the COST field for record 4, take these steps:

1. At the dot prompt, type **LIST**, and press Enter.

   Your screen should resemble figure 7.9.

```
. USE TOURS
. LIST
Record#  TOUR_CODE TO              FROM         DEPART   RETURN   COST
      1  A101      ENGLAND         NYC          07/05/94 07/12/94 1255
      2  A102      IRELAND         BOSTON       07/19/94 07/26/94 1422
      3  A103      ISRAEL          NYC          08/11/94 08/20/94 1688
      4  A104      BERMUDA         NYC          11/05/94 11/08/94  657
      5  A105      KENYA           NYC          11/15/94 11/28/94 3525
      6  A106      TANZANIA        NYC          12/06/94 12/19/94 3525
      7  A107      BRAZIL          LA           01/08/95 01/12/95 1341
      8  A108      ARGENTINA       LA           03/09/95 03/13/95 1251
      9  A109      SINGAPORE       PORTLAND     06/01/94 06/05/94 1375
     10  A110      HONG KONG       SEATTLE      06/22/94 06/27/94 1379
     11  C101      COZUMEL         NEW ORLEANS  01/17/95 01/21/95 1995
     12  C102      JAMAICA         MIAMI        02/04/95 02/08/95 1755
     13  C103      ST THOMAS       MIAMI        02/21/95 02/25/95 1615

Command Line   <A:> TOURS          Rec: EOF/13                NumCaps
                    Enter a dBASE III PLUS command.
```

Fig. 7.9 The records list from the Tours database.

2. Type **GOTO 4**, and press ↵Enter.
3. Type **REPLACE COST WITH 700**, and press ↵Enter.
4. Type **LIST**, and press ↵Enter.

The COST field for record 4 should be changed (see fig. 7.10).

```
     13  C103      ST THOMAS       MIAMI        02/21/95 02/25/95 1615

. GOTO 4
. REPLACE COST WITH 700
      1 record replaced
. LIST
Record#  TOUR_CODE TO              FROM         DEPART   RETURN   COST
      1  A101      ENGLAND         NYC          07/05/94 07/12/94 1255
      2  A102      IRELAND         BOSTON       07/19/94 07/26/94 1422
      3  A103      ISRAEL          NYC          08/11/94 08/20/94 1688
      4  A104      BERMUDA         NYC          11/05/94 11/08/94  700
      5  A105      KENYA           NYC          11/15/94 11/28/94 3525
      6  A106      TANZANIA        NYC          12/06/94 12/19/94 3525
      7  A107      BRAZIL          LA           01/08/95 01/12/95 1341
      8  A108      ARGENTINA       LA           03/09/95 03/13/95 1251
      9  A109      SINGAPORE       PORTLAND     06/01/94 06/05/94 1375
     10  A110      HONG KONG       SEATTLE      06/22/94 06/27/94 1379
     11  C101      COZUMEL         NEW ORLEANS  01/17/95 01/21/95 1995
     12  C102      JAMAICA         MIAMI        02/04/95 02/08/95 1755
     13  C103      ST THOMAS       MIAMI        02/21/95 02/25/95 1615

Command Line   <A:> TOURS          Rec: EOF/13                NumCaps
                    Enter a dBASE III PLUS command.
```

Fig. 7.10 The changed COST field in record 4.

7

Exercise 5.2: Using the Replace All Command

Assume that the cost of all the tours must be increased by 10 percent. To make this change, you need to multiply the current contents of the COST field in each record by 110 percent. In dBASE, the symbols that you use for arithmetic are addition (+), subtraction (–), multiplication (*), and division (/).

To replace the contents of the COST field for all records, take these steps:

1. Type **REPLACE ALL COST WITH COST * 1.1**, and press ↵Enter.

This command tells dBASE to calculate a new value for the COST field by multiplying the original value of the COST field by 110 percent. The old value in the COST field is erased, and the new value is stored in COST.

2. Type **LIST**, and press Enter.

The COST field in all the records should be changed (see fig. 7.11).

Fig. 7.11
The changed COST field for all records.

```
. REPLACE ALL COST WITH COST * 1.1
    13 records replaced
. LIST
Record#  TOUR_CODE TO                FROM         DEPART   RETURN    COST
      1  A101      ENGLAND           NYC          07/05/94 07/12/94  1380
      2  A102      IRELAND           BOSTON       07/19/94 07/26/94  1564
      3  A103      ISRAEL            NYC          08/11/94 08/20/94  1857
      4  A104      BERMUDA           NYC          11/05/94 11/08/94   770
      5  A105      KENYA             NYC          11/15/94 11/28/94  3878
      6  A106      TANZANIA          NYC          12/06/94 12/19/94  3878
      7  A107      BRAZIL            LA           01/08/95 01/12/95  1475
      8  A108      ARGENTINA         LA           03/09/95 03/13/95  1376
      9  A109      SINGAPORE         PORTLAND     06/01/94 06/05/94  1513
     10  A110      HONG KONG         SEATTLE      06/22/94 06/27/94  1517
     11  C101      COZUMEL           NEW ORLEANS  01/17/95 01/21/95  2194
     12  C102      JAMAICA           MIAMI        02/04/95 02/08/95  1931
     13  C103      ST THOMAS         MIAMI        02/21/95 02/25/95  1777
.
Command Line      |<A:>|TOURS           |Rec: EOF/13      |      |NumCaps

                    Enter a dBASE III PLUS command.
```

7

Exercise 5.3: Using the Replace For Command

To decrease the contents of the COST field by $50.00 for any tours leaving from New York City, take these steps:

1. Type **REPLACE COST WITH COST - 50 FOR FROM = "NYC"**, and press Enter.

   This command tells dBASE to calculate a new value for the COST field by subtracting 50 from the original COST field value *if* the FROM field contains *NYC*.

2. Type **LIST**, and press Enter.

The COST field for all tours leaving from New York City should be changed (see fig. 7.12).

```
. REPLACE COST WITH COST - 50 FOR FROM = "NYC"
     5 records replaced
. LIST
Record#  TOUR_CODE TO               FROM          DEPART   RETURN    COST
      1  A101      ENGLAND          NYC           07/05/94 07/12/94  1330
      2  A102      IRELAND          BOSTON        07/19/94 07/26/94  1564
      3  A103      ISRAEL           NYC           08/11/94 08/20/94  1807
      4  A104      BERMUDA          NYC           11/05/94 11/08/94   720
      5  A105      KENYA            NYC           11/15/94 11/28/94  3828
      6  A106      TANZANIA         NYC           12/06/94 12/19/94  3828
      7  A107      BRAZIL           LA            01/08/95 01/12/95  1475
      8  A108      ARGENTINA        LA            03/09/95 03/13/95  1376
      9  A109      SINGAPORE        PORTLAND      06/01/94 06/05/94  1513
     10  A110      HONG KONG        SEATTLE       06/22/94 06/27/94  1517
     11  C101      COZUMEL          NEW ORLEANS   01/17/95 01/21/95  2194
     12  C102      JAMAICA          MIAMI         02/04/95 02/08/95  1931
     13  C103      ST THOMAS        MIAMI         02/21/95 02/25/95  1777

.
Command Line   <A:> TOURS              Rec: EOF/13              NumCaps

                    Enter a dBASE III PLUS command.
```

Fig. 7.12
Only the NYC records have been changed.

Objective 6: To Use the Count, Sum, and Average Commands

Database programs do not have many of the built-in number crunching capabilities that spreadsheet programs have. The purpose of a database program is to store and retrieve data, not perform calculations. dBASE, however, does have the capability of adding, subtracting, multiplying, and dividing, as you learned when reading about the Replace command. dBASE also has two commands—Average and Sum—that are designed to perform calculations on Numeric type fields in a database. The Average command calculates the arithmetic mean of a field. In other words, Average sums the field, and then divides the sum by the number of records. The Sum command adds the values in a Numeric type field. As you use these commands in the following exercises, you will understand their functions.

Many options that you first learned about in the discussion of the List command also apply to the Average and Sum commands. The default for these calculation commands is to display a result for all the Numeric type fields in the database. This default is similar to the default for the List command, which is to list all the fields in a record. Just as in the List command, when you use the Average and Sum commands, you can limit the fields for which a result is produced. You simply list the fields that you want averaged or summed after the command. For example, suppose that you have in your database three Numeric type fields named FIELD1, FIELD2, and FIELD3. If you want averages for FIELD1 and FIELD3 only, you use the following command:

```
AVERAGE FIELD1, FIELD3
```

You also have the capability to set a criterion (a condition) for averaging and summing. You describe the conditions following the word *FOR* just as you set conditions in the List For command. Then, only the records that meet the criterion are averaged or summed. You can use .OR. and .AND. just as you did in Chapter 3 when you used the List For command.

The Count Command

The Count command tallies the number of records in your database. When you use this command, the field listing option does not have a purpose. Therefore, dBASE does not recognize what you mean if you follow the word *COUNT* with a field name because the Count command doesn't apply to fields as do the List, Average, and Sum commands. The Count command applies to the whole record.

You can, however, set a condition for which records should be counted by using the word *FOR*. This capability is very useful. For example, suppose that you want to know how many customers in the Customer database live in Portland. The command that gives you the answer is

```
COUNT FOR CITY = "PORTLAND"
```

Again, the power of commands such as Count, Average, and Sum is more apparent when you work with hundreds or thousands of records in a large database. Then, human error and the time involved makes accurately averaging, counting, or summing records nearly impossible. With dBASE, however, you can perform these operations quickly and correctly.

In the following exercises, you use the Customer database. Make sure that this database file is in use before you begin the exercise.

Exercise 6.1: Using the Average, Count, and Sum Commands

To use the Average, Count, and Sum commands on the records in the Customer database file, take these steps:

1. At the dot prompt, type **CLEAR**, and press Enter.

   This command clears the screen and makes the results of the following commands easier to see.

2. Type **AVERAGE**, and press [↵Enter].
3. Type **COUNT**, and press [↵Enter].
4. Type **SUM**, and press [↵Enter].

Now, your screen should resemble figure 7.13.

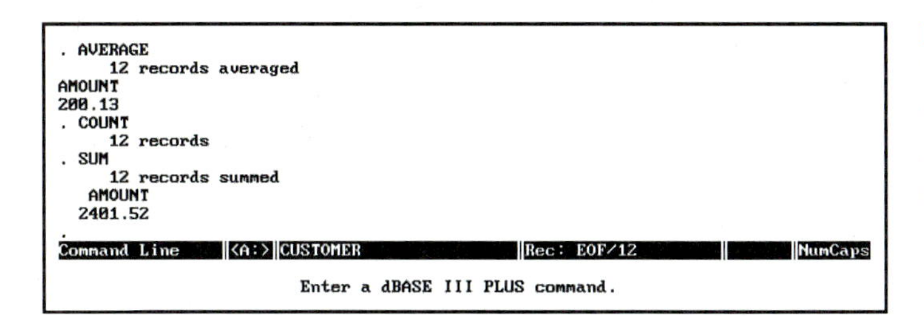

Fig. 7.13
The results of the commands appear on-screen.

The Customer database has only one Numeric type field. You can see that the results of the Average and Sum commands are displayed under the field name AMOUNT. If the Customer structure contained more Numeric type fields, the name of each numeric field would be displayed in order from left to right on-screen. Then the sum or average of that field would display under the field name. This display makes very clear the association between the field name and the sum or average.

Exercise 6.2: Using the Average For, Count For, and Sum For Commands

To use the Average For, Count For, and Sum For commands on the records in the Customer database file, take these steps:

1. At the dot prompt, type **CLEAR**, and press [↵Enter].

   This command clears the screen and makes the results of the commands easier to see.
2. Type **AVERAGE FOR STATE = "WA"**, and press [↵Enter].
3. Type **COUNT FOR CITY = "MERCER" .AND. STATE = "WA"**, and press [↵Enter].
4. Type **SUM FOR DTOC(DATE) > "12/10/94"**, and press [↵Enter].

Now, the screen should resemble figure 7.14.

Fig. 7.14
The results of the commands appear on-screen.

```
. AVERAGE FOR STATE = "WA"
      7 records averaged
AMOUNT
200.77
. COUNT FOR CITY = "MERCER" .AND. STATE = "WA"
      2 records
. SUM FOR DTOC(DATE) > "12/10/94"
      3 records summed
   AMOUNT
   664.36
.
Command Line     ||<A:>||CUSTOMER          ||Rec: EOF/12      ||    ||NumCaps

                  Enter a dBASE III PLUS command.
```

Objective 7: To Use the Find Command

In Chapter 3, you learned how to list records that meet a selection condition by using the List For command. The command searches sequentially through a database file from top to bottom and displays the record(s) that meet the criterion. dBASE can do this search very quickly when you have only ten or twenty records in your file. However, if you have ten or twenty *thousand* records in your database, you can wait ten or more minutes for the result because dBASE does not know whether it has listed all the records until it has checked through to the very last record.

7

If the record for which you are searching has a primary key field, such as a Social Security number or an invoice number, the List For technique for finding the record in a large database is unacceptably inefficient and slow. Even after the one record with that key field value is found and displayed, the List command keeps searching through the database until it comes to the bottom. This searching ties up your computer, so you still have to wait until dBASE reaches the last record.

Both the Find and Seek commands are efficient commands to use when searching for records. These commands are especially useful if you search for a record with a particular primary key field value. These two commands both have the following requirements:

- The file you are using must have an index for (be indexed on) the field you are asking dBASE to search.
- That index must be the only active index.
- You must use a Display or a special List command to see the contents of the record.

In the following exercise, you use the Find command with the Display command to extract the single record with the last name LOPEZ.

Exercise 7.1: Using the Find Command

To use the Find command, you need to have an active index. You use the Customer database and index it on the LAST field.

To use the Find command, take these steps:

1. At the dot prompt, type **INDEX ON LAST TO LASTNDX**, and press ↵Enter.
2. Type **FIND LOPEZ**, and press ↵Enter.

   Typing the field name is unnecessary because dBASE knows that the active index uses the key field LAST. You also don't need to use quotation marks because dBASE knows that LAST is a Character type field. An equal sign is unnecessary because FIND always searches for an *equal* condition.

   Notice that the record indicator in the status bar changes to Lopez's record number.
3. Type **DISPLAY**, and press ↵Enter.

   Now, your screen should resemble figure 7.15.

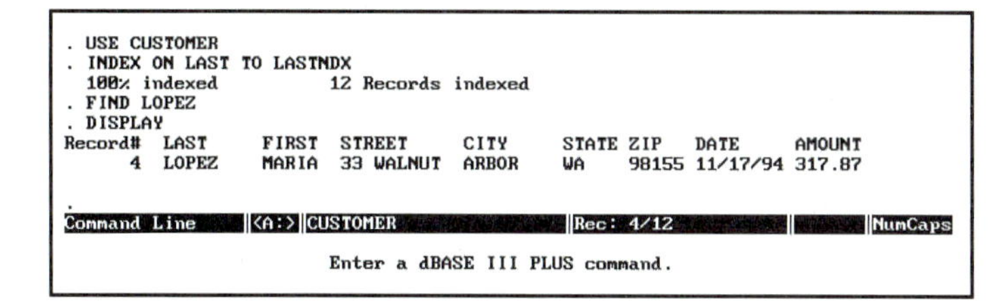

Fig. 7.15 The results of the Find command.

If dBASE does not find a record to match your request, the program displays the message `No find`.

Using the Find Command to Find and Display All Records with a Particular Value

Even when you are using the Find or Seek command to retrieve records that do not have primary key fields, you can use one of these commands to find the first record containing a particular value. Then, you use the List Next command or List While command to see any other records with the same value in that field. This technique works because the active index file causes all records with the same value in a field to be grouped together—in other words, to follow one after the other. You need to list the records only until you see the value for the key field change; then you know that you have seen all the records with that particular value. Using this "Find and then List" or "Search and then List" technique, you go directly to the first record and then list a few records sequentially. Using Find or Seek in this manner is similar to employing the Fast Forward button on a tape recorder or VCR to move quickly to the place where you want to begin viewing. If you type *TO PRINT* at the end of a List Next or List While command, you get a printout of the results.

In the following exercise, you use the Find command with the List Next command to extract the group of records for customers from Mercer.

Exercise 7.2: Using the Find Command and the List Next Command

You are going to use the CITY field to find records, and your first step is to create an index on this field.

To use the Find command and the List Next command, take these steps:

1. At the dot prompt, type **INDEX ON CITY TO CITYNDX**, and press Enter.
2. Type **FIND MERCER**, and press Enter.
3. Type **DISPLAY**, and press Enter.

   Now, your screen should resemble figure 7.16.

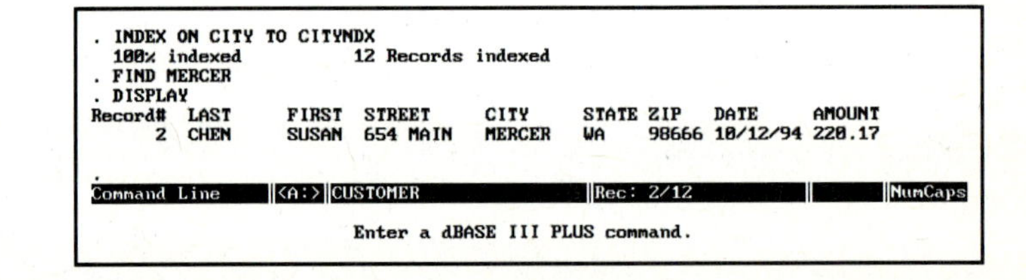

```
. INDEX ON CITY TO CITYNDX
  100% indexed          12 Records indexed
. FIND MERCER
. DISPLAY
Record#  LAST     FIRST  STREET    CITY    STATE ZIP   DATE     AMOUNT
      2  CHEN     SUSAN  654 MAIN  MERCER  WA    98666 10/12/94 220.17

.
Command Line  |<A:>|CUSTOMER          |Rec: 2/12    |    |NumCaps
                 Enter a dBASE III PLUS command.
```

Fig. 7.16
The results of the Find command.

   What happened to the other MERCER records? They are in a group immediately following the first MERCER record located by the Find command. Remember, the Find command finds only the first occurrence of a field value.

4. To list a group of five records, type **LIST NEXT 5**, and press Enter.

   Now, your screen should resemble figure 7.17.

```
. INDEX ON CITY TO CITYNDX
  100% indexed          12 Records indexed
. FIND MERCER
. DISPLAY
Record#  LAST      FIRST  STREET     CITY     STATE ZIP   DATE     AMOUNT
      2  CHEN      SUSAN  654 MAIN   MERCER   WA    98666 10/12/94 220.17

. LIST NEXT 5
Record#  LAST      FIRST  STREET     CITY     STATE ZIP   DATE     AMOUNT
      2  CHEN      SUSAN  654 MAIN   MERCER   WA    98666 10/12/94 220.17
      5  IWASAKI   JULIE  1312 MAIN  MERCER   WA    98666 10/27/94 186.55
     11  NGUYEN    MAI    10 JAMES   MERCER   OR    97054 11/10/94 105.27
      3  PETERS    KENT   81 HILL    PORTLAND OR    97299 12/10/94 102.52
      6  WILLS     BILL   312 JAMES  PORTLAND OR    97211 12/11/94 251.39

.
Command Line  |<A:>|CUSTOMER          |Rec: 6/12        |      |NumCaps
                  Enter a dBASE III PLUS command.
```

Fig. 7.17
The remaining Mercer records on-screen.

Typing *DISPLAY* before typing *LIST NEXT* was unnecessary. However, entering the commands in this way showed that the Find command locates only the first MERCER record.

This example database is a small one, and you know that listing a group of five records will show all the MERCER records in the database. The whole point of Find and Seek, however, is to get to records in a large database very quickly. But how can you be sure that you list all the records with a particular value in a field when you don't know what number should follow the word *NEXT*? One method is to keep using the LIST NEXT 10 command until the key field changes. When the key field changes, you know that you are done. A more efficient solution exists, however. You can use the List While command. This command tells dBASE to keep listing for as long as the key field value does not change.

In the following exercise, you use the Find command with the List While command to extract the group of records for customers from Portland.

Exercise 7.3: Using Both the Find and List While Commands

You are going to use the CITY field to find records. Your Cityndx must be active.

To use the Find command and the List While command, take these steps:

1. At the dot prompt, type **FIND PORTLAND**, and press Enter.

   Notice that the record indicator in the status bar shows that the first of the Portland records was found.

2. To list all the Portland customers, type **LIST WHILE CITY = "PORTLAND"**, and press Enter.

Now, your screen should resemble figure 7.18.

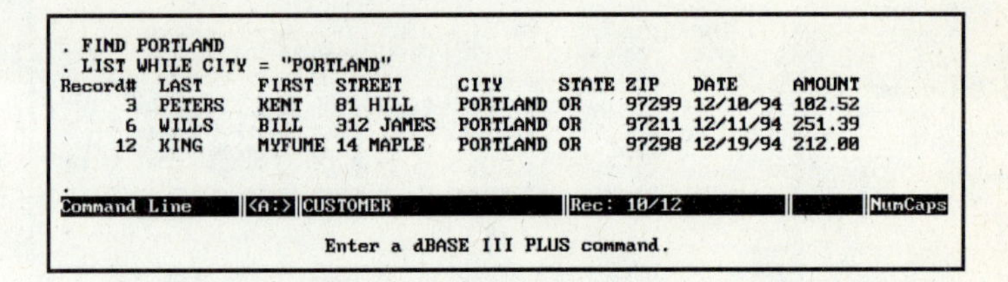

Fig. 7.18
The PORTLAND records on-screen.

Objective 8: To Use the Seek Command

The Find and the Seek commands are similar in the way they are used. For your purposes, Seek differs from Find in two ways. First, Seek requires you to place quotation marks around conditions that involve Character type fields. Second, Seek actually is more powerful than Find because Seek can locate Date type data, and Find cannot. When you use Seek for a Date type field, you must use the function that converts the characters inside the quotation marks to a Date type value. The function that does this is the Character To Date function CTOD(). For example, if you are seeking a record with "12/07/94" in the DATE field, you type the command *SEEK CTOD("12/07/94")*.

In the next set of exercises, you use Seek to find one record. Remember that the List Next and List While commands also can be used to display groups of records after Seek has located the first record in the group.

Exercise 8.1: Using the Seek Command

To use the Seek command, you need to have an index active. You use the Customer database and index it on the AMOUNT field.

To use the Seek command, take these steps:

1. At the dot prompt, type **INDEX ON AMOUNT TO AMOUNTX**, and press Enter.
2. Type **SEEK 105.27**, and press Enter.
3. Type **DISPLAY**, and press Enter.

   Now, your screen should resemble figure 7.19.

```
. INDEX ON AMOUNT TO AMOUNTX
  100% indexed          12 Records indexed
. SEEK 105.27
. DISPLAY
Record#  LAST     FIRST  STREET    CITY    STATE ZIP   DATE     AMOUNT
     11  NGUYEN   MAI    10 JAMES  MERCER  OR    97054 11/10/94 105.27

Command Line  ||<A:>||CUSTOMER          ||Rec: 11/12      ||    ||NumCaps
                  Enter a dBASE III PLUS command.
```

Fig. 7.19 The results of the Seek command.

Exercise 8.2: Using the Seek Command with Date Type Fields

To use the Seek command, you must have an index active. You use the Customer database, and index it on the DATE field.

To use the Seek command, take these steps:

1. At the dot prompt, type **INDEX ON DATE TO DATEX**, and press ↵Enter.
2. Type **SEEK CTOD("10/27/94")**, and press ↵Enter.
3. Type **DISPLAY**, and press ↵Enter.

   Now, the screen should resemble figure 7.20.

```
. INDEX ON DATE TO DATEX
  100% indexed          12 Records indexed
. SEEK CTOD("10/27/94")
. DISPLAY
Record#  LAST     FIRST  STREET    CITY    STATE ZIP   DATE     AMOUNT
      5  IWASAKI  JULIE  1312 MAIN MERCER  WA    98666 10/27/94 106.55

Command Line  ||<A:>||CUSTOMER          ||Rec: 5/12       ||    ||NumCaps
                  Enter a dBASE III PLUS command.
```

Fig. 7.20 The results of the Seek command for a Date field.

In the exercises, you indexed before you issued a Find or a Seek command to ensure that your index was up-to-date. If you already have an index on a field you want to use in a Find or a Seek command, just open the database file and the appropriate index as you did in Chapter 6, "Sorting and Indexing Database Files."

Chapter Summary

In this chapter, you have learned how to work efficiently with large databases. You have learned how to move around in the database by using the Goto command. You know how to insert a record in any place in the file. You can mark groups of records for deletion and recall a group of marked records. You have used the Replace command to place a new value in a field and replaced old field values with new calculations. You worked with the Average, Count, and Sum commands. You have learned how to go directly to a record by using the Find or Seek command. You also now know how to use the List Next and List While commands.

In the following chapter, you learn how to produce a printout of your database. You learn how to format a printout of data records in a report that has a professional appearance so that other employees in an organization can use the file. You also learn how to print mailing labels from the information in a database.

Testing Your Knowledge

True/False Questions

1. The Seek command finds only the first record that matches a condition.
2. The Replace command can be used to calculate a new value for a field.
3. If the DATE field is a Date type field, the command DELETE FOR DATE = "11/20/94" marks all records with a date of 11/20/94.
4. The Replace command can be used on the current record only.
5. When using the Count command, you must specify a field name.

Multiple-Choice Questions

1. Before you can use the __________ command on a field, an index on that field has to be active.
   a. List
   b. Replace
   c. Delete
   d. none of these answers

2. The command to place a record between other records in a database file is __________.
   a. Replace
   b. Move
   c. Insert
   d. none of these answers
3. The symbol for division in dBASE is __________.
   a. +
   b. –
   c. *
   d. none of these answers
4. With which type of field can the Find command *not* be used?
   a. Character
   b. Date
   c. Numeric
   d. none of these answers
5. Which command can be used only with Numeric type fields?
   a. Average
   b. Count
   c. Replace
   d. none of these answers

Fill-in-the-Blank Questions

1. The command to go directly to record 17 is __________.
2. The command to unmark all records marked for deletion is __________.
3. The command to list the current record and the next four records is __________.
4. The command to increase the PRICE field (a Numeric type field) of a record by 75 dollars is __________.
5. The command to average each of the Numeric type fields in all records with SEATTLE in the CITY field is __________.

Review: Short Projects

For these Sort Projects, copy the Customer database to a file named Cust. Then, use Cust to complete the projects.

1. Inserting a Record and Replacing a Field
   a. Insert the following record as the third record in the CUST file:

Field	*Data*
LAST	**SCHRADER**
FIRST	**JACK**
STREET	**98 VESTAL**
CITY	**ARBOR**
STATE	**WA**
ZIP	**98155**
DATE	**11/17/94**
AMOUNT	**124.75**

   b. Use the Replace command to change Julie Iwasaki's ZIP code to 98676. Print the file.

2. Deleting and Recalling Records
   a. Use the Delete For command to mark for deletion all the records of customers from Arbor or Renton. Print the file.
   b. Use the Recall For command to unmark the records of customers from Arbor. Print the file.

3. Using the Sum and Average commands

   Use the Sum and Average commands to determine the total amount spent by customers from Arbor and the average amount spent by customers from Seattle or Portland.

7

Review: Long Projects

1. Working with the Tours Database
   a. Use the Insert command to insert a record for a tour from Seattle to the town in which you live. The new record should be record number 11.
   b. Reduce the cost of all tours leaving from LA or MIAMI by 10 percent by using the Replace command.

c. Index the database using the FROM field. Use the Seek command to locate the start of the NYC records. Then use either the List Next or the List While command to list the NYC records on the printer.

d. Use the Average command to determine the average cost of a tour from SEATTLE or LA.

e. Use the Average command to determine the average cost of a tour leaving after 11/16/94.

2. Working with the Climate Database

   Copy the Climate database to the file Climate1. Use Climate1 to do this project.

   a. Use the Average command to find the average of each of the numeric fields.

   b. What is the average maximum temperature for stations with an elevation above 1000?

   c. Use the Count command to determine the number of records with a maximum of less than 80 and a minimum above 50.

   d. Mark for deletion all the records with a maximum of less than 80 and a minimum above 50. List the file on the printer.

   e. Unmark all records with an elevation above 3,000. List the file on the printer.

Printing Reports and Mailing Labels

8

In previous chapters, when you worked with your database, the appearance of the displayed or printed data was determined by the name, size, and type of the fields in a record. You created your database and entered the data. Therefore, this display was meaningful and useful to you. If, however, you want to present the data to others, for example, other employees in your office, you usually need to give them the information in a more polished or understandable form. The term that is usually used to refer to data output in an organized form is *report*. A report is normally printed on a printer, and copies are distributed as needed.

The information in a report consists of titles, column headings, and data. The data is printed down the page in columns under the headings. Totals are often produced at the bottom of the columns of numeric data. The use of a standard size printer for a report generally limits to 80 characters the amount of information that can be printed across a page. Some wide carriage printers can print up to 132 characters across a page. Your computer screen can display 80 characters in one line.

dBASE can print a report from your database, display the report on-screen, or save the report in a disk file for later printing. Before dBASE can produce the report, however, you need to define the way you want the report to look. You also need to indicate which data fields should be printed or totaled. In this chapter, you learn how to create report forms. A *report form* controls the printing of the data in the active database so that the report produced has a professional appearance.

In this chapter, you also learn how to define a *label form*, which can be used to print addresses from a database on the standard sheets of mailing labels available from office supply stores. You can use label forms to address business correspondence. You can also use label forms to print mailing labels for Christmas cards, wedding announcements, or mailings for student organizations or clubs. In fact, most of the mail you receive, junk mail included, is addressed by a computer running a database program like dBASE III Plus. You, too, can now enjoy the benefits of label forms.

Objectives

1. To Create and Use a Mailing Label Form
2. To Modify a Mailing Label Form
3. To Create and Use a Report Form
4. To Modify a Report Form

	Key Terms in This Chapter
Format	The physical organization or layout of data on a page. The format determines the way data is printed or displayed. The pattern that controls how data is printed or displayed is referred to as *the format*.
Report	Formatted output, usually printed, of database records. A report often contains headings, group subtotals, and overall totals for numeric fields.
Form	A file that contains the pattern (format) according to which data from the active database is to be displayed or printed. The layout you create for a report or for mailing labels is stored in a form. You need both a database file and a form file to print a report or mailing labels. dBASE gives report-form files the extension FRM. Label-form files are given the extension LBL.

Objective 1: To Create and Use a Mailing Label Form

Generating mailing labels is a frequent activity, and dBASE is set up to make printing labels easy. The sheets of gummed address labels that you can load in your printer come in five standard sizes. Table 8.1 lists the five standard (or predefined) label sizes. dBASE automatically adjusts its label printing options when you select a predefined size. To print mailing labels from a database, all you have to do is tell dBASE which standard size sheets you are using and which database fields to print on each line of the labels. Then dBASE usually prints your labels perfectly. If you need to fine-tune the label printing, you can alter some of the standard label printing options. One database record provides the data for one label.

Assume that you have regular printer paper loaded in your printer so that you can use any standard (predefined) label sheet size. If your instructor has loaded mailing label sheets in your printer, the instructor will explain which predefined size to select. If you do not have a printer connected to your computer, you can still do the exercises and view the results on your screen.

Table 8.1 Predefined Sizes for Sheets of Address Labels

Width	*Height*	*Number of Labels across Sheet*
3 1/2"	15/16"	1
3 1/2"	15/16"	2
3 1/2"	15/16"	3
4"	1 7/16"	1
3 2/10"	11/12"	3 (Cheshire style)

The Create Label Command

You use the Create Label command to create a new label form file. Before you issue this command, a database file should be in use. If a database file is not open, dBASE displays the message `No database is in USE. Enter filename`, and waits for you to enter the name of the database to use. The label-form file you create should be used only with the database that was in use when you created the label form. In other words, the database and the label form are a matched pair that work together.

dBASE assigns the file name extension LBL to label-form files. A good practice is to give both the database file and the associated label form file the same name. This convention helps you remember the name of the label-form file that goes with the database file. dBASE assigns the extension DBF to the database files. dBASE does not become confused if you use the name Customer for your label file that goes with the Customer database. To list all your label form files, at the dot prompt, type **LIST FILES LIKE *.LBL**, and press ↵Enter.

In the exercises in this chapter, you use the Customer database. Remember that you must open the database file with the address fields that you want to use before you begin to create a label form. One database record provides the data for each label.

Exercise 1.1: Using the Create Label Command to Access the Create Label Screen

To begin creating a form to print mailing labels from the data in the Customer database, do the following:

1. If CUSTOMER is not in use, at the dot prompt, type **USE CUSTOMER**, and press ↵Enter. Your status bar should show that Customer is in use before you continue this exercise.
2. At the dot prompt, type **CREATE LABEL**, and press ↵Enter. dBASE then prompts you for the name of the label form file.
3. Type **CUSTOMER**, and press ↵Enter.

   Note: You could have typed **CREATE LABEL CUSTOMER**, and pressed ↵Enter in step 2. The methods are equivalent. You can now use CUSTOMER.LBL to save the form that you create.

Your screen should now resemble figure 8.1; note the name of the form file in the status bar. The screen you see is the Create Label screen. You use menu choices to define the format for your labels. The Options menu, from which you choose the standard label sheet size to use, is open (see fig. 8.1). The highlight is on Option. Within the Option menu, the Predefined Size choice is highlighted. Now, continue to define your label format.

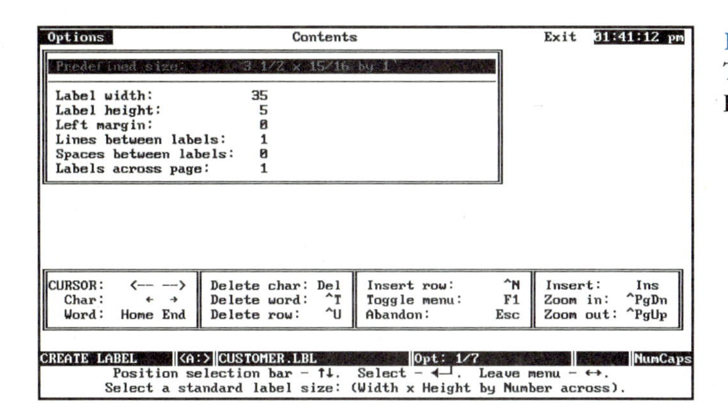

Fig. 8.1
The Create Label Form screen.

Exercise 1.2: Using the Create Label Screen to Select a Standard Label Size

To indicate which standard size label sheets you use, do the following:

1. Press ↵Enter. Notice that the Predefined Size option changes.
2. Press ↵Enter to cycle through the five standard label sheet sizes.

   Notice that as the predefined size changes, some of the other options that are below it in the menu also change. You cannot alter the five predefined sizes themselves; you can only select the one that you want.
3. Press ↵Enter until the predefined size changes back to `3 1/2 x 15/16 by 1`. Refer to table 1.1 for the meaning of this choice. Again, your screen should resemble figure 8.1.

dBASE now knows the size and the number of the labels on the sheet in your printer. Next, you need to tell dBASE what should be printed on each label.

The Label Contents Menu Box

The Label Contents menu box is the menu through which you tell dBASE which fields from your database to print on a label. This menu is different from any that you have previously used. The box is meant to represent one label, and the lines on which you can print on the label are numbered 1 through 5. To enter a field name in a line (1–5) of the menu box, you first move the highlight to the line in which you want the field to appear. Then, you press ↵Enter. A black arrowhead and blinking black cursor appear in that menu line. Now you can type one or more field names separated by commas. When you have finished defining the contents of the line, press ↵Enter.

To help remember the names of the fields in the database, press F10. You will see a menu from which you can select fields for each line of the label. If you remember the field names, you can simply type them in the Label box. Remember to separate the field names by a comma if more than one field is to be printed on a line of the label.

Exercise 1.3: Using the Create Label Screen to Define the Contents of a Label

To indicate which fields should be printed in each line of the label, do the following:

1. Leave the Options menu, and move to the Contents menu by pressing → once.

   Your screen should now resemble figure 8.2. The highlight is on the first line at the top of the label.

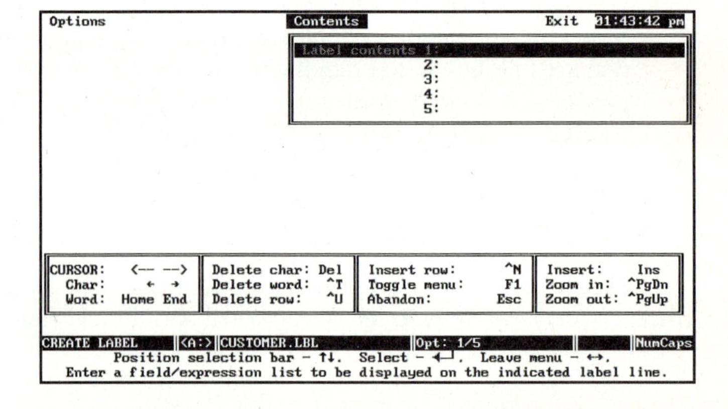

Fig. 8.2 The Contents menu, used for establishing the form of a label.

2. Press ↵Enter. A black arrowhead and a blinking cursor appear in the highlight; these symbols indicate that you can type in the line (see fig. 8.3. Note that colors in this figure are reversed so that you can see more easily.).

3. Press F10 for a list of the fields in the Customer database (see fig. 8.4).

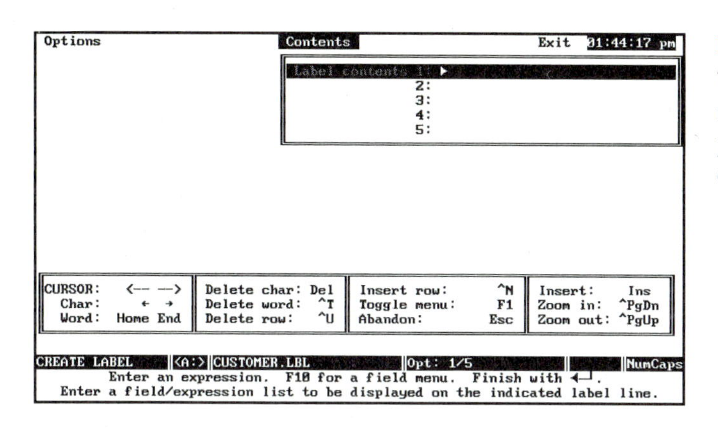

Fig. 8.3 The arrowhead indicating the place where you can type.

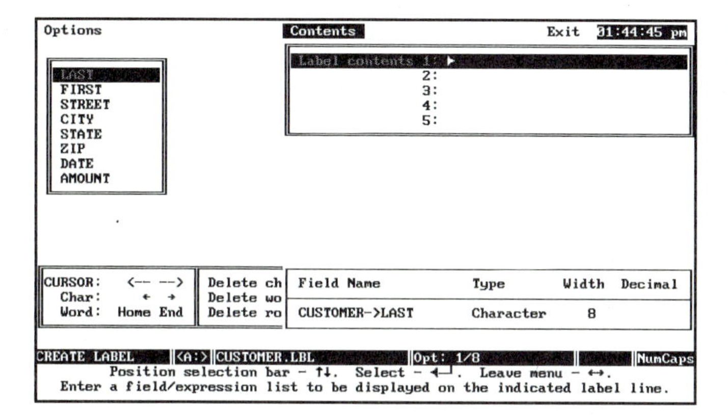

Fig. 8.4 The Customer database fields.

8

4. Move the field name list highlight to the FIRST field by pressing ↓ once.
5. Press ↵Enter. The top line in the label form shows that the label will begin with data from the FIRST field (see fig. 8.5).
6. You also need the last name in the top line of the mailing label. Type a comma (,) to separate the fields.
7. Press F10 to see the list of field names again.
8. Press ↵Enter to select the LAST field.

   Your screen should now resemble figure 8.6.
9. Press ↵Enter to finish your formatting of the top line in the mailing label.
10. Press ↓ to move the highlight to the second line of the label.

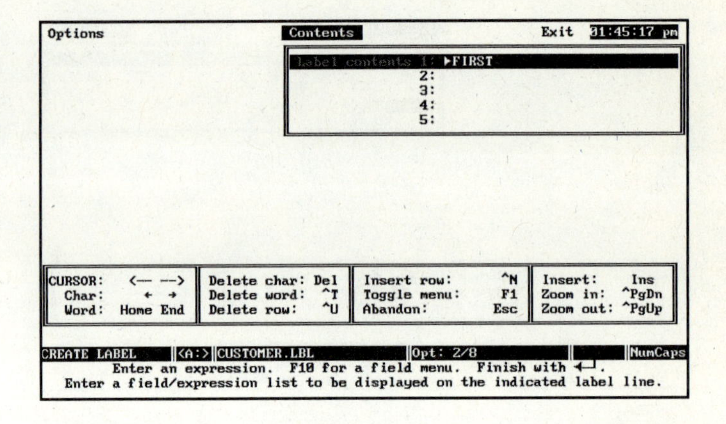

Fig. 8.5 The FIRST field data will print in the top line of the label.

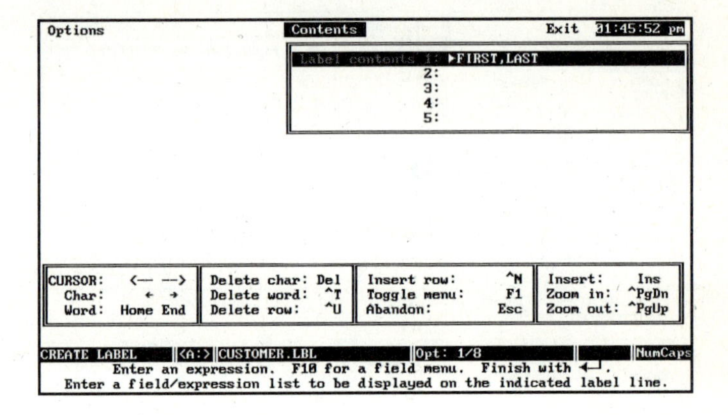

Fig. 8.6 These fields' contents will print in the label's top line.

11. Press ↵Enter to display the black arrowhead and the blinking cursor so that you can format the second line in the label.

    If you can remember the field names, you can dispense with the field name list. You can type the field names in the appropriate line when you see the black arrowhead. Remember to move to a line by using ↑ or ↓. Then activate the line by pressing ↵Enter. When you are finished defining the contents of the line, press ↵Enter.

12. In line 2, type **STREET**, and press ↵Enter.
13. In line 3, press ↵Enter to display the arrowhead. Type **CITY,STATE**, and press ↵Enter.
14. In line 4, press ↵Enter to display the arrowhead. Type **ZIP**, and press ↵Enter.

    Your screen should now resemble figure 8.7. You have completed the formatting of your label.

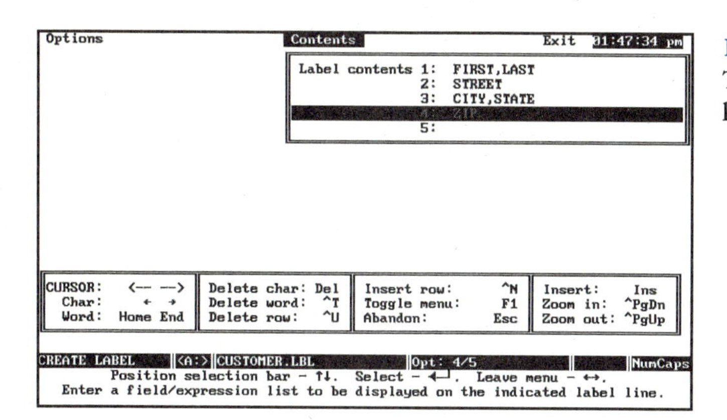

Fig. 8.7 The completed label format.

15. Press → to move the highlight to the Exit menu.
16. Press ↵Enter to save CUSTOMER.LBL and return to the dot prompt.

Printing Your Labels

Now you are ready to display your labels on-screen and then print them. Usually, you should check the results of your work before you actually print the labels. To display or print the labels, you use the Label Form command. This command is an abbreviation for *produce labels from the data in the active database by using the label-form file ...* . . In the following exercise, you use the form file CUSTOMER.LBL that you just created.

Exercise 1.4: Displaying and Printing Your Labels

Make sure that Customer, the database that supplies the data to the Customer label form file, is active. To produce your labels, follow these steps:

1. At the dot prompt, type **LABEL FORM CUSTOMER**, and press ↵Enter.

   You have more labels than can be displayed on one screen. Therefore, the first few labels will scroll off your screen. Your screen should now resemble figure 8.8. Notice that each database record produces one mailing label.

   If your computer is connected to a printer, do the following:

2. Type **LABEL FORM CUSTOMER TO PRINT**, and press ↵Enter.
3. Type **EJECT**, and press ↵Enter.

8

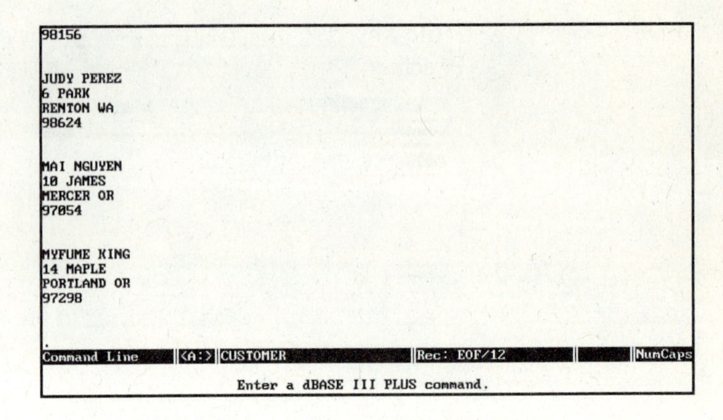

Fig. 8.8
The labels displayed on-screen.

This chapter has discussed producing mailing labels from label-form files. You can use this method to produce any kind of labels you need. Labels for storage bins in warehouses, item labels for shelves in retail stores, and name tags for conferences or large meetings are examples of labels often printed using dBASE.

Objective 2: To Modify a Mailing Label Form

Once you have created a label-form file, you can use it as many times as necessary because the file is stored on disk. If the database changes or if your labeling needs change, you do not need to create a new form file from scratch. You can modify a form file to fine-tune it. The command used to modify a label-form file is the Modify Label command. In the next exercise, you learn how to use this command to make a change to a different type of standard label sheet. You can also change the contents of the label itself.

Exercise 2.1: Modifying a Label-Form File

In this exercise, you change from the standard sheet type to a sheet with three labels across. Then you insert a comma between the CITY and STATE fields in the third line of the label. First, make sure that the Customer database file is in use. Then, do the following:

1. At the dot prompt, type **MODIFY LABEL CUSTOMER**, and press Enter.

Your screen should now resemble figure 8.9. This screen is similar to the Create Label screen, and you use it in the same way.

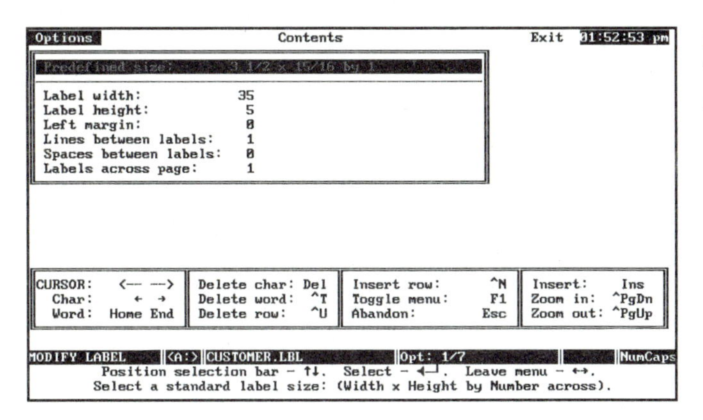

Fig. 8.9
The Modify Label form screen.

2. Press ↵Enter until 3 1/2 x 15/16 by 3 appears in the highlight.
3. Press ↓ once to highlight Label Width.
4. Press ↵Enter to display the black arrowhead.
5. Press Del three times to delete the 35. Then type **30**, and press ↵Enter.

   Your screen should now resemble figure 8.10.

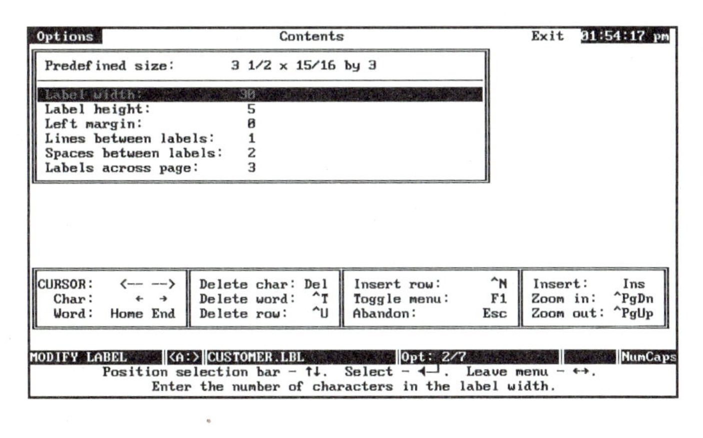

Fig. 8.10
Modifications made to the standard sheet settings.

6. Press → to move to the Contents menu.
7. Press ↓ twice to move to line 3. Then press ↵Enter.
8. Press ←Backspace until *STATE* is erased. Then type **",",STATE**, and press ↵Enter.

Verify that your screen resembles figure 8.11. Notice that you should type the quotation marks.

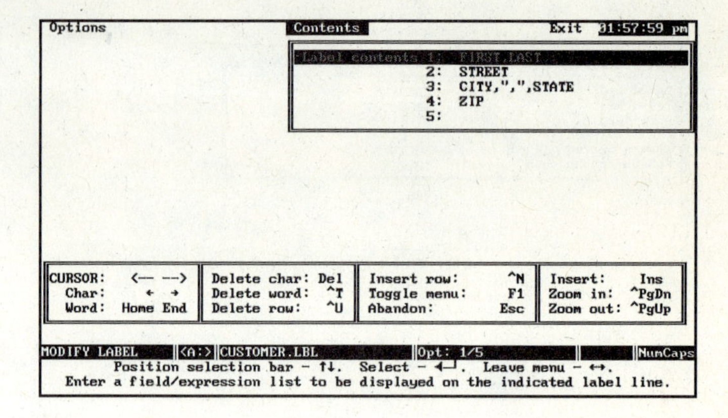

Fig. 8.11
The modifications to a label appear on-screen.

9. Press → to move to the Exit menu, and press ↵Enter to save the modified form.

You are now ready to print the modified labels on the sheets with three labels across. Before you do that, index the Customer database on the ZIP field. The post office charges a reduced rate for bulk mailings when the letters are sorted in ZIP code order. The index does this ordering for you.

Exercise 2.2: Displaying and Printing Your Modified Labels

Make sure that Customer, the database that supplies the data to the modified Customer label-form file, is active. To produce your labels, take these steps:

1. Type **INDEX ON ZIP TO ZIPINDX**, and press ↵Enter.
2. At the dot prompt, type **LABEL FORM CUSTOMER**, and press ↵Enter.

   Your screen should now resemble figure 8.12. Notice that each database record produces one mailing label.

If your computer is connected to a printer, follow these steps:

1. Type **LABEL FORM CUSTOMER TO PRINT**, and press ↵Enter.
2. Type **EJECT**, and press ↵Enter.

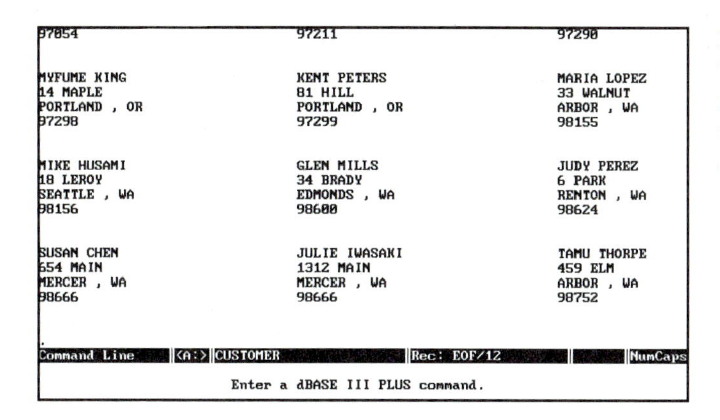

Fig. 8.12
The modified label form will print these Customer database records.

Now you know the basics of creating and modifying label-form files. In the next section, you are introduced to the techniques for creating a report form file.

Objective 3: To Create and Use a Report Form

In the first part of this chapter, you learned that dBASE can print mailing labels if you provide a guide or template that explains how the data should be formatted and printed. This guide to the layout of your output from the database is stored on disk in a form file that is designed to work with one database. The form molds the database data into the shape you want for your output. Reports are created through report forms in the same way that label forms produce labels.

You build a report form by designing a report template using the Create Report screen. This screen, displayed by the Create Report command, is sometimes called the Report Form Generator screen. It consists of a series of menu choices with which you can create a report form. When you first use the report form generator, it seems very complex. However, you will proceed carefully through the task of building a report form one step at a time. It is especially important for you to work slowly and to *read the messages* displayed at the bottom of your screen just below the status bar. dBASE uses these messages to tell you what you should do next.

Building the Report Format

You design the form file for a report in the same way that you create the label form—by making selections from a series of menus. dBASE displays a representation of the layout of your report in the Report Format box. This box shows you how your report will look. As you set up the report, you can see how your form is progressing by checking the Report Format box. Its use is similar to that of the Label box on the Create Label screen. In the Label box, you can place five lines of data (numbered 1 through 5) when you are creating the format for a label. The Report Format box representation is an approximation of how a page of the finished output will appear. As you make choices from menus, the representation changes to reflect your selections.

Creating a report form is more complicated than creating a label form. The concept, however, is the same—you are creating a layout specification for the output of data from your database. The completed report form is stored on disk in a special file with the extension FRM. The database that provides the data for the report must be in use while you create the report specification. dBASE can then make your work easier because the program knows the names, types, and sizes of all the fields you will print in the report. In the following exercises, you build, one step at a time, a simple report from the Customer database. In the first exercise, you add two records to provide more data for the report.

Exercise 3.1: Adding More Data to the Customer Database

First, make sure that the Customer database file is in use. Then, to add two more records to the database, do the following:

1. At the dot prompt, type **APPEND**, and press Enter.
2. Add the following two records:

LAST:	**BURNS**	**WRIGHT**
FIRST:	**MARY**	**HEIDI**
STREET:	**23 FIRST**	**61 REED**
CITY:	**REDWOOD**	**YORK**
STATE:	**CA**	**CA**

ZIP:	**98067**	**98470**
DATE:	**11/24/94**	**12/09/94**
AMOUNT:	**103.55**	**592.20**

3. Press Ctrl+End to return to the dot prompt.

You are now ready to create your report form. The first time you use the Report Form Generator screen, you may sometimes be unsure of the next step. Remember to *read the messages* displayed at the bottom of your screen just below the status bar. If you do become confused or make a mistake, you can stop building the form at any time by pressing Esc. dBASE then asks you whether you want to abandon the operation. Type **Y** to stop what you are doing. Then, you can start over again from the beginning, and no harm has been done.

Exercise 3.2: Setting the Options

Make sure that the Customer database is in use. To begin creating a report form, do the following:

1. At the dot prompt, type **CREATE REPORT**, and press ↵Enter.

   dBASE asks you to enter a name for the report-form file.

2. Type **EXAMPLE**, and press ↵Enter.

   The Create Report screen is displayed (see fig. 8.13). The name of the report format file EXAMPLE.FRM displays in the status bar.

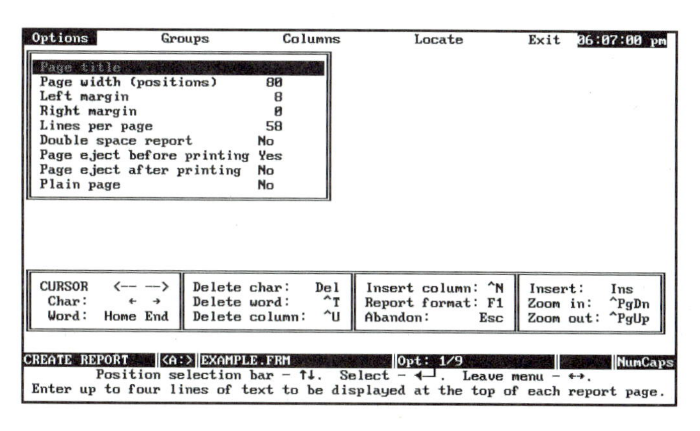

Fig. 8.13
The Create Report screen.

3. To enter a title to be printed on the report, press ↵Enter. A black arrowhead appears in the Page Title highlight, and a box displays with a blinking cursor.

   Type **CUSTOMER PURCHASES REPORT**.

   Your screen should now resemble figure 8.14.

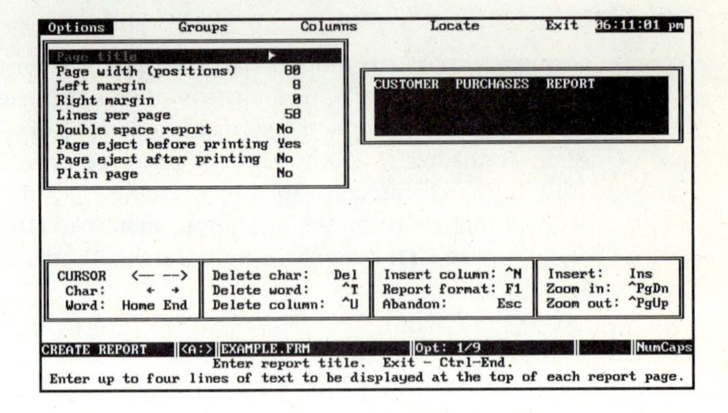

Fig. 8.14
The page title is highlighted.

8

4. Press Ctrl+End to signal that you are done entering a page title.
5. Press ↓ to move the menu highlight to Double Space Report, and press ↵Enter to change No to Yes.

   This option causes the lines in the report to be double-spaced and therefore easier to read.
6. Press ↓ to move the menu highlight to Page Eject after Printing, and press ↵Enter. This option causes the sheets of the report to be ejected from the printer so that you won't have to use the Eject command when the report is finished.

   Your screen should now resemble figure 8.15.

The Columns Menu

The next step in creating your report-format file is to specify which fields you want to appear in the report. The data from each field will print in one column down the report page. The majority of the lines in the report consist of the data from the database records. You also need to enter the column heading you want to print for each column of data. The Columns menu enables you to select the data and type the headings. You must complete a Columns menu for each column you want printed on your report.

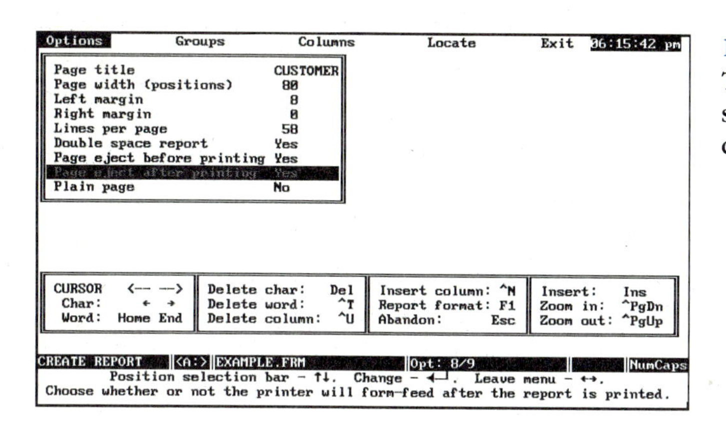

Fig. 8.15
The Options settings are completed.

Exercise 3.3: Defining the First Column in the Report

To format the first column of data that is to appear on the report, do the following:

1. Press → to move the highlight to the Columns menu. The Contents choice should be highlighted.

   Notice the messages at the bottom of the screen. The Contents line in the Columns menu is the place where you enter the name of the database field whose data is to be printed in this column of the report.

2. Press ↵Enter to display the black arrowhead.

   You can now press F10 if you need a list of the database's field names. You can select the fields from this list. You used this list when you were constructing your label form. Don't use this technique here because you are already familiar with Customer's field names. The first column in your report will contain data from the FIRST field in your database.

3. Type **FIRST**, and press ↵Enter.

   Now, type a heading for this field.

4. Press ↓ to highlight the Heading choice; then press ↵Enter.

   Your screen should now resemble figure 8.16. Notice the messages at the bottom of the screen.

5. Press ↓ twice.
6. Type **FIRST**, and press ↵Enter.
7. Type **NAME**, and press ↵Enter.

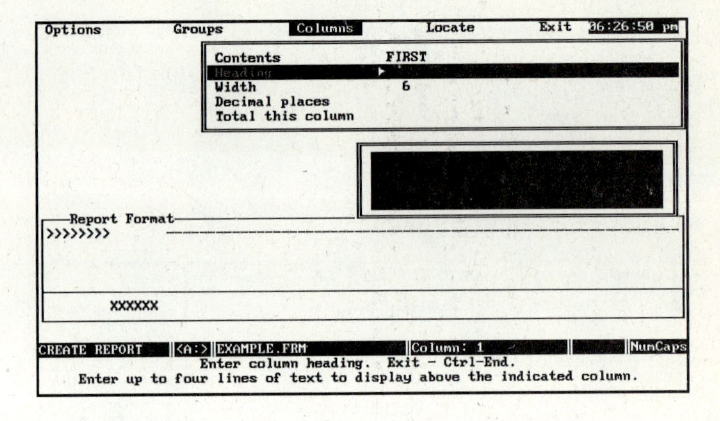

Fig. 8.16 The data content of the first column has been set.

Your screen should now resemble figure 8.17. You have finished setting up the first column of your report.

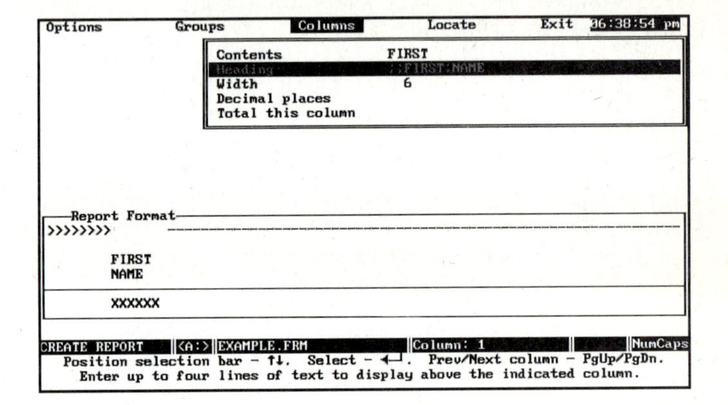

Fig. 8.17 The completed first-column settings.

Note that you did not have to enter a column width (refer to fig. 8.17). The width was automatically set to 6, the width of the FIRST field in your database. Decimal Places and Total This Column do not apply because FIRST is a Character type field.

The Report Format box (refer to fig. 8.17) has changed as a result of your menu selections. This representation of your report layout gives you some idea of what your report looks like at this stage. You can see the heading and the six X's that represent data in the field.

Exercise 3.4: Defining the Second Column in the Report

In this exercise, you continue the report form by defining the second column.

To define the second column, follow these steps:

1. Press PgDn to move to the next column to begin the definition. PgUp and PgDn enable you to move left and right between the columns of your report.

   Your screen should now resemble figure 8.18. Notice that the status bar indicates that you are defining column 2.

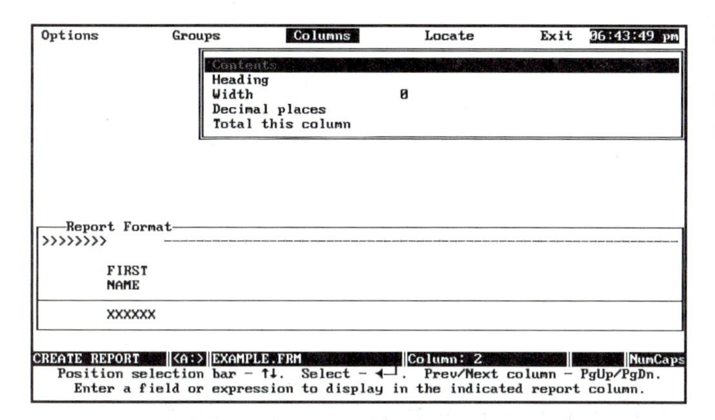

Fig. 8.18 Defining columns by using the Column menu.

2. Press ↵Enter. Type the field name **LAST**, and press ↵Enter.
3. Press ↓ to move the highlight to the Heading line.
4. Press ↵Enter.
5. Press ↓ twice.
6. Type **LAST**, and press ↵Enter.
7. Type **NAME**, and press ↵Enter.

Your screen should now resemble figure 8.19. Notice that the column width has been set to 8, the width of the database field.

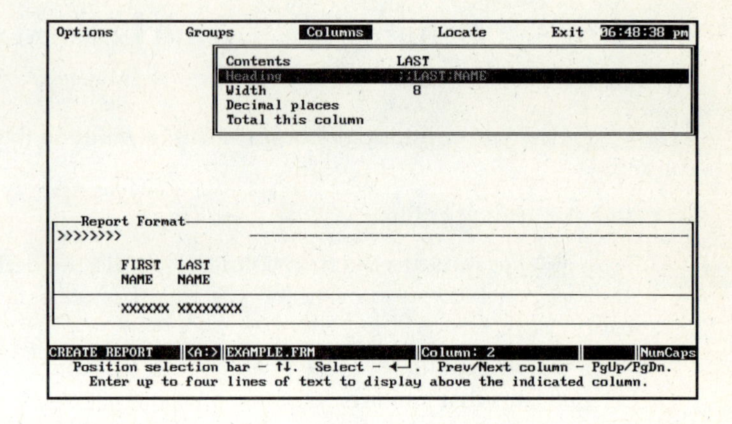

Fig. 8.19 The second-column settings are completed.

Remember that you can move between columns by pressing the PgUp and the PgDn keys. You can return to a column definition and make changes if necessary. All changes will be shown in the Report Format box.

Exercise 3.5: Defining the Remaining Columns in the Report

To define the rest of the columns, do the following:

1. Use the Columns menu to define the remaining columns:

Column #	3	4	5	6	7
Contents	**STREET**	**CITY**	**STATE**	**ZIP**	**AMOUNT**
Heading	**STREET**	**CITY**	**STATE**	**ZIP CODE**	**AMOUNT OF PURCHASE**

When you have finished with column 7, your screen should resemble figure 8.20. For columns containing Numeric type fields, dBASE inserts the number of decimal places and automatically produces totals for this field on your report.

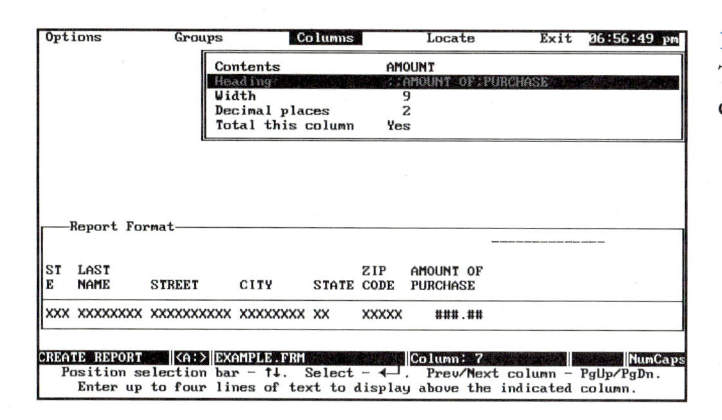

Fig. 8.20
The completed column settings.

2. You have completed your report design. Press → twice to move to the Exit menu.
3. Press ↵Enter to save the report-form file and return to the dot prompt.

Your report-format file is now saved to a disk file named EXAMPLE.FRM.

If you forget the names of your report files, you can list them. At the dot prompt, type **LIST FILES LIKE *.FRM**, and press ↵Enter. All your report-form files will be listed.

8

Exercise 3.6: Printing the Report

In this exercise, you print your report. Your computer must be connected to a printer for you to complete this exercise. The Customer database also must be in use.

To print the report using the form file you just designed, do the following:

1. At the dot prompt, type

   REPORT FORM EXAMPLE TO PRINT

2. Press ↵Enter. Your report should resemble figure 8.21. The date will be the one on which you print the report. (The date has to be set properly on your computer.)

When you have printed a report, you (or another employee) may see something that should be changed or improved. In the next section, you learn how to modify a report form by using the Modify Report command. This command works similarly to the Create Report command. You will use many techniques that you have already learned.

Fig. 8.21
The Customer Purchases Report is completed.

```
Page No.      1
07/10/94
                         CUSTOMER  PURCHASES  REPORT


FIRST  LAST                                        ZIP   AMOUNT OF
NAME   NAME      STREET     CITY      STATE  CODE   PURCHASE


GLEN   MILLS     34 BRADY   EDMONDS   WA     98600     100.95

SUSAN  CHEN      654 MAIN   MERCER    WA     98666     220.17

KENT   PETERS    81 HILL    PORTLAND  OR     97299     102.52

MARIA  LOPEZ     33 WALNUT  ARBOR     WA     98155     317.87

JULIE  IWASAKI   1312 MAIN  MERCER    WA     98666     186.55

BILL   WILLS     312 JAMES  PORTLAND  OR     97211     251.39

TAMU   THORPE    459 ELM    ARBOR     WA     98752     115.48

CHRIS  OWEN      43 TAFT    ENDWELL   OR     97290     324.95

MIKE   HUSAMI    18 LEROY   SEATTLE   WA     98156     263.40

JUDY   PEREZ     6 PARK     RENTON    WA     98624     200.97

MAI    NGUYEN    10 JAMES   MERCER    OR     97054     105.27

MYFUME KING      14 MAPLE   PORTLAND  OR     97298     212.00

MARY   BURNS     23 FIRST   REDWOOD   CA     98067     103.55

HEIDI  WRIGHT    61 REED    YORK      CA     98470     592.20

*** Total ***
                                                      3097.27
```

8

Objective 4: To Modify a Report Form

The report you created in the preceding section is a simple one designed to give you a general idea of the steps involved in creating a report with dBASE. In this section, you make an addition to the report form so that you can obtain subtotals for each of the states in which your customers live. To get subtotals, you must group together the records from each state. The best way to group the records is to index the Customer database file on the STATE field. In Exercise 4.1, you modify the EXAMPLE.FRM format file. In Exercise 4.2, you index the database and print your report.

Exercise 4.1: Modifying the Report-Form File

The Customer database must be in use. To modify the Example report form so that AMOUNT subtotals for each state are produced, do the following:

1. At the dot prompt, type **MODIFY REPORT EXAMPLE**, and press ↵Enter.

   Your screen should now resemble figure 8.22. You use this screen in the same way that you use the Create Report screen.

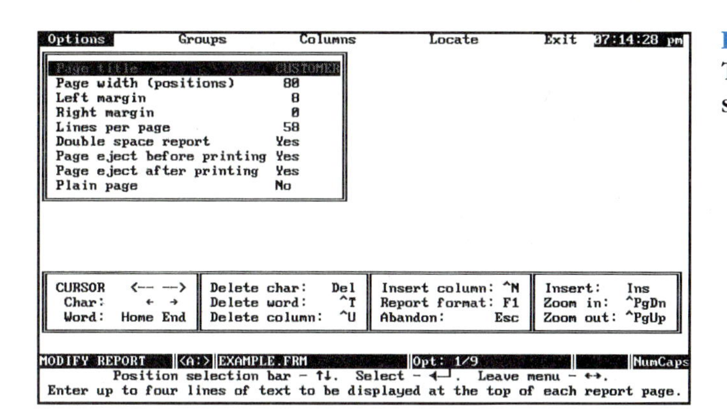

Fig. 8.22 The Modify Report screen.

2. Press → to move to the Groups menu (see fig. 8.23). You use this menu to tell dBASE the groups for which you want subtotals calculated.

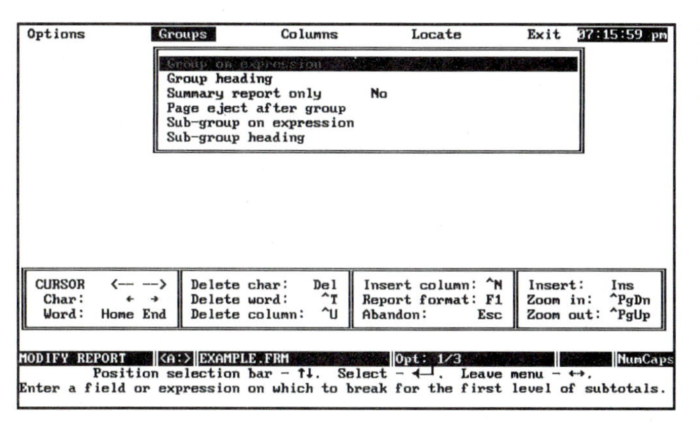

Fig. 8.23 The Modify Report Groups menu.

3. Press ↵Enter.

   You are going to separate the output of the report into separate subgroups by using the contents of the STATE field.

4. Type **STATE**, and press ↵Enter.
5. Press ↓.
6. Now, type a short heading for each group. Press ↵Enter.
7. Type **Customers from:**, and press ↵Enter.

   Your screen should resemble figure 8.24.

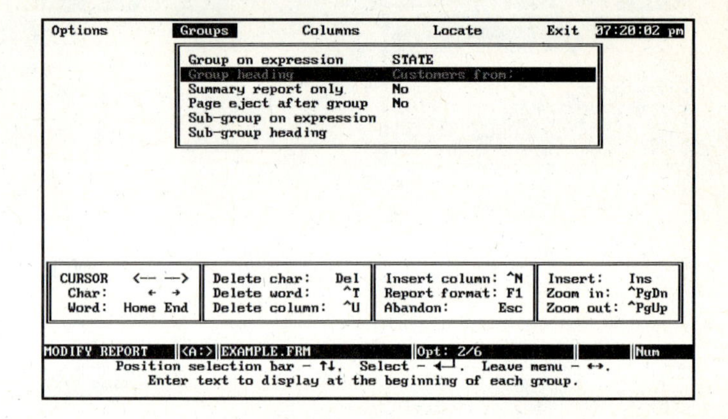

Fig. 8.24
The completed Groups menu.

8. Press → to move the highlight to the Exit menu.
9. Press ↵Enter to save your format modifications and return to the dot prompt.

Printing Your Completed Report

Now you have finished your report and are ready to print it. First, you index the Customer database file on the STATE field so that the records from each state are grouped together in subgroups. Then, you print the report using the Example report format file.

Exercise 4.2: Printing the Report

Make sure that the Customer database is in use. To print the modified report, do the following:

1. At the dot prompt, type **INDEX ON STATE TO STATEIND**, and press [Enter].
2. Type **REPORT FORM EXAMPLE**, and press [Enter].

   Your report should resemble figure 8.25.

```
Page No.     1
07/10/94
                        CUSTOMER  PURCHASES  REPORT


FIRST  LAST                                      ZIP    AMOUNT OF
NAME   NAME      STREET       CITY       STATE  CODE    PURCHASE

** Customers from: CA
MARY   BURNS     23 FIRST     REDWOOD    CA     98067      103.55

HEIDI  WRIGHT    61 REED      YORK       CA     98470      592.20

** Subtotal **
                                                           695.75

** Customers from: OR
KENT   PETERS    81 HILL      PORTLAND   OR     97299      102.52

BILL   WILLS     312 JAMES    PORTLAND   OR     97211      251.39

CHRIS  OWEN      43 TAFT      ENDWELL    OR     97290      324.95

MAI    NGUYEN    10 JAMES     MERCER     OR     97054      105.27

MYFUME KING      14 MAPLE     PORTLAND   OR     97298      212.00

** Subtotal **
                                                           996.13

** Customers from: WA
GLEN   MILLS     34 BRADY     EDMONDS    WA     98600      100.95

SUSAN  CHEN      654 MAIN     MERCER     WA     98666      220.17

MARIA  LOPEZ     33 WALNUT    ARBOR      WA     98155      317.87

JULIE  IWASAKI   1312 MAIN    MERCER     WA     98666      186.55

TAMU   THORPE    459 ELM      ARBOR      WA     98752      115.48

MIKE   HUSAMI    18 LEROY     SEATTLE    WA     98156      263.40

JUDY   PEREZ     6 PARK       RENTON     WA     98624      200.97

** Subtotal **
                                                          1405.39
*** Total ***
                                                          3097.27
```

Fig. 8.25 The completed report showing subtotals for each state.

8

You can create many subgroupings for a report. For example, with a larger database, you might want to report subtotals first for each city, then for each state. You would use the Groups menu to set up these groupings. You would also have to index the database on all the fields that you use for subgroupings.

Chapter Summary

In this chapter, you have learned how to create the format files that enable dBASE to print labels and reports from the data in your database. You also learned how to print a database using the two different kinds of forms. Finally, you learned how to make changes to label- and report-form files and how to print the revised labels and report.

In the next chapter, you learn how to extract related information from two different database files. You will learn how to do this in two different ways: by creating a view file and by using the Join command. You learn how to link two or more files together to create a new database from which you can print reports.

Testing Your Knowledge

True/False Questions

1. When you use the Create Report screen, dBASE explains the possible actions that you can take by displaying messages below the status bar.
2. To abandon the creation of a report format file, press and hold Ctrl and then press End.
3. When you create a format file, the database used with that format file need not be in use.
4. By default, Numeric type fields are automatically totaled on a report.
5. To move between columns when creating or modifying a report form using the Columns menu, press ← or →.

Multiple-Choice Questions

1. The extension that dBASE uses for all label format files is ________.
   a. LAB
   b. LBL
   c. FOR
   d. none of these answers
2. The extension that dBASE uses for all report format files is ________.
   a. FOR
   b. FMT
   c. RPT
   d. none of these answers
3. The Create Report screen menu that enables you to indicate which data fields should print on the report is the ________ menu.
   a. Fields
   b. Columns
   c. Options
   d. none of these answers
4. dBASE can print labels on ________ different standard size sheets of labels.
   a. 3
   b. 4
   c. 5
   d. none of these answers
5. Before you can print subtotals on a report, the database must be ________.
   a. active
   b. in order on the field that groups the subtotaled records
   c. both a and b
   d. none of these answers

Fill-in-the-Blank Questions

1. The command to set up a label-form file is __________.
2. The command to set up a report-form file is __________.
3. The command to print labels using a form file named Labl1 is __________.
4. The command to print a report from a format file named Report1 is __________.
5. The command to alter the contents of a report-form file named Report1 is ____________________.

Review: Short Projects

1. Modifying a Label File

   Modify the Customer label-form file to print two labels across the page and put a period after the name of the state.
2. Printing a Grouped Report without Indexing the Database

   Use the Customer database without an active index on the STATE field. Print a report from the Example report-form file you modified in Exercise 4.1.
3. Modifying a Report File

   Make the following changes to the EXAMPLE.FRM file. Then, print a report using this report-form file.
   a. Change the page title to an appropriate title for this report.
   b. Change one of the column headings.
   c. Change the report to single-spacing.
   d. Do not print group subtotals.

Review: Long Projects

1. Printing Both Mailing Labels and a Report from the Student Database
   a. Print mailing labels from the data in the Student database file.
   b. Print a report from the data in the Student database file. The report should contain a title and columns for the student number, first and last names, address data, and phone number.

2. Printing Reports from the Tours Database
   a. Print a single-spaced report that contains all the data fields and does not total the COST field.
   b. Modify the report you created in step a so that it is double-spaced and prints subgroup totals for each of the different cities from which tours depart.
   c. Print the Tours data using the form you modified in step b. The output should have the data grouped by the cities from which the tour departs. Subtotals should be printed.
3. Printing Reports from the Climate Database
   a. Print a double-spaced report with columns for COUNTRY, STATION, and ELEVATION (in that order). Do not total the ELEVATION field.
   b. Modify the report you created in step a to include all the fields in the database in the order in which they occur in the structure of the database. Total only the PRECIP and ELEVATION fields.
   c. Print the report using the form you modified in step b.

Retrieving Data from Multiple Linked Databases by Using Views and Joins

9

Chapters 1 and 2 discuss the basics of database design. One point made is that a database system consisting of several smaller database files is more efficient than one big file containing all your data. If you are setting up a database system for a college, for example, you should have one database file for each entity—students, classes, and instructors—for which you must store data. The structures for the files then are simpler because each record in a given file contains data on the same kind of entity. You lose this simplicity if you try to design one large file in which you mix records with student data, instructor data, and class data.

To visualize this situation, jot down the structure of one big database file to store the information on students, classes, and instructors at your school, and then add some sample records of each kind. Imagine how complicated data entry and listing would be and how complicated the reports would be from this database. Your databases, then, should consist of several small database files, although the records in the different database files may be related.

Organizations want to store not only data in a database system but also the relationships among the different entities. A college, for example, needs to store the relationships among its students, classes, and instructors. Students are enrolled in classes that are taught by instructors. The three entities are *linked* by their relationships in the college. The college personnel need to be able to find out which students are taking a particular class and which instructor teaches this class. These relationships have to be stored so that the college can produce such reports as class rosters and grade sheets for the instructors and registration forms and transcripts for the students.

In the previous chapters, you worked with data records in only one database file at a time. In this chapter, you learn how relationships among entities—such as students, classes, and instructors—are stored and how you can retrieve and use information on these relationships.

Objectives

1. To Understand the Concept of Related Database Files
2. To Use the Select Command to Open Multiple Database Files Simultaneously
3. To Create a View File
4. To Use a View to Retrieve Data from Two Linked Files
5. To Modify a View File
6. To Create a New Database File by Using the Join Command

Key Terms in This Chapter	
Primary key field	A field that contains a unique identifier, such as a Social Security number, that identifies a record in a database file.
Link field	A field that occurs in more than one database file. A link field is used to match (join) and extract related records from the two or more database files. In dBASE, link fields should be the same type and width in both files.
Relational database	A group of database files that can be linked (joined) by using a shared link field or fields.
Work area	An area of computer memory, also called a *select area*. dBASE can open one database file and all its associated indexes in a work area. Ten work areas, numbered 1 through 10, are available. Work area 1 is the default work area. You access other work areas by using the Select command.
Select command	Chooses a work area from the ten available. You use Select to switch from one work area to another.
Current work area	The selected, or active, work area; the name of the database file in this work area appears in the status bar.
View file	A file that enables dBASE to select and display fields from a record in one database and fields from a related record in a second database. The two databases must be linked by a common field. Opening a view opens the linked databases and all associated indexes. View files have the extension VUE.

Objective 1: To Understand the Concept of Related Database Files

Remember that dBASE III Plus is known as a relational database management system because of the way in which data is stored and because of the way that related pieces of information from different files can be brought together.

Relational Databases

A *relational database* consists of one or more related database files. For an example of related database files, assume that you create a database file which contains information about your clients—name, address, phone, and so on. You create another database file that contains information about the tours your company offers. As your business develops, these database files become *related* because you sell tours to clients. This relationship should appear in the database system.

You want to know which clients will be traveling together on a particular tour. You also want to know which tour a client has already booked so that you do not embarrass yourself by trying to sell the client the same tour again. You need to be able to cross-reference the two files so that you can use data from both files. Your database system is not successful if it tells you all about your clients or all about the costs, stops, restaurants, and hotels on a particular tour but nothing about which clients are booked on that tour.

Relationships among Data Files

Notice that these client-tour relationships, like relationships among students, teachers, and classes in a school, are not an artificial product of using a database program. Rather, these relationships exist in the real world, and just as your database system must contain data about real-world entities like students or tours, the system also must contain information about their relationships in the real world.

This requirement doesn't mean that you must set up a special database file that stores relationships like other files store data. Of course, you can set up this kind of file in some situations. For example, a sales invoice file would—by the data it contains—store the relationship between a customer and the products the customer purchased on a given day. Often, however, by designing databases with a common (or link) field, you allow the relationship to be stored without the need for a separate file to store the relationship. When you use this technique with dBASE, you then can use a view or the Join command to make the relationship apparent and work with the related data.

You can link two database files by using a field that exists in both database files. If a field value in one database file's record also occurs in a record in the other database file, a relationship exists between records in the two database files. If a customer identification number field is included as a link field in both database files, for example, information about a particular customer can be extracted from both an invoice database file and a customer database file. In dBASE, link fields should be the same type and width in both files.

Using a Primary Key Field as a Link Field

Often, one field in a database file is designated as a *primary key field*. Key fields are optional in a database file, but these fields do have advantages. Only one record in a database file can have a particular value in the primary key field. Primary key field values, therefore, uniquely identify records. In your school's database, for example, information about you is one record and your Social Security number or student number uniquely identifies your record.

As you know, dBASE also uses *key* to refer to a field on which an index file was created. This usage of the term *key*, however, is different from the meaning of *key* in the phrase *primary key field*. A primary key value is uniquely associated with a single entity—as your Social Security number is uniquely associated with you.

If your Social Security number occurs in a record in a school class file, a retail store billing file, an insurance company's policies file, a hospital file, or a bank file, or any file, that record is your record. Because the records are identified by your unique Social Security number, the primary key field, a database program can look for your records in a variety of different files. This capability is what is meant by the phrase "related information in separate database files." Primary key fields, therefore, are useful as link fields between different files. All records that are related in the different files, because they involve you, contain your number and can be joined by the database program. This capability is how, for example, a government tracks the taxes owed by its citizens.

By using this capacity for connecting different but related records in database files, you can keep small, simple database files—each file containing a particular set of data. This connectivity makes updating and changing the database files in a database simpler and more efficient. Because related data records can be retrieved from linked files, the data is not fragmented into separate files that cannot be integrated. For example, a retail store does not get in the position of having information on sales staff, products, and customers but being unable to learn which sales person sold a product to a particular customer.

Retrieving Related Data from Multiple Databases

dBASE III Plus has the capability of linking related records in multiple database files. For dBASE to link records, you have to design your database file structures with the appropriate common identifier (link) fields. Link fields should be the same type and width in both files. If you haven't followed this rule, you can restructure the files later and add the link fields. If, however, you want to store the relationships between the records in different entities, you must include link fields in the files of these entities. You can use these link fields to retrieve related records from different files in two ways in dBASE. You can use the dBASE Join command, or you can create a *view*. If you want to link files using a view, the link field must be the same name in both files. If you use the Join command, the fields can have either the same or different names.

When you use the Join command, you create a new database file. This file results from the join operation and contains fields from all related records in the two original joined database files. The database file that results from the join can be used like any other dBASE database file. In fact, the join file can be joined to a third database if the proper link fields were designed into the databases.

A *view file* also can link two database files by using a common field if the fields have the same name, type, and width. You can create and use the view file to display and edit records from more than one database file at a time. You also can print the view file data in a report. Views, however, are not databases. A view is a way of seeing the data in one or more files and cannot be joined with database files.

Objective 2: To Use the Select Command to Open Multiple Database Files Simultaneously

So far in this text, everything that you have done with databases—listing, editing, sorting, indexing, reporting—has required that you have only one database file open at a time. In this chapter, you need to have more than one database file open at a time. To do this, open the database files in different work areas. These work areas are referred to by dBASE as *select areas*. The select areas are referred to by number (1 through 10) or by letter (A through J). A view file automatically opens the linked database files in different select areas.

Select Areas

Ten select areas (1–10 or A–J) are available; in each of these areas dBASE can open a database file and the associated indexes. Only one select area—referred to as the *current* work area (or select area)—can be active at a time. Until now, you have used only select area 1 because this area is the active work area when you start dBASE. If you open another database, any database that you were working with is closed before the second database is opened.

To have more than one database file open at a time, open each database file in a different select area. You make one of the other nine select areas active by using the Select command. For example, you can open one database file in select area 1 and another database file in select area 2. You cannot open the same database file in two work areas; you can open a database file only once.

The Current Select Area

Only one select area (and the database file) can be active (current) at a time. If you use the List command, the records listed are records in the *active* database file only. The name of the active database file always appears in the status bar. You move between select areas and make them active by using the Select command. For example, if select area 1 is active and you type *SELECT 2*, work area 2 becomes the active (current) select area.

When you open multiple databases, you can easily become confused about which databases you already opened in which work area, which database is active, which index is the master index, and what field is this index's key. To help keep these very important issues clear, press F6 (Display Status). To close the database files in all the work areas at once, use the Clear All command. To close only one database file, select the work area with this database open, type **USE**, and press ↵Enter. In the next exercise, you open three database files in different work areas.

Exercise 2.1: Using the Select Command to Open Multiple Database Files

To begin this exercise, start dBASE and make sure that you have your data disk in the proper drive. To open three different database files, take these steps:

1. Press F6 to verify that no database files are in use and that select area 1 is the current work area.
2. Type **USE STUDENT**, and press ↵Enter.
3. Type **INDEX ON ITEM TO INDEX1**, and press ↵Enter.
4. Press F6 to determine the status of your work areas. Notice that the database is open and the index is active.
5. Type **SELECT 2**, and press ↵Enter.
6. Type **USE COURSES**, and press ↵Enter.
7. Type **INDEX ON ITEM TO INDEX2**, and press ↵Enter.
8. Type **SELECT 3**, and press ↵Enter.
9. Type **USE TOURS**, and press ↵Enter.
10. Press F6.

    Your screen should resemble figure 9.1.

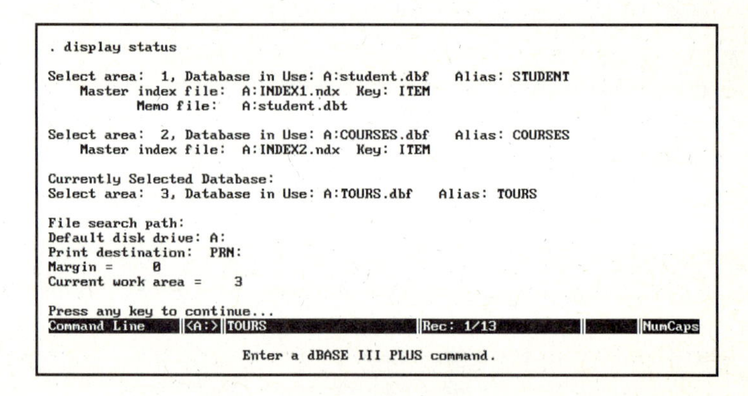

Fig. 9.1 The three database files open in three different work areas.

You now have three database files open simultaneously, and work area 3 is the active (or current) work area. As you see from the status bar, Tours is the active database file. In the next exercise, you use the Select command to switch between open databases.

Exercise 2.2: Using the Select Command to Move between Work Areas

To move between work areas, take these steps:

1. Type **SELECT 1**, and press Enter.

   Student is now the active database.

2. Type **LIST**, and press Enter. The Student records should be listed.
3. Press F6. Your screen should resemble figure 9.2.

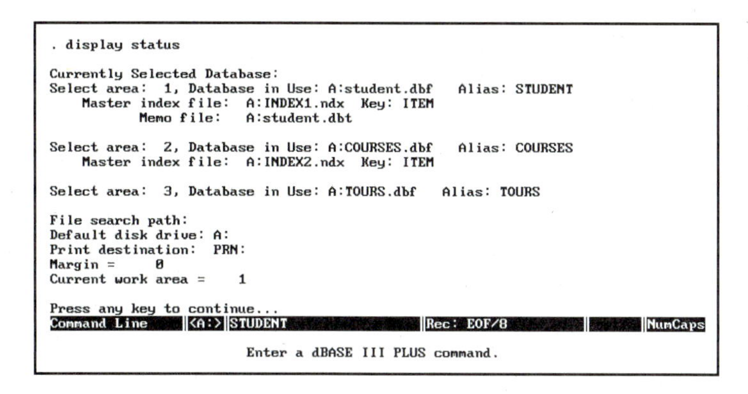

```
. display status

Currently Selected Database:
Select area:  1, Database in Use: A:student.dbf    Alias: STUDENT
    Master index file:  A:INDEX1.ndx  Key: ITEM
           Memo file:   A:student.dbt

Select area:  2, Database in Use: A:COURSES.dbf    Alias: COURSES
    Master index file:  A:INDEX2.ndx  Key: ITEM

Select area:  3, Database in Use: A:TOURS.dbf    Alias: TOURS

File search path:
Default disk drive: A:
Print destination:  PRN:
Margin =      0
Current work area =    1

Press any key to continue...
Command Line      |<A:>|STUDENT          |Rec: EOF/8        |     |NumCaps

                        Enter a dBASE III PLUS command.
```

Fig. 9.2 Work area 1 (or A) is the current work area.

4. Type **SELECT 2**, and press Enter.
5. Type **LIST**, and press Enter. The Courses records should be listed.
6. Press F6. Your screen should resemble figure 9.3.

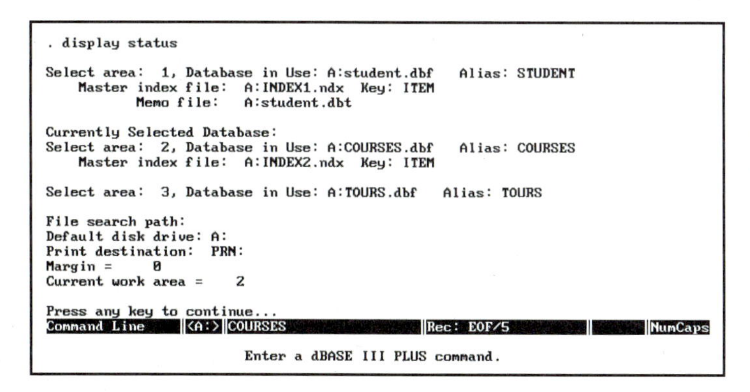

```
. display status

Select area:  1, Database in Use: A:student.dbf    Alias: STUDENT
    Master index file:  A:INDEX1.ndx  Key: ITEM
           Memo file:   A:student.dbt

Currently Selected Database:
Select area:  2, Database in Use: A:COURSES.dbf    Alias: COURSES
    Master index file:  A:INDEX2.ndx  Key: ITEM

Select area:  3, Database in Use: A:TOURS.dbf    Alias: TOURS

File search path:
Default disk drive: A:
Print destination:  PRN:
Margin =      0
Current work area =    2

Press any key to continue...
Command Line      |<A:>|COURSES          |Rec: EOF/5        |     |NumCaps

                        Enter a dBASE III PLUS command.
```

Fig. 9.3 Work area 2 (or B) is now the current work area.

Exercise 2.3: Using the Clear All Command to Close All Open Database and Index Files

To close all open database files and indexes, take these steps:

1. Type **CLEAR ALL**, and press ↵Enter.
2. Press F6 to verify that all databases are closed.

Objective 3: To Create a View File

The Create View command creates a file known as a view file. A view file links multiple database files so that you can edit, list, or print data from more than one database. The database files linked by the view must contain a common field—the link field. Memo type fields cannot be used as link fields. When you create a view, you specify the two databases to link, the common (link) field that relates records in both files, the index files whose key is the common field, and the names of the fields from the two databases that you want to see together. You then save the view file.

You use a view file by using the Set View To command. Then when you type *LIST*, you see records that consist of fields from both databases. In this book, you link only two database files, but you can link up to ten database files in one view. You can see fields from ten database files on one screen, printer listing, or report. If you want to change a view file, you use the Modify View command.

The Student database file (from Chapter 3 Long Project 3) and the Courses database file (from Chapter 3 Short Project 3) have a common field, the ITEM field. This field is a primary key field in the Courses database file. In the Student database file, this field is used to indicate in which course a student is enrolled. The ITEM field is a perfect example of a link field because you can use it to create a relationship with a view file that enables you to see related fields from the two databases.

In the following exercises, you create a view file that relates Student and Courses, and then you use the view. Next, you modify the view and use the modified view. The first time you create a view, the process may seem complicated, and it is, but the following text breaks the creation into parts, taking you through it step by step, and explains what you are doing.

Exercise 3.1: Naming the View File

To begin the creation of a view file, take these steps:

1. At the dot prompt, close all open database files by typing **CLEAR ALL** and pressing Enter.
2. Type **CREATE VIEW FIRST1**, and press Enter.

   The name of the view file will be FIRST1.VUE.

   The screen now should resemble figure 9.4. The database files listed may differ somewhat depending on the files on your disk. Make sure that STUDENT.DBF and COURSES.DBF are in the list because you will link these files in the view.

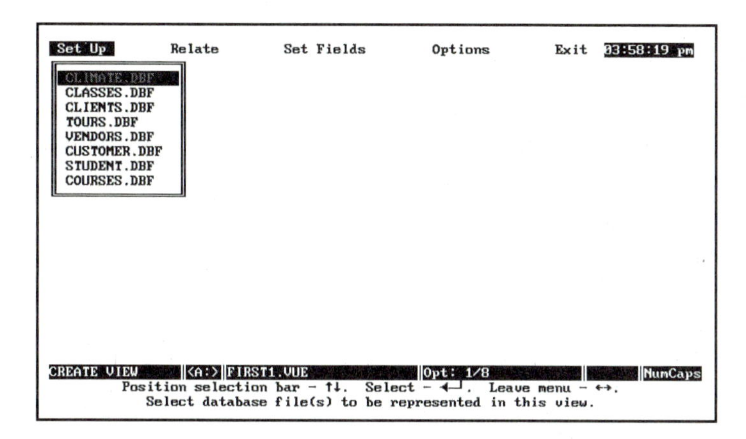

Fig. 9.4 The Create View screen.

The screen shown in figure 9.4 is the Create View screen. You now have started the view creation process. If you make a mistake and want to start over, just press Esc until you are back at the dot prompt. The next step is to use the Set Up menu to tell dBASE which database files to use and which index files to open.

Exercise 3.2: Selecting the Database Files to Link and Their Index Files

To use the Set Up menu to select the database and index files, follow these steps:

1. From the list of database files, select Student by moving the highlight over the file name (with the arrow keys) and pressing Enter. A black arrowhead appears before the file name.

   A box listing the index files on your disk also appears.

2. From the index list, select Index1 by highlighting it and pressing ↵Enter. You created this index in Exercise 2.1. Its key is the ITEM field.

   Your screen should resemble figure 9.5.

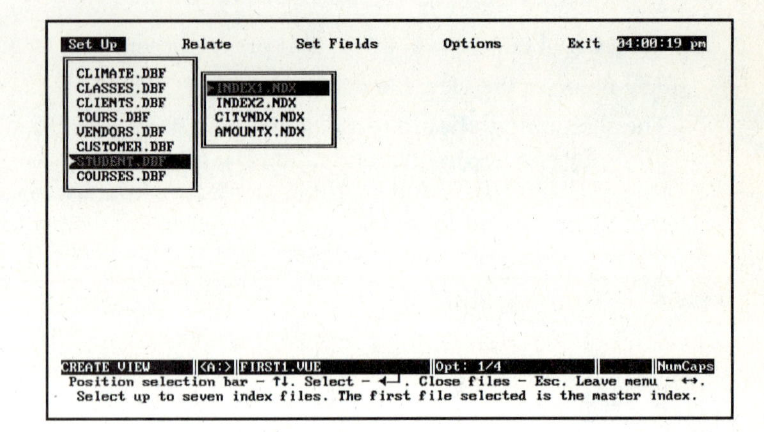

Fig. 9.5 The Student database and Index1 are selected.

3. Leave the index file list by pressing →.
4. From the list of database files, select Courses by moving the highlight over the file name (with the arrow keys) and pressing ↵Enter. A black arrowhead appears before the file name, and the index files are listed.
5. From the index list, select Index2 by highlighting it and then pressing ↵Enter. You created this index in Exercise 2.1. Its key is the ITEM field.

   Your screen should resemble figure 9.6.

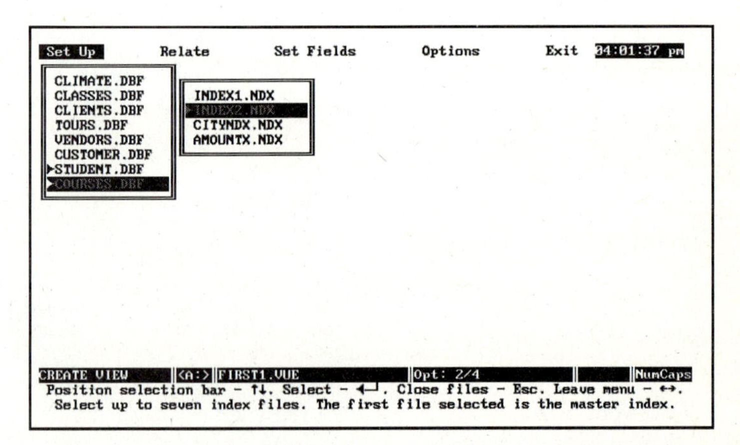

Fig. 9.6 The Courses database and Index2 are selected.

You now have finished selecting files and can leave the Set Up menu. Next you need to explain to dBASE which field in the Student and Courses databases is the link field. To do this, you use the Relate menu.

6. Leave the index file list by pressing →. Press → again to select the Relate menu.

Exercise 3.3: Using the Relate Menu to Define the Linkage between the Two Database Files

To use the Relate menu to define the linkage between Student and Courses, take these steps:

1. Select Student by pressing ↵Enter.
2. Press ↵Enter a second time.

   Your screen should resemble figure 9.7.

   Now, you need to tell dBASE the name of the link field that relates Students and Courses.

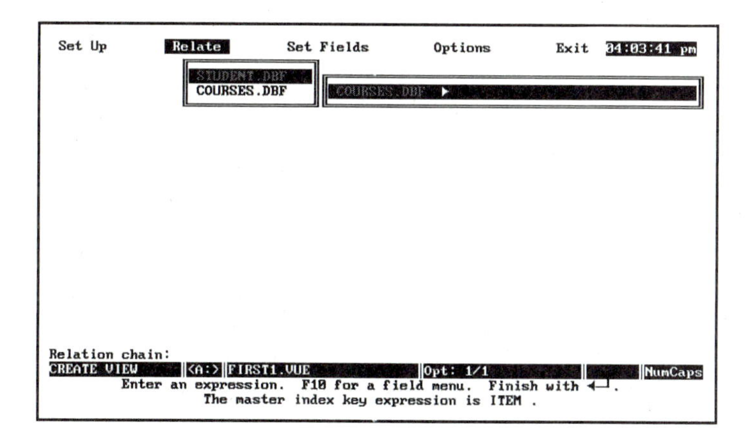

Fig. 9.7
You now can enter a link field name.

3. Press F10 for a list of fields.
4. Select ITEM in the list of fields by moving the highlight over it and pressing ↵Enter. You also can dispense with pressing F10 and just type the field name.

   Your screen now should resemble figure 9.8.

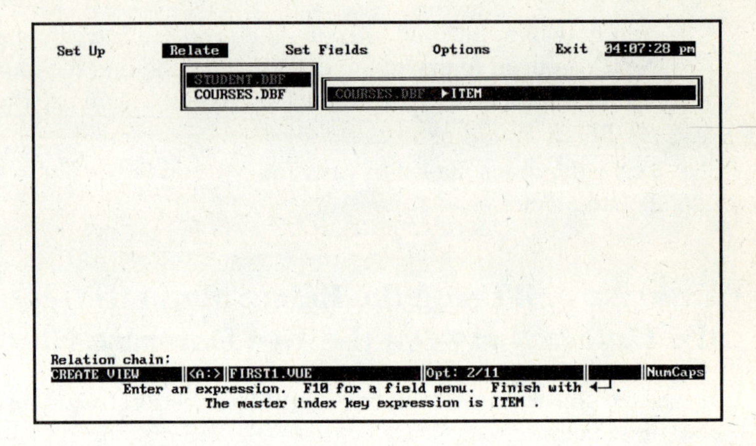

Fig. 9.8 The link field name is entered.

5. Press ↵Enter.
6. Press → to move to the Set Fields menu.

   The screen now should resemble figure 9.9.

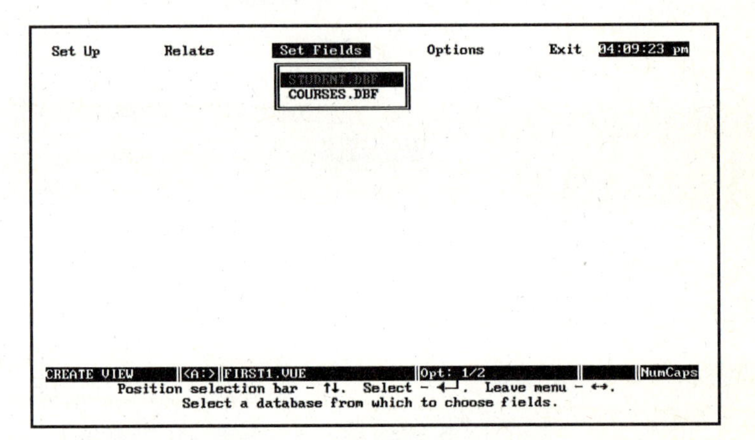

Fig. 9.9 The Set Fields menu.

9

Exercise 3.4: Selecting the Fields to Include in the View

You use the Set Fields menu to tell dBASE which combination of fields from the two databases you want to see together. In the following exercise, you use the Set Fields menu to select the fields from Student and Courses.

To select the fields for inclusion using the Set Fields menu, take these steps:

1. Select the Student database file by pressing ↵Enter.

   The default is to include all the fields in the view. Every field, therefore, is marked (with a white arrowhead) for inclusion. To unmark fields for inclusion, highlight the field name, and press ↵Enter.

2. Unmark the following fields:

   STREET, CITY, ZIP_CODE, GPA, ADVISED, NOTES.

   The screen now should resemble figure 9.10.

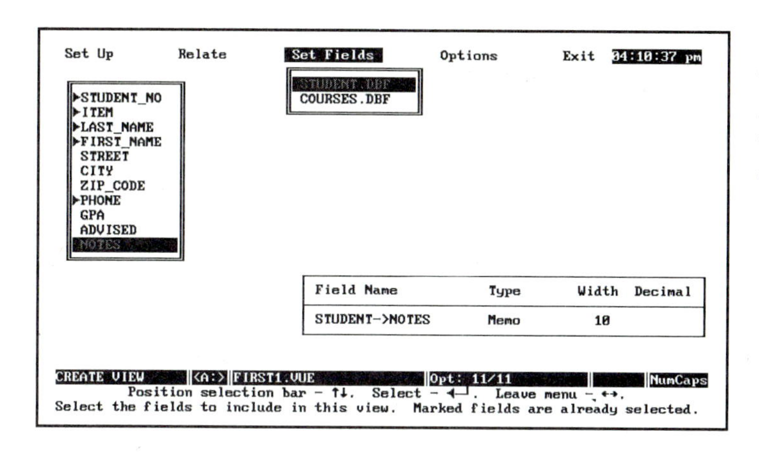

Fig. 9.10 The selected fields from the Student database file.

3. Press →.
4. Select Courses by highlighting the word and pressing ↵Enter.
5. Unmark the fields ITEM, ROOM, and ENROLLMENT by highlighting the field name and pressing ↵Enter.

   The screen now should resemble figure 9.11.

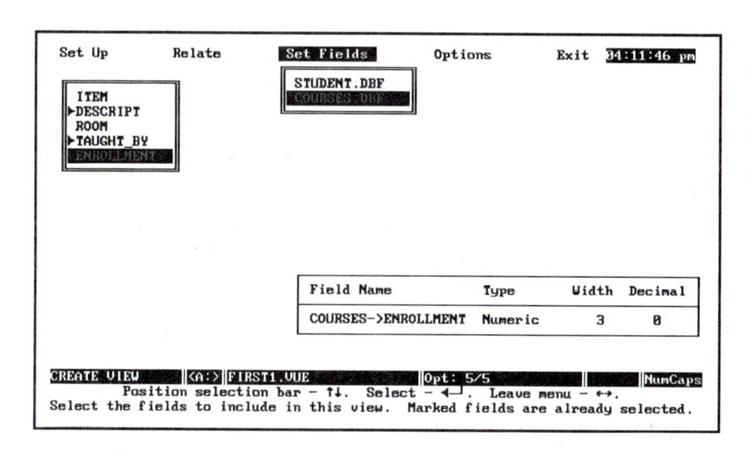

Fig. 9.11 The selected fields from the Courses database file.

Exercise 3.5: Saving the View

To save the view, take these steps:

1. Press → twice to open the Exit menu.
2. Press ↵Enter to save the view and return to the dot prompt.

Now that you have created and saved the view file, you are ready to use the new file. The following section explains how to use a view file.

Objective 4: To Use a View to Retrieve Data from Two Linked Files

To use a view file, you first close all open database files by using the Clear All command. Then you use the Set View To command to open the view file. When you open the view file, the linked database files and the indexes on the common (link) field are opened in separate work areas. The view then is created by extracting the fields you marked from the two database files. If no related records exist in the two files—if no matching values occur in the link field—no data from the second file is displayed on-screen. In this case, however, matching values do exist in the Student and Courses database files because each of the students is registered in one of the courses. In the following exercise, you use the view file FIRST1.VUE, which you just created.

Exercise 4.1: Using the View File

To use the new view file, follow these steps:

1. At the dot prompt, close all open files by typing **CLEAR ALL** and pressing ↵Enter.
2. Type **SET VIEW TO FIRST1**, and press ↵Enter.
3. Type **LIST**, and press ↵Enter.

   The screen now should resemble figure 9.12.

```
. SET VIEW TO FIRST1
. LIST
Record#  STUDENT_NO  ITEM LAST_NAME       FIRST_NAME PHONE        DESCRIPT
                     TAUGHT_BY
      2  077-33-2535 C001 Whitman         Ashante    305-331-7198 African Civili
zations             Sands, Thomas, & Wilcox
      6  133-07-1324 C002 Spencer         Allison    305-211-3456 Chinese Though
t & Art             Hwang, Simmons, & Winters
      7  133-77-2636 C002 Lopez           Lupe       305-177-3602 Chinese Though
t & Art             Hwang, Simmons, & Winters
      1  060-56-0237 C003 Becker          Ken        305-296-0864 Philosophies o
f India             Corbett, Merick, & Narwa
      4  101-73-5923 C003 Mariscos        Julio      305-198-1911 Philosophies o
f India             Corbett, Merick, & Narwa
      8  527-80-3029 C003 Wong            Claudia    305-855-9742 Philosophies o
f India             Corbett, Merick, & Narwa
      5  125-78-1256 C004 Benoit          Shaka      305-363-2416 Japanese Cultu
re                  Ishii, Kimura, & Mikawa
      3  151-45-9427 C005 Flores          Gloria     305-754-3485 Civilizations
of Mexico           Accursio, Corona, & Hernandez

.
Command Line    |<A:>|STUDENT          |Rec: EOF/8    |    |NumCaps
                  Enter a dBASE III PLUS command.
```

Fig. 9.12 The listing of the combined fields.

Notice that the first five fields are from the Student database and the last two fields are from the Courses database.

4. To see what the view has done, press F6.

   The screen now should resemble figure 9.13.

```
. display status

Currently Selected Database:
Select area:  1, Database in Use: A:STUDENT.DBF   Alias: STUDENT
    Master index file:  A:INDEX1.NDX  Key: ITEM
           Memo file:   A:STUDENT.dbt
    Related into: COURSES
    Relation: ITEM

Select area:  2, Database in Use: A:COURSES.DBF   Alias: COURSES
    Master index file:  A:INDEX2.NDX  Key: ITEM

File search path:
Default disk drive: A:
Print destination:  PRN:
Margin =      0
Current work area =    1

Press any key to continue...
Command Line    |<A:>|STUDENT          |Rec: EOF/8    |    |NumCaps
                  Enter a dBASE III PLUS command.
```

Fig. 9.13 The databases and indexes opened by the view file.

Notice that both database files are in use in different work areas and that dBASE notes the fact that Student is related into Courses by using the ITEM link field.

5. Close all the files involved in the view by typing **CLEAR ALL** and pressing Enter.

Objective 5: To Modify a View File

Once you have created a view, if you need to make changes in the view, use the Modify View command. If you forget the name of a view file, you can see a list of all view files by typing the command **LIST FILES LIKE *.VUE**.

Exercise 5.1: Modifying the View File

To modify the view file First1, take these steps:

1. At the dot prompt, type **MODIFY VIEW FIRST1**, and press Enter.

   The screen should resemble figure 9.14.

   You now will modify the view file by unselecting two fields contributed by the Student database to the original view.

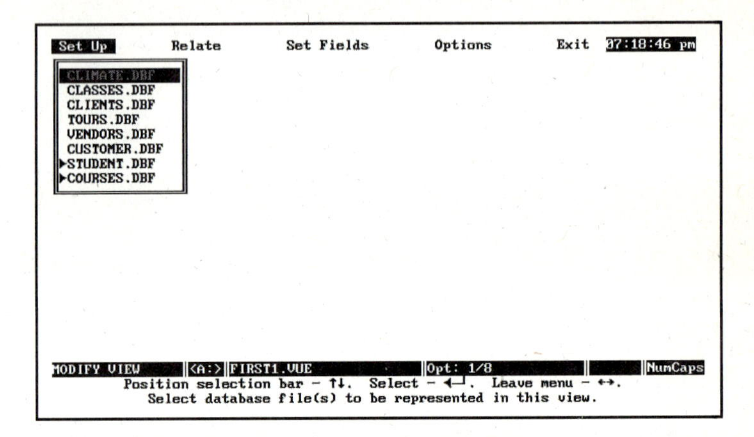

Fig. 9.14 The Modify View screen.

2. Press → twice to move the highlight to the Set Fields menu.
3. Press Enter to select STUDENT.DBF.

   The screen now should resemble figure 9.15.

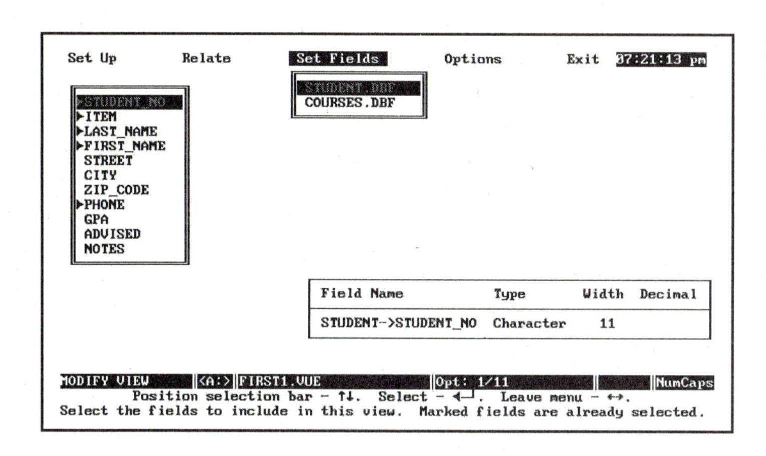

Fig. 9.15 The screen that enables you to deselect fields.

4. Deselect the STUDENT_NO and PHONE fields by placing the highlight on each field and pressing ↵Enter.

   Now your screen should resemble figure 9.16.

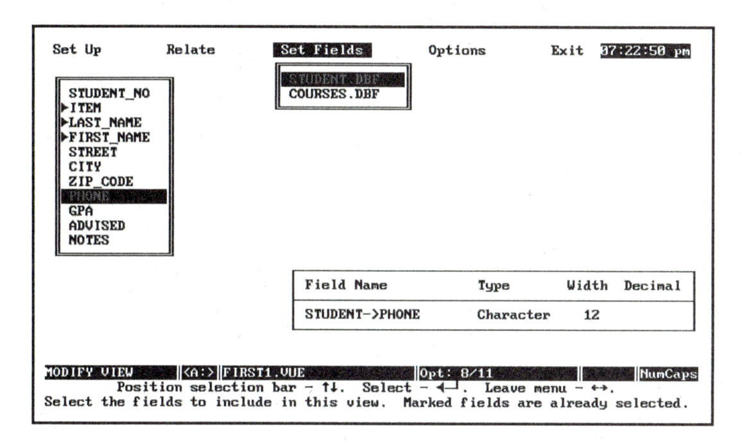

Fig. 9.16 STUDENT_NO and PHONE are no longer fields in the view.

9

5. Press → three times to move the highlight to the Exit menu.
6. Press ↵Enter to save the modified view.

Exercise 5.2: Using the Modified View File

To use the modified view file First1, take these steps:

1. Type **CLEAR ALL**, and press ↵Enter.
2. Type **SET VIEW TO FIRST1**, and press ↵Enter.
3. To see the fields now in the view, type **LIST**, and press ↵Enter.

   Notice that you still have access to fields from both databases, but you now have only three fields from Student.
4. Type **LIST FIRST_NAME, LAST_NAME, DESCRIPT**, and press ↵Enter.

   The screen should resemble figure 9.17.

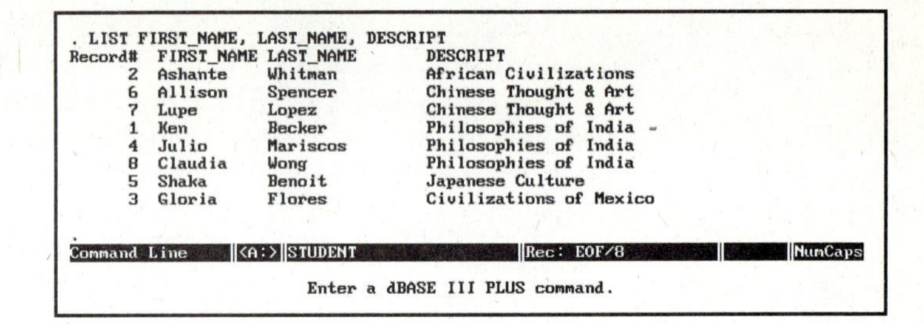

```
. LIST FIRST_NAME, LAST_NAME, DESCRIPT
Record#  FIRST_NAME LAST_NAME       DESCRIPT
     2  Ashante    Whitman          African Civilizations
     6  Allison    Spencer          Chinese Thought & Art
     7  Lupe       Lopez            Chinese Thought & Art
     1  Ken        Becker           Philosophies of India
     4  Julio      Mariscos         Philosophies of India
     8  Claudia    Wong             Philosophies of India
     5  Shaka      Benoit           Japanese Culture
     3  Gloria     Flores           Civilizations of Mexico

Command Line  <A:> STUDENT          Rec: EOF/8          NumCaps
                 Enter a dBASE III PLUS command.
```

Fig. 9.17 Fields from the two database files.

9

5. To finish working with the view, type **CLEAR ALL**, and press ↵Enter.

   If you finish a view file but want to delete it, use the Delete File command. For example, to delete a view file named BAD1, close all files with the Clear All command. Then type **DELETE FILE BAD1.VUE**, and press ↵Enter.

Objective 6: To Create a New Database File by Using the Join Command

The second method you can use to link two database files is the Join command. In some ways, linking the files using Join is easier than creating a view. For example, you don't have to index either of the databases, and the link field can have different names in the two database files. The Join command creates a new database that contains the linked records. You can edit and print this new database. Memo type fields cannot be used as a link field.

Joining two database files is a two-step process. First, in separate work areas, open the two databases that you want to join. Usually, you use work areas 1 and 2 (also designated A and B). Second, type the Join command. To see the results of the join, you have to open the new database file that resulted from the join.

The only complicated aspect of using the Join command is that you *always* must be aware of which of the two databases is the active database (in the currently selected work area). Luckily, this information is easily found; just press F6. Fields from the database open in the *not currently selected work area* are preceded by a designator that indicates which work area the fields are in. The designator consists of the letter (A through J) of the work area, followed by an arrow symbol made from the - and the > symbols.

The field NAME from the database open in the *currently selected work area*, for example, is referred to as NAME, regardless of which work area that contains the field. If a field is from a not currently selected work area, however, and this work area is work area 1, the field is referred to as `A->NAME`. If a field is from a not currently selected work area and this work area is work area 2, the field is referred to as `B->NAME`. This symbolism means, respectively, "NAME from work area A" or "NAME from work area B". Remember that if you just use a field name, dBASE assumes that the field is from the database open in the currently selected (or active) work area.

When the new database file is created from the join, all fields from the two joined databases are by default written to the new file. If you want only some of the fields from the two files to appear in the new database, use the optional FIELDS statement at the end of the Join command statement. This option is illustrated in Exercise 6.2.

9

In the following exercise, you join the Student and Courses database files by using the link field ITEM to create a new database file named Stu_cor. Stu_cor will contain all the fields from the two joined databases.

Exercise 6.1: Joining the Student and Courses Databases

To join these databases, writing all fields to the new database Stu_cor, take these steps:

1. At the dot prompt, type **CLEAR ALL**, and press Enter.
2. Type **USE STUDENT**, and press Enter.
3. Type **SELECT 2**, and press Enter.
4. Type **USE COURSES**, and press Enter.

5. You now have a choice.

   If you *like* being frustrated, get in the habit of *not* pressing F6 so that you can see which databases are open in your work areas and which is the currently selected database. You always know what you are doing—right?

   If you *don't like* being frustrated, get in the habit of *frequently* pressing F6 so that you can see which databases are open in your work areas and which is the currently selected database. You sometimes get confused when you are trying something new—right?

   Press F6.

   The screen should resemble figure 9.18.

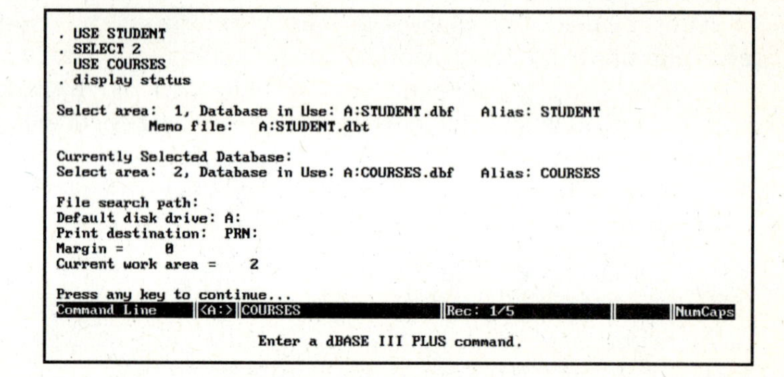

Fig. 9.18
The status before the join.

   Which work area, A or B, is Student in? Which is the currently selected database? Press ↵Enter to complete displaying the status. If you made a mistake, type **CLEAR ALL**, and start the exercise again.

6. At the dot prompt, type the command **JOIN WITH STUDENT TO STU_COR FOR ITEM = A->ITEM**, and press ↵Enter.

   dBASE displays the message `8 records joined` at the bottom of the screen.

7. Type **USE STU_COR**, and press ↵Enter.

8. Type **LIST**, and press ↵Enter.

   The screen should resemble figure 9.19.

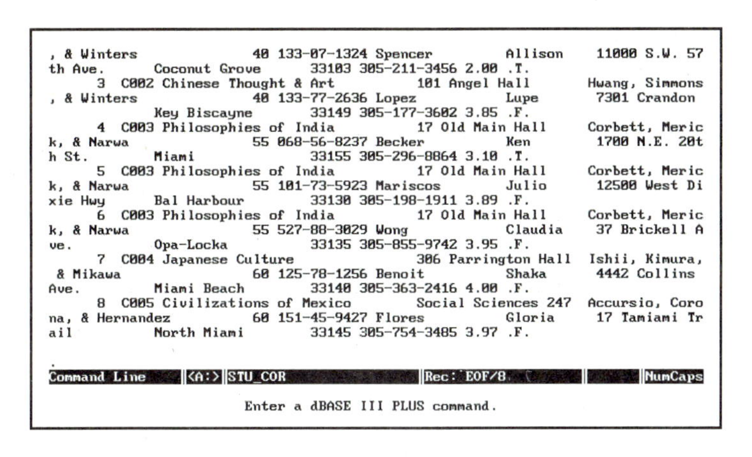

```
, & Winters              40 133-07-1324 Spencer        Allison    11000 S.W. 57
th Ave.      Coconut Grove      33103 305-211-3456 2.00 .T.
     3  C002 Chinese Thought & Art          101 Angel Hall        Hwang, Simmons
, & Winters              40 133-77-2636 Lopez          Lupe       7301 Crandon
             Key Biscayne       33149 305-177-3602 3.85 .F.
     4  C003 Philosophies of India          17 Old Main Hall      Corbett, Meric
k, & Narwa               55 068-56-8237 Becker         Ken        1700 N.E. 20t
h St.        Miami              33155 305-296-8864 3.10 .T.
     5  C003 Philosophies of India          17 Old Main Hall      Corbett, Meric
k, & Narwa               55 101-73-5923 Mariscos       Julio      12500 West Di
xie Hwy      Bal Harbour        33130 305-198-1911 3.89 .F.
     6  C003 Philosophies of India          17 Old Main Hall      Corbett, Meric
k, & Narwa               55 527-88-3029 Wong           Claudia    37 Brickell A
ve.          Opa-Locka          33135 305-855-9742 3.95 .F.
     7  C004 Japanese Culture               306 Parrington Hall   Ishii, Kimura,
 & Mikawa                60 125-78-1256 Benoit         Shaka      4442 Collins
Ave.         Miami Beach        33140 305-363-2416 4.00 .F.
     8  C005 Civilizations of Mexico        Social Sciences 247   Accursio, Coro
na, & Hernandez          60 151-45-9427 Flores         Gloria     17 Tamiami Tr
ail          North Miami        33145 305-754-3485 3.97 .F.

Command Line   <A:> STU_COR          Rec: EOF/8                   NumCaps
                    Enter a dBASE III PLUS command.
```

Fig. 9.19 Fields from the joined database files.

9. Press F5.

   The screen should resemble figure 9.20. Notice that fields 1 through 5 are from Courses and fields 6 through 14 are from Student.

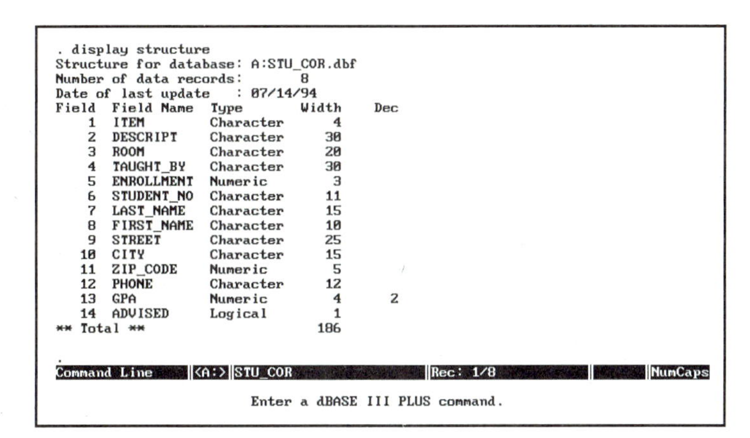

```
. display structure
Structure for database: A:STU_COR.dbf
Number of data records:       8
Date of last update   : 07/14/94
Field  Field Name  Type       Width    Dec
    1  ITEM        Character      4
    2  DESCRIPT    Character     30
    3  ROOM        Character     20
    4  TAUGHT_BY   Character     30
    5  ENROLLMENT  Numeric        3
    6  STUDENT_NO  Character     11
    7  LAST_NAME   Character     15
    8  FIRST_NAME  Character     10
    9  STREET      Character     25
   10  CITY        Character     15
   11  ZIP_CODE    Numeric        5
   12  PHONE       Character     12
   13  GPA         Numeric        4      2
   14  ADVISED     Logical        1
** Total **                     186

Command Line   <A:> STU_COR          Rec: 1/8                     NumCaps
                    Enter a dBASE III PLUS command.
```

Fig. 9.20 The structure of the database file that resulted from the Join.

10. Press F6. Notice that Courses no longer is open in area 2.

Exercise 6.2: Joining Student and Courses in a New Database with Three Fields

In this exercise, you create a new database Stu_cor2 that contains only three of the joined database fields: FIRST_NAME, LAST_NAME, and DESCRIPT.

1. At the dot prompt, type **CLEAR ALL**, and press Enter to make sure that all databases are closed before you begin.
2. Type **USE STUDENT**, and press Enter.
3. Type **SELECT 2**, and press Enter.
4. Type **USE COURSES**, and press Enter.
5. Type the following command:

   JOIN WITH STUDENT TO STU_COR2 FOR ITEM = A->ITEM FIELDS FIRST_NAME, LAST_NAME, DESCRIPT

   The screen now should resemble figure 9.21. Notice that the command is too long to display on one line of the screen. Don't worry; dBASE keeps all the characters you type.

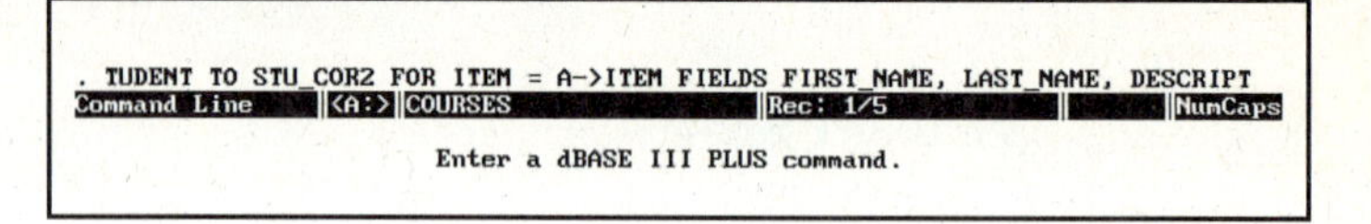

```
. TUDENT TO STU_COR2 FOR ITEM = A->ITEM FIELDS FIRST_NAME, LAST_NAME, DESCRIPT
Command Line    <A:> COURSES             Rec: 1/5                 NumCaps

                     Enter a dBASE III PLUS command.
```

Fig. 9.21 The Join command scrolls because it is so long.

6. Press Enter.
7. Type **USE STU_COR2**, and press Enter.
8. Type **LIST**, and press Enter.

   The screen now should resemble figure 9.22.

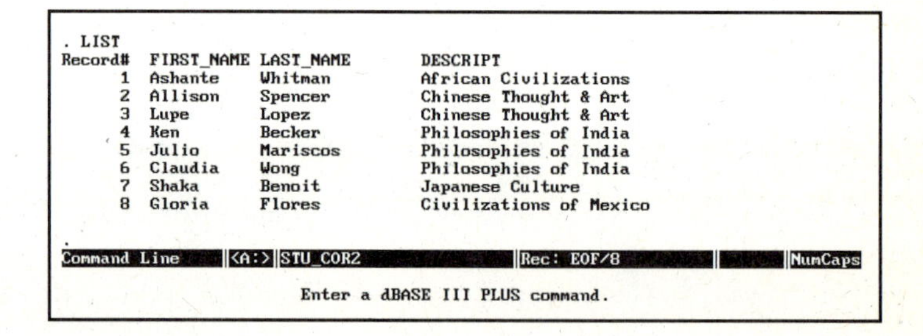

```
. LIST
Record#  FIRST_NAME LAST_NAME     DESCRIPT
      1  Ashante    Whitman       African Civilizations
      2  Allison    Spencer       Chinese Thought & Art
      3  Lupe       Lopez         Chinese Thought & Art
      4  Ken        Becker        Philosophies of India
      5  Julio      Mariscos      Philosophies of India
      6  Claudia    Wong          Philosophies of India
      7  Shaka      Benoit        Japanese Culture
      8  Gloria     Flores        Civilizations of Mexico
.
Command Line    <A:> STU_COR2            Rec: EOF/8               NumCaps

                     Enter a dBASE III PLUS command.
```

Fig. 9.22 Three fields in the new database that resulted from the join.

Chapter Summary

In this chapter, you have learned how to extract related information from two different database files by creating a view and by using the Join command. You also learned how to open database files in different work areas by using the Select command.

Testing Your Knowledge

True/False Questions

1. A database must be indexed on the link field before it can be made part of a view.
2. Two view files can be joined by using the Join command.
3. Memo fields cannot be joined.
4. The result of a Join command is a new database file.
5. A->CITY refers to the CITY field from the database file open in work area 1.

Multiple-Choice Questions

1. Work area 1 also can be referred to as __________.
   a. work area A
   b. select area 1
   c. both a and b
   d. none of these answers

2. The command to close all open views, database files, and index files is __________.
   a. Use
   b. Clear
   c. Clear All
   d. Close
3. To see which work area is the current work area, press __________.
   a. F1
   b. F10
   c. PgUp
   d. none of these answers
4. The menu in the Create View screen that you use to state the name of the link field is the __________ menu.
   a. Set Up
   b. Options

c. Relate

d. none of these answers

5. Before you can join two database files, they must be ___________.

a. indexed

b. open

c. current

d. all these answers

Fill-in-the-Blank Questions

1. Before you can open a database file in work area 3, you must first enter the command __________________.
2. To move from using a database open in area 2 to a database open in area 1, you enter the command __________________.
3. To abandon the creation of a view file, press the _________ key.
4. To alter an existing view file, use the __________________ command.
5. The menu in the Create View screen that enables you to select the fields that appear in the view is the _____________ menu.

Review: Short Projects

1. Modifying a View File

   Modify the First1 view file so that all the fields in both database files are included in the view.

2. Joining the Student and Courses Databases

   Join the Student and Courses databases so that all the fields from both databases are included in the new database file resulting from the join.

3. Learning the Differences between Linking Files by Creating a View and Using the Join Command

   a. List the steps involved in linking two files with a view.

   b. List the steps involved in linking two files with a join.

   c. What procedures or data requirements differ when you link a file using a view as opposed to using a Join command?

Review: Long Projects

1. Linking the Tours and the Climate Databases
    a. Create a view that displays the destination, departure, and cost data from the Tours database and the STATION and COUNTRY fields from the Climate database.

       Note: This project requires some thought. Print the view that contains this data.

    b. Use the Join command to create a new database that contains the same data shown in the view you created in step a. Print the structure of the new database, and list the records in the new database.
2. Linking the Tours and the Clients Databases
    a. Create a view that displays the destination, departure, and cost data from the Tours database and the NAME and INTERESTS fields from the Clients database. Print the view that contains this data.
    b. Try to create a view that displays all the fields from the Tours database and all the fields from the Clients database. Print the view.
    c. Use the Join command to create a new database that contains all the fields from the Tours and Clients databases. Print the structure of the new database, and print the records in the new database.
3. Linking the Tours, Climate, and Clients Databases

    Linking three databases is a challenging project.

    a. Use a series of Join commands to produce a new database that contains all the fields from the Tours, Climate, and Clients databases. Print the structure and the data from the database.
    b. Create a view that contains two fields from each of the Tours, Climate, and Clients databases. Display status to print. List the view to print.

Index

Symbols

< (less than) comparison operator, 99
<= (less than or equal to) comparison operator, 99
<> (not equal to) comparison operator, 99
= (equal to) comparison operator, 99
> (greater than) comparison operator, 99
>= (greater than or equal to) comparison operator, 99

A

American Standard Code for Information Interchange, *see* ASCII
AND operator, 97-98, 176
Append command
  dot prompt, 85
  Update menu, 54, 125
appending records, 50, 53-57, 85
ascending order (sorting records), 143
ASCII (American Standard Code for Information Interchange), 136
Assistant, 10-11, 26-27
Average command (dot prompt), 175-176
Average For command (dot prompt), 177

B

backups, 108-111
Browse command (Update menu), 64, 67

C

character fields, 96, 99, 137-138
Clear All command, 228
Clear command (dot prompt), 87
clearing monitor, 87
closing database files, 228
columns
  defining, 204-209
  width, 206
Columns menu, 204
commands
  Append, 125
  Clear All, 228
  Copy, 17
  Create Label, 191-192
  Create Report, 203
  dot prompt, *see* dot prompt commands
  entering, 10-11
  Join, 16, 224, 238-242
  listing, 86
  menus, 22, 26
  Modify Structure, 16, 112
  Rename, 17
  Retrieve menu, 51, 58
  saving dot prompt commands, 82
  Select, 226-227
  selection bars, 22, 26
  Set Up menu
    Open, 50
    Quit, 36
    View, 51
  Set View To, 228
  Sort, 11
  Tools menu
    List Structure, 34
    Set drive, 24

Update menu
Append, 54
Browse, 64, 67
Delete, 65-67
Edit, 61
Pack, 65, 71
Recall, 69
comparison operators, 99
Copy command, 17
copying database files, 17, 110-111
Count commands, 176-177
Count For command (dot prompt), 177
Create Label command, 191-192
Create Label screen, 192-193
Create Report command, 203
current work area, 221

D

data entry (custom screens), 17
data type mismatches, 96
data types
logical, 122
entering text, 126-127
inserting, 124
listing field contents, 128
memo, 122-124
entering text, 125-127
inserting, 124
listing field contents, 127-128
database files, 5-8, 28-29
calculations, 175-177
closing, 228
copying, 17, 110-111
deleting files, 129-130
designing, 28-34, 40-43
objectives, 41
output, 42
restructuring, 43
size, 42-43
editing, 50, 61-63
exiting, 102-103
fields, 28, 39-40, 53
Character, 39-40
Date, 39-40
defining, 28
link fields, 22
listing, 90
Logical, 39-40
Memo, 39-40
naming, 38
Numeric, 39-40
width, 40
indexing, 146-147
index files, 145-148, 152-155
multiple fields, 156-157
joining, 238-242
linking
defining links, 231-232
records, 22
selecting, 229-231
listing, 84, 91
multiple databases, 225-226
naming, 37-38
opening, 50-52, 83, 225-226
printing, 145-146
records
appending, 50, 53-57, 85
counting, 176
deleting, 65-71, 87-88
displaying, 58-61
editing, 86
listing, 89, 94-99
marking for deletion, 66-68
printing, 60-61, 100-101
selecting, 164-166
unmarking for deletion, 69-70
relational, 6-9
renaming, 17, 128-129
restructuring, 43, 108-112, 119
changing field type, 117-119
deleting fields, 114
inserting fields, 113
moving fields, 115-116
naming fields, 120-122
sizing fields, 116-117
viewing changes, 120
saving sorted files, 143
searches, 13-14

settings, 91-92
sorting, 139-140, 144-145
structures, 8, 28-29, 40-41
displaying, 34-35
listing, 84
modifying, 16-17
printing, 36
see also relational databases
date fields, 96-97
deleting, 169-170
searching, 183
sorting, 138
default directory, 22-23
default disk, 22-24
default drive, 102
defining
label contents, 194-197
links, 231-232
report columns, 205-209
Delete command
dot prompt, 87
Update menu, 65-67
Delete For command (dot prompt), 168-170
deleting
database files, 129-130
fields, 114
records
marking for deletion, 87, 168-170
unmarking for deletion, 88, 170-172
descending order (sorting records), 142-143
designing database files, 28-34, 40-43
objectives, 41
output, 42
restructuring, 43
size, 42-43
directories (disks)
default directory, 22-23
paths, 24
Disk Operating System, *see* DOS
disks
default drive, 22-24, 102
directories, 22-23
drives, 24
Display command (dot prompt), 88
Display Status commands, 93
DOS (Disk Operating System), 22-24
dot prompt commands, 82-88
Append, 85
Average, 175-176
Average For, 177
Clear, 87
Count, 176-177
Count For, 177
Delete, 87
Delete For, 168-170
Display, 88
Display Status, 93
Edit, 86
Find, 178-182
Goto, 164-166
Insert, 166-168
List, 84, 88-93
List Files, 91
List For, 94-99
List History, 86
List Next, 180-181
List Status, 91-93
List to Print, 100-101
List While, 181-182
Pack, 87
Quit, 103
Recall, 88
Recall All, 171-172
Recall For, 171
Replace, 172-174
Replace All, 173-174
Replace For, 174
Seek, 178, 182-183
Set Bell Off, 102
Set Default To, 102
Sum, 175-176
Sum For, 177
Use, 83
DTOC (Date To Character) function, 96

E

Edit command
  dot prompt, 86
  Update menu, 61
editing
  database files, 50, 61-63
  records, 65-71, 86, 172-174
entering
  commands, 10-11
  text
    Logical fields, 126-127
    Memo fields, 125
  see also data entry
equal to (=) comparison operator, 99
exiting dBASE, 36

F

fields, 6-8, 28, 39-40, 53
  Character fields, 39-40, 96, 99, 137-138
  Date fields, 39-40, 96-97
    deleting, 169-170
    searching, 183
    sorting, 138
  defining, 28
  deleting, 114
  editing, 172-174
  indexes, 149-151, 156-157, 178
  inserting, 113
  key fields, 6, 8, 136
  link fields, 6, 22, 221-224
  listing, 90
  Logical fields, 39-40, 122
    entering text, 126-127
    inserting, 124
    listing contents, 128
  major sort fields, 141
  Memo fields, 39-40, 122-124
    entering text, 125-127
    inserting, 124
    listing contents, 127-128
  moving, 115-116
  naming, 38, 120-122
  Numeric fields, 39-20, 96, 99
    calculations, 175-177
    sorting, 138
  primary key fields, 164, 178, 221-224
  sizing, 116-117
  types, 117-119
  width, 40
file name extensions, 192
files
  backups, 108-111
  closing all files, 228
  copying, 110-111
  database files, 6-7
    copying, 17
    renaming, 17
  default directory, 22-23
  default disk, 22-24
  deleting, 129-130
  directories, 22-23
  index files, 12-13, 136, 145-148, 152-155, 229-231
  label-form files, 15, 191
  Memo fields, 123
  opening multiple files, 225
  renaming, 128-129
  report-format files, 15
  saving, 24
  view files, 16, 221, 224, 228, 232-235
    including fields, 232-233
    modifying, 236-238
    naming, 229
Find command (dot prompt), 178-182
finding, *see* searching records
formats, 190, 202
forms, 190
  labels, 190-191
  mailing labels, 198-200
  report forms, 190
    modifying, 210-214
    options, 203-204
function keys, 92-93
functions, 96

G

Goto command (dot prompt), 164-166
greater than (>) comparison operator, 99
greater than or equal to (>=) comparison operator, 99

I

indexing
  database files, 146-147
  index files, 12-13, 136, 145-148, 152-155, 229-231
  indexes, 145-153, 168, 172, 178-179, 182
    fields, 149-151
    multiple fields, 156-157
    multiple indexes, 154-156
  records, 12-13
Insert command (dot prompt), 166-168
inserting
  fields, 113
    Logical fields, 124
    Memo fields, 124
  records, 166-168, 202-203

J

Join command, 16, 224, 238-242
joining databases, 238-242

K

key fields, 6, 8, 136
  primary key field, 164, 178, 221-224

L

Label Contents menu box, 193-194
label-format files, 15
labels, 14-15
  defining contents, 194-197
  mailing labels
    forms, 191-198
    modifying form, 198-200
  printing, 193-194, 197-201
  selecting, 193-194
  size, 193
LBL (label) file name extension, 192
less than (<) comparison operator, 99
less than or equal to (<=) comparison operator, 99
link fields, 6, 221-224
linking
  databases
    defining links, 231-232
    selecting, 229-231
  index files, 229-231
  records, 16, 22
  see also joining databases
List command
  dot prompt, 84, 88-93
  Retrieve menu, 58
List Files command (List Files), 91
List For command (dot prompt), 94-99
List History command (dot prompt), 86
List Next command (dot prompt), 180-181
List Status command (dot prompt), 91-93
List Structure command (Tools menu), 34
List to Print command (dot prompt), 100-101
List While command (dot prompt), 181-182
listing
  database files, 91
  field contents, 127-128
  fields, 90
  records, 89, 94-99
    comparison operators, 99
    conditions, 94-95

data type mismatches, 96
date fields, 97
multiple conditions, 97-98
logical fields, 122
entering text, 126-127
inserting, 124
listing contents, 128
logical operators
AND, 97-98, 176
OR, 97-98, 176

M

mailing labels, 14-15
forms, 191-198
modifying, 198-200
major sort fields, 141
Memo fields, 122
entering text, 125-127
inserting, 124
listing contents, 127-128
memo files, 123
menus, 22, 26
Columns menu, 204
Relate menu, 231-232
selection bars, 22
Set Fields menu, 232
Modify Structure command, 16, 112
modifying
forms
mailing labels, 198-200
reports, 210-214
view files, 236-238
monitor, 87
moving
between select areas, 227
fields, 115-116

N

naming
database files, 37-38
fields, 38, 120-122
view files, 229
not equal to (<>) comparison operator, 99
Numeric fields, 96, 99
calculations, 175-177
sorting, 138

O

opening
databases, 50-52, 225-226
multiple files, 225
options (report forms), 203-204
OR operator, 97-98, 176

P

Pack command
dot prompt, 87
Update menu, 65, 71
primary key fields, 164, 178, 221-224
printing
database file structures, 36
database files, 145-146
dot prompt commands, 100-101
labels, 193-194, 197-201
records, 60-61
reports, 209, 212-213
prompt (entering commands), 10-11

Q

Quit command
dot prompt, 103
Set Up menu, 36
quitting from dot prompt, 102-103

R

Recall All command (dot prompt), 171-172
Recall command
dot prompt, 88
Update menu, 69
Recall For command (dot prompt), 171

records, 6-7
- appending, 50, 53-57, 85
- counting, 176
- deleting, 65-71
  - marking for deletion, 66-68, 87, 168-170
  - unmarking for deletion, 69-70, 88, 170-172
- displaying, 58-61
- editing, 86, 172-174
- fields, 53, 90
- index files, 136, 145-148
- indexing, 12-13
- inserting, 166-168, 202-203
- linking, 16
- listing, 89, 94-99
  - comparison operators, 99
  - conditions, 94-95
  - data type mismatches, 96
  - Date fields, 97
  - fields, 90
  - multiple conditions, 97-98
- printing, 60-61, 100-101
- searching, 13-14, 178-182
- selecting, 164-166
- sorting, 11-13, 136, 137-138, 139-140
  - ascending order, 136, 143
  - descending order, 136, 142-143
  - fields, 139-140
  - index files, 148
  - key fields, 136
  - multiple fields, 140-142
  - problems, 144-145

Relate menu, 231-232
relational databases, 6, 8-9, 221-222
relationships, 222-223
Rename command, 17
renaming database files, 17, 128-129
Replace All command (dot prompt), 173-174
Replace command (dot prompt), 172-174
Replace For command (dot prompt), 174
report-format files, 15
report forms, 190, 201-209
- modifying, 210-214
- options, 203-204

reports, 14-15, 189-190
- columns, 204-209
- formats, 202
- printing, 209, 212-213

restructuring databases, 43, 108-112, 119
- changing field type, 117-119
- deleting fields, 114
- field names, 120-122
- inserting fields, 113
- moving fields, 115-116
- sizing fields, 116-117
- viewing changes, 120

Retrieve menu commands, 51, 58

S

saving
- files, 24
- sorted files, 143
- views, 234

screen components
- dot prompt, 82
- status bar, 26-27, 31

Screen Painter, 17
screens, 192, 193
searching records, 13-14, 178-182
Seek command (dot prompt), 178, 182-183
select area
- current, 225
- moving between, 227
- *see also* work area

Select command, 226-227
selecting
- databases, 229-231
- labels, 193-194

selection bars (menus), 22, 26
Set Bell Off command (dot prompt), 102
Set Default To command (dot prompt), 102

Set drive command (Tools menu), 24
Set Fields menu, 232
Set Up menu commands, 50
  Quit, 36
  View, 51
Set View To command, 228
size (labels), 193
sizing fields, 116-117
Sort command, 11
sorting
  database files, 139-140
  index files, 145-148
  records, 11-13, 136-140, 168
    ascending order, 136, 143
    Character fields, 137-138
    Date fields, 138
    descending order, 136, 142-143
    fields, 139-140
    index files, 148
    key fields, 136
    multiple fields, 140-142
    Numeric fields, 138
    problems, 144-145
start-up, 23-25
status bar, 26-27, 31
structure, 6, 8, 16-17
structures (database files), 29, 40-41
  displaying, 34-35
  listing, 84
  printing, 36
Sum command (dot prompt), 175-176
Sum For command (dot prompt), 177

T

tables, *see* database files
text, 125-126
Tools menu commands
  List Structure, 34
  Set drive, 24

U

Update menu commands
  Append, 54
  Browse, 64, 67
  Delete, 65-67
  Edit, 61
  Pack, 65, 71
  Recall, 69
Use command (dot prompt), 83

V-Z

View command (Set Up menu), 51
view files, 16, 221, 224, 228
  including fields, 232-233
  modifying, 236-238
  naming, 229
  retrieving linked data, 234-235
views, 16
  linking files, 224
  saving, 234

warning bell, 102
work area, 221
  see also select area